GREAT WESTERN RV TRIPS

Great Western RV Trips

A YEAR-ROUND GUIDE TO THE BEST RVING IN THE WEST

Jan Bannan

RAGGED MOUNTAIN PRESS/MCGRAW-HILL

Camden, Maine • New York • San Francisco • Washington, D.C. • Auckland
Bogotá • Caracas • Lisbon • London • Madrid • Mexico City • Milan • Montréal
New Delhi • San Juan • Singapore • Sydney • Tokyo • Toronto

The **McGraw·Hill** Companies

34567890DOCDOC01098765432

Library of Congress Cataloging-in-Publication Data
Bannan, Jan Gumprecht.
   Great western RV trips : a year-round guide to the best RVing in the West / by Jan Bannan.
      p.   cm.
   ISBN 0-07-006722-8 (pbk.)
   1. Recreational vehicle living—West (U.S.)—Guidebooks. 2. West
(U.S.)—Guidebooks. I. Title.
TX1110.B36 1998
796.7'9'0978—dc21   98-24107
                                           CIP

Questions regarding the content of
this book should be addressed to

Ragged Mountain Press
P.O. Box 220
Camden, ME 04843
Visit us on the World Wide Web
at www.raggedmountainpress.com

Questions regarding the ordering of
this book should be addressed to

The McGraw-Hill Companies
Customer Service Department
P.O. Box 547
Blacklick, OH 43004
Retail customers: 1-800-262-4729
Bookstores: 1-800-722-4726

This book is printed on 60lb. Finch
Printed by R.R. Donnelly & Sons, Crawfordsville, Indiana
Design by Paul Uhl/Design Associates
Production by Dan Kirchoff, Eugenie Delaney, and Shannon Thomas
Edited by Jeff Serena and Tom McCarthy
All photographs by Jan Bannan

Contents

Introduction

Years ago, when I was on my way to becoming a professional photographer, I quickly learned that the best outdoor photographs were taken in scenic wild places in early morning and late evening. I needed to be there when the slanted sunlight was spreading color and clarity on the mountain peaks and when the calm waters of lakes and rivers became reflecting pools. And I saw how beautiful the world could be at these special times. Every day was different and unexpected in the light of changing weather. And I learned the easiest way to be there at the right time was to camp near the action.

You don't have to be a photographer to enjoy this spectacular light and time of day. Anglers fish at such times, canoeists glide through the morning mist, and anyone can see the same images with obvious pleasure. Choosing your campground judiciously puts you near the best trails. After returning from a hike or other self-propelled activity, you can relax at a temporary home without driving anywhere. Isn't this what recreation time in the outdoors is about?

If you're just interested in visiting and exploring the urban environment, campgrounds and RV rigs are not the smart choice. But if you are traveling in the rural and wild countryside while pursuing activities close to nature, then camping is really the only satisfying approach. (Traveling with your pet is another reason for preferring an RV.) Camping puts you among wildlife, plants, wetlands, geology, waterways, culture, and history; you are bound to go home with a more intimate awareness and knowledge of places visited, in addition to having lots of fun. Motels are not the answer if your goal is to feel the pulse of the natural world. Although millions of campers visit state and national parks annually, such numbers can't express the emotional appeal of immersing yourself in wild places.

My memories are rich with experiences that happened by walking out from my campsite—sometimes only a couple a steps. Some of these places are included in this book. Let me toss out a few to whet your urge to wander.

- Watching egrets, brown pelicans, and Mexican fishermen as a fiery sunrise colored Bahia Concepcion in Baja
- Hiking to hot springs along the Rio Grande River in Big Bend National Park in Texas
- Scanning for bighorn sheep while walking to a palm oasis in Anza-Borrego Desert State Park in California
- Wandering along a cliff trail watching winter surf and gray whales on the southern Oregon coast
- Observing white pelicans skimming over the Arkansas River in Oklahoma's Cherokee Strip
- Tracing the path carved by the Colorado River through Utah's Canyonlands National Park from a viewpoint high atop Dead Horse Point
- Finding a Roosevelt elk herd near a campsite in northern California redwoods
- Walking from the campground at Colter Bay in the Grand Tetons and finding a moose, trumpeter swans, and a beaver family tutoring their young

- Sauntering beneath "Ponytail" Falls in the Columbia River Gorge of Oregon
- Riding a gondola to the "top-of-the-world" in Oregon's Wallowa Mountains
- Gliding across Lightning Lake in a canoe at sunrise in British Columbia's Manning Provincial Park
- Throwing a fishing line into the stream near the spectacular Rogue River Gorge in Oregon
- Wandering through a cathedral of old-growth trees in the Hoh River Rain Forest of the Olympic Peninsula
- Exploring North America's highest sand dunes adjacent to autumn foliage in the Rocky Mountains of Colorado
- Watching Skyline Arch in Utah's Arches National Park catch the morning light and then scampering over red rock formations
- Hiking to see Anasazi Indian ruins at Bandalier National Monument in New Mexico

Why Travel with the Seasons?

To really enjoy the best experiences while wandering the diverse and fascinating western United States, you need to be attuned to the weather of place as well as to the best times to savor the wildness of our most popular parks. And by being alert to the habits of wildlife and the seasonal blooming of plants, you can catch the profusion of creamy flowers bursting from tall saguaro cactus and visit wildlife refuges when great flocks of snow geese, sandhill cranes, and endangered whooping cranes are in the area.

Being there at the right time means you can winter in a pleasant climate—even in Death Valley—and explore in comfortable weather. (During a trip to discover spring wildflowers in Anza-Borrego Desert State Park, I made a side trip and took a tram to the summit of Mount San Jacinto, where I was surprised with enough snow for a snowman, yet I slept snug that night in the desert.) RV travelers might be surprised to find that the winter climate of the Oregon coast is very temperate. (I've had more trou-

ble with snow on the Mexican border.) Sure, there's rain and winter storms, but look at the many rewards.

Summers can be spent at high elevations that are snowed-in during winter but pleasant when other places are having heat waves. Coordinating this information with special events is also possible, such as visiting the waterfalls of the Columbia Gorge during the peak windsurfing season when hot-shot international talent participates in events on the Columbia River (and you can do your own windsurfing right from your campground). Or you can visit the famed Britt Music Festival in Jacksonville, Oregon, and the Shakespeare Festival in nearby Ashland on your trip to Crater Lake National Park.

Autumn travel means colorful foliage trips, and Colorado aspens supply that beautifully at a time when Rocky Mountain elk are in rut and bugling for mates. Imagine yourself in a campground when everyone is listening to this music. Or consider harvesting fruit in Capitol Reef National Park in orchards that Mormon pioneers planted amid dazzling red rock cliffs.

How can we value this country of ours if we know little of it? The tours described here will edge you a bit closer to how the West was settled, the courage it took, and the richness of the landscapes that are now national treasures.

Some Thoughts about Recreational Vehicles

I have camped my way around the West on a seven-month trip in a motorhome, used a pickup camper for another long excursion, used a Volkswagen Vanagon for a long trip as one-half of a couple, pulled a folding camper trailer, set up many a tent, and had a unique setup in a small pickup canopy, complete with sink and running water. So I've been there and done it for some seventeen years now, usually traveling solo because of my vocation as a travel writer-photographer. Since I want to be able to go anywhere that lures me, I have some opinions about RV travel.

If you're in the process of obtaining a

Delicate Arch, Arches National Park, Utah.

RV rig, consider your travel expectations very carefully. Obviously, full-time RVers need enough space to carry the essentials for a pleasant life, although what is essential is debatable and personal. But do you, even for a trip of a month or more, really need a rig so big that it prohibits you from getting everywhere you want to go and also entices you inside too much of the time? If you want to stay inside, why not stay home where you've got everything you need and want? Shouldn't travel be a different experience than your regular routine?

Long and wide rigs are prohibited on some of the roads to special places; they are not easy to park and they usually consume enormous amounts of fuel. These big rigs are simply not advisable on many of the national forest or backcountry roads. I can tell you that a pickup camper, conversion van, or a small motorhome is a joy to drive, easy to back up, and gets you anywhere except on the worst sort of road.

The seven months of travel while circling the West were done in an 18-foot motorhome, complete with a specially installed setup for my computer, 3,000 slides needed for work along the way, a shelf of reference books, camera gear, music equipment, all the clothes I needed, and the usual kitchen and tool paraphernalia. It even had a nice shower and bathroom, although I also enjoyed the massaging power of showers in campgrounds. I know, I traveled alone—well, not quite, my cat went along—but surely most couples can be comfortable in a rig of that size for a short time, or a 21- or 24-foot motorhome, or in a fifth-wheel or trailer unit of the same overall length. My point is that you'll miss a lot if you're accommodating your rig and not your recreation destinations. And how about forgetting the television and microwave? It's hard to resist needing electricity and being indoors if you cave in to these addictions. I disagree with what Sherman Goldenberg wrote in *Modern Maturity*: "On the road, you can take the comforts of home with you." That's fine for full-timers who spend considerable time in one place.

Economics does enter into some choices of a rig, but the price is so variable—and can be so expensive—that only those buying inexpensive rigs can use price as a reason to camp and avoid motels. Other reasons are more to the point of what the outdoor experience involves, and I think you need to be sure about why you're traveling.

I realize this is personal information—I'm certainly writing this book for all kinds of RVers—so I'll contribute some general information about RV rigs. Here are your basic choices:

1. A folding camping trailer, also called a pop-up or tent camper, is an economical way to travel. You can leave the camper behind while you're out doing activities, but such a rig is not likely to have a toilet or shower.

2. Truck campers—camper shells on trucks—are growing in appeal and some have all the conveniences. They will go almost anywhere, especially when mounted on a four-wheel-drive truck, and the truck can be upgraded or changed at any time. The camper can be removed when not in use, even in campgrounds if you want to go to the trouble.

3. Conventional travel trailers come in many styles, weights, and lengths, some old, some new, and fully equipped. The lighter ones can be pulled by passenger cars and small pickups. Their advantage is that you can leave them in campgrounds and in parking lots when exploring places where they are prohibited on the road. Their disadvantages are backing them and the parking space they require.

4. Fifth-wheel trailers are said to be easier to tow than trailers—I can't attest to that—and also have the same advantages as other trailers; that is, they can be parked when not needed or not allowed. They come in various sizes with a range of amenities. They do take up slightly less road length because a bedroom can project over the truck bed.

5. Motorhome sales are booming, with every type from class A's with a cabover bed, to the flowing lines of class C rigs, which are constructed as a unit rather than installed on a separate chassis. The problem with the larger motorhomes is that you must either tow a

Grand Tetons, Jackson Lake, WY.

small vehicle for getting around or drive the motorhome everywhere (bicycles are handy for some errands); this could require putting things away and unhooking everything for even a short trip to the store, if you opt for electrical, water, and sewer conveniences at campgrounds.

6. Conversion vans can work well and are great if you're the outdoor type who likes to go anywhere. Some even have toilets, and they certainly get better fuel economy than most rigs. They're also fine for driving at home. I inspected a custom four-wheel-drive van in a campground that was designed for real comfort and utility.

7. Buses are another choice. Any type of bus can be used, from an old, converted, small school bus or delivery truck (I've seen about everything during my travels) to those elegant $400,000 custom numbers. Driving such a rig and its costs are the factors to consider.

8. Any vehicle carrying a tent and cooking equipment and taking a recreational trip is an RV, isn't it?

I've talked to travelers with small rigs that include electronic global positioning devices, and buses with high-tech surround-sound stereo systems, so it's out there if you think you have to have it.

I strongly urge you to obtain a rig with sufficient power for mountain travel. The West has numerous mountain passes that put stress on an underpowered vehicle. And going downhill from these passes requires good brakes. This comes as a surprise to some travelers from the Midwest and the East, so be forewarned. Richard Miller, an experienced trucker, has written *Mountain Directory for Truckers, RV, & Motorhome Drivers* that you might find helpful. (See Appendix for details.)

Finally, when you're in your RV, give some thought to the other traffic. I live in a tourist community along the Oregon coast, where residents are trying to keep appointments on time. This sometimes means traveling between coastal towns. We love our visitors and put up with slow traffic in summer, but expect all drivers to show respect for others on the road. Particularly distressing are those drivers going much slower than allowed on highways because they are not in a hurry—or perhaps their rigs are not in good shape. Even other RVers appreciate it if vehicles pull over and let others pass if they're slowing down a line of traffic; it's much less dangerous than having people trying to pass where it's not safe. It's also considerate to use the slow lane except when passing or turning—in town also. Long rigs take a lot of room in a busy traffic area.

At all times, drivers of vehicles should consider the environment. Don't drive off-road unless permitted; it disturbs grasses and other vegetation, even young trees. It's even preferable to avoid driving on soft, muddy roads rather than tearing them up. Do obey all posted vehicle restrictions.

Choosing a Campground

All of us have a preference about what sort of campground we prefer, and the assortment out there today covers the spectrum of possibilities. I sometimes feel I've been in almost every public campground in the West and even a few private ones. I prefer a campsite with some privacy, some space, and natural surroundings, and I'd like a shower available if possible. But even when I traveled on extended trips in a motorhome, hookups were not a concern. Certainly, they're nice when I'm staying a while (I don't have a generator and don't want to inflict its noise on others) or when I need to use my computer (on my last trip I had a Powerbook), but I'm not out there to watch TV or stay in my rig except to sleep or eat when it's raining. Somewhere along the line we've forgotten that most of these rigs are self-contained; they have batteries for electricity and lights, running water without hooking up, even hot water, and a stove and refrigerator that use propane. Obviously, the battery needs recharging, so these comments only apply when we're driving every day or so. So what's the problem? Let's be self-contained at least some of the time and get into the wild spirit. For that reason, I cannot understand using private campgrounds where the RVs are parked close together, unless you find one with attractive recreation features or you're doing a winter trip and run into inclement weather. Most of the recommended campgrounds in this book are public, quiet, and close to activities and great scenery. Private campgrounds are more often near busier areas; take along a guide book for these if you must hook up.

I've gotten into the habit of stopping at chambers of commerce and national forest ranger stations to obtain free handouts for campgrounds. These often tell me a lot about the facilities. Forest camps and Bureau of Land Management campgrounds—and other public affairs—run the gauntlet from primitive sites with no water, carry out your garbage, and vault toilets (some of these are free), to nicer ones with water, flush toilets, and even showers. The latter are more often state parks. Handouts further inform me if there's hiking, fishing, swimming, and other activities available at the camp. This book will answer lots of those questions about some campgrounds, but I can't tell you about all of them or there would not be room for touring information.

If you are 62 years old, stop at a ranger station to obtain a Golden Age Pass for $10. This is a lifetime pass to all federal fee areas, and it allows you to pay half-fare for camping and other activities. A Golden Access Pass is available for the blind or permanently disabled.

Sometimes it's an interesting experience to try one of the new resorts with a swimming pool—I even found reasons to include one on the southern Oregon coast tour described here. On the flip side is camping in the boondocks. The mapping-America's-back-roads-people, DeLorme, define boondocks as "the back woods, wild country, the kind of place, whether far or near, where you need an *Atlas & Gazetteer*." I've enjoyed doing this a few times in a scenic place, although I'm very cautious as a single woman traveling alone; I consider whether friendly campers are also in the area. Be sure camping is permitted, however, and don't trespass. At those times when the end of the day comes and you're not where you want to be, with no campground in sight, consider a space at a mobile home park that welcomes overnighters.

While staying in a campground, practice some pertinent etiquette. A campsite should be a place of privacy, so try to not disturb others by strolling through the middle of their site. Respect quiet hours so others can sleep. Some of them plan to be out in that special early time of day. Do not leave a campfire unattended. Must I mention fireworks? They are incompatible with the outdoor experience.

Safety and Wisdom in the Outdoors

WILDLIFE ENCOUNTERS

When we go outdoors for recreation, we invade habitats populated by wildlife. If we go gently and quietly, with respect for both plants and animals, we can experience natural connections that are part of our heritage. Edward O. Wilson called the hunger for other life "biophilia," and believes it to be a basic part of the human psyche. Who would want to live in a world where we were the only life-forms?

Yet, it's amazing how often travelers fail to respect the wildness of the animals they see. In some parks, wildlife is acclimated to humans, but their lives are disturbed by approaching them too closely, so keep your distance, especially from nests and dens. A raised head and pointed ears, skittish movement, or alarm calls mean you are causing distress. Never feed, chase, or try to capture animals or even pet a friendly deer; it causes them to lose their ability to live wild and safe. Where will you be in the midst of winter when those animals you fed must rely on their own resources? The outdoors is not a Walt Disney theme park.

Learn more about the lives of the indigenous animals for the best viewing; read up on their behavior and go to natural history museums. Usually, the best wildlife viewing times are early morning or late afternoon; birding is best during spring and fall migrations. To some extent, binoculars and spotting scopes have replaced hunting equipment, and taking photographs is an excellent technique (and a good conservation tool) for identifying plants, birds, and butterflies. It's not a good idea to wear perfume, and your clothing should be of muted colors to avoid alerting wildlife to your presence (although I like my photography models to wear something red as they hike the trail, so I'm ambivalent about that).

Wildlife consists of all living animals, not just the charismatic ones—even that scary rattlesnake has its place in the ecosystem. Learn about nontoxic ways to fight insects—citronella and other herbs, for example—or if you use DEET, use a solution that has a concentration of less than 30 percent for your own sake. Know the symptoms of Lyme disease if you are in tick country.

If you fish, think of the future and practice catch-and-release techniques at least part of the time. Avoid walking on or running boats through gravel bars, which are often spawning areas for fish. If you gather clams, crabs, mussels, mushrooms, or

Castle crest wildflowers at Crater Lake National Park.

other edibles, be sure doing so is legal in that area, that it's a safe time to do it, and that you collect only the limit. To conserve fish populations for the future, know the local fishing restrictions and carry the appropriate licenses.

ON THE TRAIL

Whether traveling a trail by foot, horse, or bicycle, if it's a hike of any length or difficulty, it's best to be prepared for the unexpected: a change in the weather, getting lost, or whatever. Take along drinking water, a map, a walking stick, sunscreen lotion, a sweater, insect repellent, sunglasses or a sun hat, dry matches, a compass, a knife, a flashlight, a snack (add an extra high-energy bar just in case), and mini-first-aid kit (include forceps for tick removal and aspirins). New disposable gear that takes little room includes toe and hand heaters (flat 3-inch squares), ponchos (a flat 3 x 5 inches), and insulating blankets (2 x 4 inches). One of the pleasures of outdoor recreation is a picnic at the foot of a waterfall or some other scenic spot along the trail. All these items are easily carried, with hands

free, in a knapsack on your back. Be sure to throw in an extra roll of film.

When hiking, fit your shoes to the terrain, using lug soles only when necessary. Walk single file—and go in small groups—in the center of the trail and do not shortcut or cut new trails; this will minimize erosion and damage to the natural habitat. Stay on the trails in fragile terrain and avoid muddy trails, if possible, to reduce erosion damage. (Never jog on these; if you jog, do so in developed areas.) Riparian areas are sensitive; do not trample banks where beaver, otter, and mink live.

Respect all natural features and do not collect, trample, or deface them. Flowers can be photographed and trees can be touched, even hugged, but leave no graffiti on trees or rocks, nor blackened rocks or burned logs from fires. If visiting a wilderness area, be sure you have a permit if required. The only wheeled devices allowed in wilderness areas are wheelchairs—no bicycles.

Where they are allowed on trails, mountain bikers should not skid or ride on rain-soaked ground; stick to established trails and do not speed. Never drive or mountain bike cross-country. Wear a protective helmet and carry a tire pump and patch kit. Bikers should yield to hikers and equestrians.

There is nothing quite like the joy of hiking a trail in solitude or quiet company, watching for wildlife, and seeing what nature is doing at the moment. But such joy is easily shattered by the loud noises of other hikers or their radios, or by an unexpected, uncontrolled approach of a pet, just when you have discovered a fawn near the path. Please respect the enjoyment of others.

Unless you know the water is potable, do not drink it without first treating it by boiling it, filtering it, or adding a chemical purifier. The days of trusting a cool mountain stream are gone. And do not trespass on private property without permission.

You would think that by now we'd all know to never litter, but the truth is that some people are still tossing trash around our wonderful landscapes—some even toss cigarettes in a dry forest. Leave no food remains, including banana or orange skins; do not even bury them. Use zipper-type plastic bags to carry food and pack out what's left. Carry out all you carry in, including fishing line, hooks, and lures. The phrase "Leave nothing but footsteps" cannot be said too often.

Please don't litter, and pick up any you find. For more details on the Leave No Trace program, contact the National Outdoor Leadership School. And please recycle whenever possible.

Risk is always a factor in outdoor expeditions, although a little knowledge certainly helps to lessen it. Parks with grizzly bears offer good handouts on what to do, and you need to be alert for rattlesnakes and other poisonous creatures. Some cactus can be pretty painful if you get impaled. Check for ticks after hiking. I've found, however, that more problems arise from drastic weather conditions, steep hazardous cliffs, and accidental falls than from wildlife encounters. Life cannot be lived fully without some calculated risktaking.

I'm not going to tell you to never hike alone. If I abided by that rule my experiences would be greatly diminished. Be prepared to accept what happens, however, if you do go alone—the good and the bad. There are both pluses and minuses to solo hiking.

IN THE WATER

Whether canoeing, kayaking, rafting, swimming, or waterskiing, if you choose to enter the water, make it a fun experience. If it's to be a safe undertaking, match your skills to the local conditions and consider the weather; it can change quickly. Ask locally about specific water routes. Wear Coast Guard-approved personal flotation devices (PFDs) and don't drink alcoholic beverages while enjoying water sports. If waterskiing, two people should be in the boat—one to drive and one to observe the skier. If your boat capsizes, stay with your boat for easier rescue. Know the regulations if windsurfing or boating.

Swimmers should never swim alone or during an electrical storm. Check the water depth before you dive. If swimming from a boat, be sure the boat is anchored and kept nearby by a knowledgeable operator. Nonswimmers should not go into deep water, even with a raft or inner tube, and small children should be carefully supervised. Do remember to float if you become exhausted while swimming. Swimmer's cramps are frightening, but try to stretch the muscle while you float and don't forget that you can still swim even with that cramp—it just won't be much fun.

In all water sports, know and respect your physical limits. And don't panic in an emergency. Calm, constructive thinking will give the best results.

How to Use This Book

Each of the sixteen tours in this book—four in each season—includes an itinerary that showcases special areas and destinations in the West. Mileage varies from tour to tour. Some tours require longer stops; you can do portions of any tour or you can do the entire tour. This will allow you to stay a considerable period in one area, or spend more time on the road.

This is a guide for all types of recreational vehicle travel. Some side trips will call for parking the trailer or motorhome and using the tow or pull vehicle, and I'll suggest what to do when this happens. Try the following approach in using this book:

1. If "where" and "what" are more important than "when," scan through the outline of places visited under each tour in the Table of Contents and decide which trip you'd like to do first. If you feel "when" is more important, look under the appropriate season.

2. Read the chapter on the tour you've selected to be sure it's the right one for you now; start selecting which attractions especially appeal to you. I've done the preliminary work of accumulating information, so the trip will need little organization or planning. I'll alert you to road conditions and restrictions for RVs, special attractions and activities, and a sampling of campgrounds—the

ones closest to sunsets, wildlife, and scenery—along the tour. How-to details on recreational activities—hiking, river running, fishing, geology, historic sites, scenic drives, and the like—are woven into the narrative.

3. A map will show the route and let you appreciate the area being covered, with towns and highways labeled to help you orient yourself. Outstanding stops will be shown on the map, but room doesn't exist for all the places worthy of your time, so take this book along for reference. If you're a map person, take along state maps that show all the highways and places that are impossible to put on the small pages of a book, although you probably could follow the route just with my directions. Do note that I take freeways only when absolutely necessary; you may find opportunities to use them and miss certain points along the way.

4. Several of the tours are done as loops, so you can begin at any point rather than only where I suggest. The tours vary in length. Perhaps you'll want to stay longer in some places and skip others, or do a segment of a tour rather than the complete one. It's your choice; the information is there for whatever you select. I've tried to give you an overview of possibilities. For example, you may choose to spend more days hiking or paddling in one area.

5. Check the beginning of each chapter for phone numbers for resources, certain campgrounds, attractions that need advance tickets, and other sundry information. This information is organized in trip sequence.

6. Plan your itinerary, allow time for activities along the route, and choose appropriate gear to take along. Tour mileages are approximate; they allow for some travel away from the main route.

7. Have a great trip!

Spring Trips

How can any traveler resist the burst of life that accompanies spring in the western United States? The deserts are peppered with colorful cactus blooms and wildflowers. Redwood forests are brightened by the rosy hues of huge rhododendron and the vivid green of revived vegetation. Birds are migrating, mating, and nesting. Gray whales, accompanied by their newborn calves, are heading north along the Pacific coast to the Arctic. Nature is revitalized, and it rubs off on the human spirit.

Rhododendron

Travelers may head out to walk trails in the pleasant temperatures or feel the exhilaration of running along the fast-flowing rivers of springtime. It's a time to visit popular sites such as Yellowstone National Park before they are inundated by the crowds of summer.

Scarlet columbine
(Aquilegia canadensis)

CHAPTER 1

Slicing Through Arizona's Midsection: *Flowers, Deserts, and Canyons*

MILEAGE

Approximately 700 miles (1,126 km)

RESOURCES

- Organ Pipe Cactus National Monument, Superintendent, Route 1, Box 100, Ajo, AZ 85321; (520) 387-6849.
- Saguaro National Park, 3693 South Old Spanish Trail, Tucson, AZ 85730; (520) 733-5158.
- Cottonwood/Verde Valley Chamber of Commerce, 1010 S. Main Street, Cottonwood, AZ 86326; (520) 634-7593.
- Jerome Chamber of Commerce, 50 Main Street, P.O. Box K, Jerome, AZ 86331; (520) 634-2900.
- Sedona-Oak Creek Canyon Chamber of Commerce, Forest Road and AZ 89A, P.O. Box 478, Sedona, AZ 86339; (520) 282-7722.
- Grand Canyon National Park, Superintendent, P.O. Box 129, Grand Canyon, AZ 86023; (520) 638-7888; mule trips at (520) 638-2401.

CAMPGROUNDS

ORGAN PIPE CACTUS NATIONAL MONUMENT: 5 miles (8 km) south of Why on AZ 85 to monument, 22 (35 km) more miles to campground; campsites with restrooms, reservations not accepted.

GILBERT RAY CAMPGROUND: Off McCain Loop Road, just south of Saguaro West; campsites with electrical hookups, restrooms; reservations not accepted.

PICACHO PEAK STATE PARK: 27 miles (43 km) northwest of Saguaro West; campsites with hookups, restrooms with showers, dump station; reservations not accepted.

DEAD HORSE RANCH STATE PARK: Near Cottonwood; campsites with hookups, restrooms with showers, dump station; reservations not accepted.

GRAND CANYON NATIONAL PARK: 79 miles (127 km) north of Flagstaff on US 180; tent and trailer campsites, restrooms, showers; reservations not accepted.

A southwestern state that beckons to people with its sunny skies and outdoor living, Arizona also claims wonderful stands of saguaro cactus. These treelike plants resemble giant creatures from a distance, and their spectacular flowering is missed by those who travel to Arizona in the summer, fall, or winter. If you follow this tour and arrive in saguaro country in late April or May, the enormous flowers of these cactus will be a highlight. Birds will be active and nesting, often in the cactus themselves.

North of the Sonoran Desert, with its enigmatic richness of flora and fauna, you will find ancient Indian ruins, the red rock country near Sedona, and the cool, green Oak Creek Recreation Area. Even if you can't hike down into it, just gazing into the pride of the state, the Grand Canyon, is an emotional experience. Temperatures in the southern desert are usually in the eighties in late April, with highs in the seventies in the north in May, so consider traveling from south to north. Sunny days should greet you, since spring is one of the driest seasons.

Organ Pipe Cactus National Monument

Three mountain ranges, outwash plains called *bajadas,* rocky canyons, and dry washes, or *arroyos,* provide the setting in Organ Pipe Cactus National Monument. Stretching 330,000 acres north from the Mexican border, the Monument is a place where intense sunlight, extreme temperatures, and little rain determine the vegetation. Yet, an extraordinary mix of Sonoran Desert plant species are showcased here, including the namesake, the organ pipe cactus, a plant common in Baja California. Like the saguaro, the organ pipe cactus has huge, wonderful flowers and fruit long valued by the local Indians. Other exotic plants cross the international border as well—the elephant tree, the limberbush, and the senita cactus. Although summer is scorching, April is fine; you'll be enchanted with what you find, and some of the cactus will be in bloom.

Aim first for the visitor center, where a wheelchair-accessible path will help to introduce you to the desert and its plants. The campground is nearby among the tall cactus and is a good place to stash your trailer or motorhome before exploring the park's gravel roads.

A few trails are accessible right from your parked rig. An enjoyable day hike heads across easy rolling terrain to the Victoria Mine, the monument's richest and oldest gold and silver mine. Nice mountain views are along the Paloverde Trail to the visitor center, and a 1-mile Perimeter Trail circles the campsites (pets are permitted). The Desert Loop Nature Trail is inviting at any time and provides views of the Sonoyta Valley and the pink granite Cubabi Mountains in Mexico; the ridgeline is a great place to watch the sun set among the giant saguaro.

THE AJO MOUNTAIN AND PUERTO BLANCO DRIVES

The surprise highlight of the monument is the profusion of colorful wildflowers that mix with the tall organ pipe cactus along the winding, 21-mile (34-km) Ajo Mountain Drive, a mostly one-way, graded dirt road. No motorhomes over 25 feet (7.6 m) in length or trailers are advised; guidebooks are available. Look for displays of golden poppies, pink owl clover, desert dandelions, and goldfields. Cactus flowers and huge organ pipes add to the visual magic. As you climb into the higher elevations, look for jojoba, agave, rosewood, and juniper. Accessible from the drive is the Estes Canyon-Bull Pasture Trail, a strenuous 4.1-mile (6.6-km) round-trip hike that climbs to a high plateau where ranchers once brought their cattle; you will have excellent vistas.

The other tour is the 53-mile (85-km) Puerto Blanco Drive, a good half-day trip with the same vehicle considerations. It loops around the Puerto Blanco and Sonoyta mountains, the La Abra Plain, Golden Bell Mine, Quintobaquito Spring, and has a spur leading to the Senita Basin, which is a good place to find exotic plants.

Although many of the animals in the

Organ Pipe Cactus National Monument choose to avoid the intense sun by roaming at night, you should be able to spot some hummingbirds around the flower blossoms and perhaps a roadrunner, a Gambel's quail, or a cactus wren. As you drive north out of the park, consider taking the short road into Alamo Canyon, where the remains of a fence, a brick structure, and a corral are situated near Alamo Wash at the edge of the Ajo Range.

Tohono O'odham Indian Reservation

Head east toward Tucson on AZ 86 from the curious town of Why—perhaps misnamed by the Postal Service when the locals named it "Y"—and drive through the 71,000-acre Tohono O'odham Reservation, formerly known as the Papago Indian Reservation. The historic Tohono O'odham people used 450 species of the Sonoran Desert's plants for food, revealing a remarkable knowledge of plant life in the region. The present-day Tohono O'odham are noted for their basketry and pottery.

Near the eastern edge of the reservation, the white domes of the Kitt Peak National Observatory are visible for miles. If you decide to visit, travel the road high into the Quinlan Mountains. Guided tours are conducted daily from the visitor center. Reputed to be the largest optical telescope facility in the world, the 23 major research instruments at Kitt Peak include the world's largest solar telescope and the Mayall 4-meter telescope. In the distance to the south is 7,730-foot (2,356-m) Baboquivari Peak, a sacred dwelling place of the Tohono O'odham deity I'itoi, or "Elder Brother."

SAN XAVIER DEL BAC MISSION

Also part of the Tohono O'odham Reservation, the San Xavier District contains the white, twin-towered Mission San Xavier del Bac. To visit this, turn south on Mission Street when you approach the outskirts of Tucson; the highway becomes Ajo Drive. This beautiful church, also called the "White Dove of the Desert," beckons to visitors for miles and is open to the public.

Although the mission was founded by Jesuit Father Eusebio Francisco Kino, the present structure was constructed by the Franciscans and is the main church and school for the Tohono O'odham. Step inside to view the interior murals and the altars. I still remember attending church here years ago on Easter Sunday.

Saguaro National Park: The Tucson Mountain District

Those who thrive on the Sonoran Desert experience love its clarity of light, expansive openness, the uniqueness of its plants and animals, and its blazing sunsets. The uninitiated will make their own decisions, but the Tucson Mountain District (Saguaro West) of Saguaro National Park is an excellent place to begin to discover the desert's appeal and its secrets. To reach the park, return to Ajo Drive and head west to Kinney Road and then northwest to the entrance to the park.

The new Red Hills Information Center is an architectural delight of light, color, and striped shadows on the landscape. Inside are maps, information, and a slide show. Outside is the wheelchair-accessible Cactus Garden. A mile northwest, the short Desert Discovery Trail is a place to silently walk among the accordion-pleated saguaro population, where individual plants have anywhere from two to fifty arms; one abnormal type, the cristate saguaro, has a fanlike top. Some saguaro are tall and straight, others are twisted.

The life of a saguaro plant is an amazing, slow-motion story that begins with the

Saguaro cactus, Tucson Mountain District, AZ.

incredible odds of roughly one mature plant arising from the 22 million seeds produced in the lifetime of the parent saguaro. Arms pop out as buds only after 75 to 100 years, when the plant is 12 to 20 feet high. The saguaro may grow to 50 feet (15 m) and weigh several tons, hoarding water, when available, in its interior. The many spines of these plants are vital for protection, but more so for shading the plant against the hot sun. The magnificent, creamy, yellow-centered blossoms open at night in May and last just 24 hours. The nectar attracts bats, moths, ants, wasps, bees, birds, and butterflies. Tasty fruit then develops, which is a feast for squirrels, packrats, pocket mice, coyotes, foxes, skunks, javelinas, birds, kangaroo rats, and humans. The Tohono O'odham have long used the saguaro fruit for making syrup, jam, and ceremonial wine, which they drink while dancing to invoke rain for their crops.

Continue north if you wish to drive the 6-mile (10-km) graded dirt Bajada Loop Drive past Apache Peak, two picnic areas, and the short Valley View Overlook Trail (there are no restrictions on motorhomes or trailers, but check road conditions). In addition to the saguaro flowers, look for flowers on hedgehog, fishhook, prickly pear, and cholla cactus.

As always, a longer walk will immerse you into the landscape of this basin-and-range province, and walking is a good way to envision the task of pioneer travelers who had to find the best routes. The highest point is 4,687-foot (1,429-m) Wasson Peak. The 9.8-mile (15.8-km) Hugh Norris Trail, from the trailhead past the Sus Picnic Area, will take you to the summit and back. An interesting 8-mile (13 km) loop route to the summit combines the King Canyon, Hugh Norris, and Sendero Esperanza trails. The summit is not difficult to reach, and a 360-degree view of the surrounding mountain ranges, which seem to pop up as often as freckles on a fair-skinned youngster, is the reward. Open mine shafts in this area are a hazard, but those near the trail are well marked. A map is available.

Although the park does not offer a campground, Pima County's Gilbert Ray Campground is adjacent, and a stay there provides bonuses of desert sunsets. In the midst of early- and late-day bird activities, you can check out the saguaro flowers, which will give you clues about the marvelous interconnections of nature illustrated by the saguaro cactus. White-winged doves, nurtured by the nectar and fruit of this cactus, are the major distributor of its seeds. The insulated walls and cool interior (warm in winter) of the saguaro "condo" entice an assortment of residents who live in close quarters. Gila woodpeckers and gilded flickers build nests in cavities, although they are so fussy about their homesites that they often discard some choice sites, which cactus wrens, elf owls, phainopeplas, and others are quite happy to use. Honeybees are also attracted to the holes. Red-tailed and Harris hawks assemble bulky nests in the arm joints of saguaros.

Arizona-Sonora Desert Museum

You could wander for years in the Sonoran Desert without seeing and learning what takes only a few hours to absorb at the incredible Arizona-Sonora Desert Museum. Here you can observe animal behavior that eludes you in the wild. The museum features a jaguar and mountain lion living as neighbors. The simulated rocks and crevices of the small cat canyon provide homes for the agile and secretive margay, the once-hunted spotted ocelot, and the dark-colored jaguarundi.

Visitors also can see the "scary" creatures of the desert: scorpions, lizards, rattlesnakes, Gila monsters, and tarantulas (all of which are safely contained). Underwater windows make for great viewing of the charismatic otters and beavers. The magnificent desert bighorn sheep can be seen in their cliff-and-canyon enclosure that recreates a rocky area called "White Tanks" west of Phoenix. The prairie dog community is full of playful interaction. Other animals include the tortoise, Mexican wolf, deer, javelina, badger, kit fox, and coyote.

The walk-in aviary is fabulous and houses a great variety of birds that are well adjusted to visitors. They continue their daily business of living and assembling nests within four habitats representative of those that occur naturally in the Sonoran Desert.

The Earth Sciences Center features man-made "wet" and "dry" limestone caves, complete with stalactites and stalagmites. You will learn how packrats have long built nests in caves. These nests are interesting; artifacts 10,000 to 14,000 years old have been found in limestone caves in the huge nests of packrats, who cement their nests with urine to preserve them.

The plant displays are well done and include boojum trees, grassland plots, and a Demonstration Desert Garden, which demonstrates the use of native plants for home landscaping. There is also a Tohono O'odham Indian exhibit.

Leave the park by heading north on Sandario Road and then right on Avra Valley Road to US 10 to continue the tour.

Picacho Peak State Park

Dominated by impressive Picacho Peak, a landmark used by Spanish explorers, additional spectacular Saguaro scenery is found in Picacho Peak State Park. Go northwest on Interstate 10 to exit 219. Picacho Pass was the site of one of the few battles of the Civil War fought in the Southwest. In spring the slopes of the mountain are awash with golden poppies and other wildflowers that complement the saguaro, prickly pear, and other cactus blooms. This is an excellent place to camp adjacent to hiking trails and birds joyfully announcing the day.

The self-guiding nature trail has interpretive signs that identify the desert vegetation. The paloverde trees adapt to desert conditions by harvesting sunlight in their green bark and dropping their leaves when its dry. Certain areas of the desert can go two years without rain. Look for cholla, prickly pear, and creosote bush. A short trail also leads to the Children's Cave.

The big attraction in Picacho Peak State Park is the 2-mile (3.2 km) Hunter National Recreation Trail to the 3,374-foot (1,028-m) summit of Picacho Peak. This is a difficult trail—complete with cables for handholds along the route—that climbs to the

Memorial to Mormon Battalion Trail at Picacho Peak State Park, AZ.

upper saddle of the mountain and then on to the summit. Although only experienced hikers should go for the summit, it's fun to hike a portion of the trail for the great vistas and to gain some intimacy with the mountain. Indians once scouted the territory from the summit. Check with a ranger for current weather conditions near the top.

A gentler approach to the peak is via the 3.1-mile (5-km) Sunset Vista Trail. It wanders through the quiet desert away from the highway and then finally offers a route up the back side of Picacho Peak, connecting to the Hunter Trail near the summit.

You can learn much about the myths and truths concerning the elusive animal life of the Sonoran Desert at the evening campfire talks. For example, the Gila monster, although poisonous, is so secretive that your chances of seeing one are minimal. Myth says it won't let go if it bites you when provoked or cornered, but the truth is that it takes time to grind its jaws to inject the toxin when it bites. The danger of the gentle tarantula spider is a Hollywood myth and it is highly over-rated as a scary creature. The scorpions are dangerous, although nocturnal, so you should always check for them in boots or shoes.

Valley of the Sun

Phoenix sprawls across the "Valley of the Sun" and there is little choice except to travel right through this city on Interstate 10 and then Interstate 17 to connect to destinations north. You might want to stop at the nationally acclaimed Heard Museum, the Arizona Science Center, the Phoenix Art Museum, the Pioneer Arizona Living History Museum, or the Pueblo Grande Museum while you are in the area. If so, I'd suggest stopping at an information center before reaching the busy city to obtain a copy of *Arizona Traveler,* which has a city map of Phoenix.

Montezuma Castle

Two distinct cultures left remnants of their activity in the Verde Valley north of Phoenix. In A.D. 600, the Hohokam—the first permanent settlers—were farmers who grew corn, beans, squash, and cotton, and watered them by building irrigation ditches. The Sinagua Indians lived in nearby foothills and on the plateau above the valley. When the Hohokam migrated north to more fertile land, the peaceful Sinagua moved into the valley, adopted the irrigation system, and began building large pueblos about A.D. 1150, perhaps borrowing this architectural mode from the Anasazi.

A good example of a Sinagua pueblo is Montezuma Castle, which was misnamed by early white settlers who thought it had been built by Aztecs. It is now contained in a national monument and accessible from exit 289 on Interstate 17. A paved, wheelchair-accessible walkway loops from the visitor center to good views of the 20-room dwelling recessed in the cliff some 100 feet above. It is easy to see the appeal of this area near shading sycamore trees on the bottomland by Beaver Creek. Yet for some unknown reason, the Sinagua left the valley in the early 1400s.

A few miles north, again off Interstate 17, is Montezuma Well, a turquoise-blue pond that is a limestone sink formed long ago when an underground cavern collapsed. Springs replenish the water continuously, and both the Hohokam and Sinagua used its waters for irrigation. A Hohokam pithouse, Sinagua dwellings, and traces of ditches remain in this area where 150 to 200 Sinagua lived.

The tour now leaves the Interstate and heads west to US 89A to Cottonwood and continues on toward Clarkdale.

Tuzigoot National Monument

Near Clarkdale, Tuzigoot is another Sinagua village on a long limestone ridgeline above a vast tailings pond in the Verde Valley. The walkway here brings you right among this sprawling pueblo of stones and masonry. Rising up two stories in some places, the first floor has 77 rooms. When it was an active center of civilization, entry into the pueblo was via ladders through roof openings.

The visitor center has a Sinagua Room that provides more detailed hints about the daily lives of these prehistoric Indians. They wove cloth from cotton, ground corn, constructed baskets, dried skins, and were fine artisans, making a variety of stone tools that included axes, knives, and hammers. Macaws from Mexico are evidence of trading.

Nearby Dead Horse Ranch State Park offers a fine campground along the Verde River, with a stocked fishing lagoon and

Bighorn sheep nibbling on vegetation at the Arizona-Sonora Desert Museum, AZ.

both hiking and equestrian trails winding through vegetation that includes some 350 native plants. Over 100 bird species have been identified, so the birding is good and summer bird walks are scheduled.

Special Events:
Cottonwood celebrates an International Folk Festival in late April, when professional dancers and musicians present folk ballets from various countries. The first weekend of May features the Greater Cottonwood Antique Aeroplane and Auto Show and the Sizzlin' Salsa Sunday/Cinco de Mayo at Cottonwood's Historic Old Town.

Mining History at Jerome

From Dead Horse Ranch State Park, campers can view the spectacular setting of the town of Jerome on the side of Cleopatra Hill, which overlooks the Verde Valley. Once a wild mining camp with a booming population, it is today a colony of artists and craftspersons. Steep, winding streets with historic buildings and unique shops attract visitors to Jerome, which is a National Historic Landmark.

In Jerome State Historic Park is the preserved mansion of mining developer "Rawhide Jimmy" Douglas, which overlooks Jerome and "Rawhide Jimmy's" Little Daisy Mine. Designed as a hotel for visitors

---

Special Event:
Jerome hosts the annual Paseo de Casas the third weekend of May. This home tour features historic public buildings ranging from Victorian homes to renovated miners' shacks, an art exhibition, and a display of photographs. This is a self-paced tour with continuous shuttle service.

---

and investors, the adobe-brick structure featured a wine cellar, billiard room, and marble-faced bathrooms. Visitors today can view artifacts of the Douglas family, copper mining exhibits, antique equipment, and a three-dimensional model of Jerome. A billion dollars worth of copper and other ores were extracted via the 100 miles of subterranean tunnels and shafts that honeycomb the earth beneath Jerome.

Sedona and Oak Creek Canyon

After sidetracking south to Jerome, head north on US 89A to Sedona. Situated at the southern gateway to Oak Creek Canyon, Sedona is an upscale retirement and tourism area where hundreds of artists draw inspiration from the red rock landscape of buttes and monoliths that change colors and shapes with the time of day and the weather. So dazzling is this area that it is the second most visited site in Arizona. A slew of advertisements and films are set in this

Hedgehogs blooming along Ajo Mountain Drive in Organ Pipe Cactus National Monument, AZ.

locale, and Zane Grey used the canyon as the backdrop for his novel, *Call of the Canyon,* later persuading Hollywood to film a motion picture version of it here. All this makes for a busy Sedona; the Sedona Trolley is available for getting around the town, and sightseeing narration is provided.

Three miles south of Sedona off AZ 179 is the Chapel of the Holy Cross, a contemporary Catholic shrine built of red rock and dominated by a 90-foot (27-m) cross artistically placed in a photogenic position between two large, red sandstone peaks.

Special Events:
On the second weekend in May, Sedona hosts the Annual Hopi Show, with Hopi artists (traditional and contemporary), dancers, food, and cultural activities. It also hosts the Annual Western American Week at the end of May, with air and antique auto shows, art shows, a Wild West BBQ, and a country dance.

Scenic drives in this area will let you make other discoveries. The Red Rocks/Secret Mountain Wilderness to the northwest has many hiking trails to such attractions as Devil's Bridge. Hot-air balloon rides are offered by several commercial operators in Sedona.

Oak Creek Canyon Drive

Oak Creek Canyon Drive heads north along US 89A, curving between white, red, and yellow cliffs dotted with pine, cypress, and juniper trees, creekside cabins, occasional meadows, trout streams, and rocky gorges. According to the 1991 *Rand McNally Road Atlas*, this drive is one of the nation's eight top scenic highways among "*Arizona Traveler*'s great American road trips." The American Automobile Association recommends no trailer over 20 feet (6 m) in length on the climb to Flagstaff, although the lower elevation of the drive is not difficult.

Stop at Slide Rock State Park for an unusual splash in spring-fed Oak Creek, where it curves through meadows and pours over red rocks in small waterfalls and into pools, some deep, where people flock to enjoy the cool water in the hot sun. This open, sunny space is backed by massive, brilliantly colored red rock formations. The park is the site of the historic Pendley Homestead. Where three previous homesteaders had tried to grow crops and failed for lack of successful irrigation, Pendley made his irrigation system work, after

seven years of digging and working. The "Pendley Ditch" still irrigates the apple orchard, where one of Pendley's Arkansas black apple trees continues to grow. The park system, which has restored the original house and apple barn, staffs a visitor center; conducts experimental agriculture; and oversees the apple production, a vegetable garden, and produce sales. A walkway borders old equipment including the Pendley waterwheel, a sickle-bar mower, a two-row corn planter with fertilizer attachment, and many varieties of apple trees.

The drive past Slide Rock State Park ascends gradually along the creek with a succession of inviting forest service campgrounds by the water, where yellow columbines grow and canyon wrens sing. The last miles of the drive are the steepest approaching the Oak Creek Canyon Vista Point and rest stop. From the lookout points there you can see three switchback sections of the highway. It's hard to believe that this route began as a cattle trail and then became a rough wagon road as a shortcut to Flagstaff. The drive connects to Interstate 17 and then branches off again with

Oak Creek, Slide Rock State Park, AZ.

US 89A leading to the route to the Grand Canyon via US 180.

A scenic drive, US 180 edges Arizona's highest mountains, the San Francisco peaks, as it travels through the Kaibab National Forest. A major winter sports area, 12,663-foot (3,860-m) Mount Humphreys is the state's tallest point. Summer attracts hikers to the high country, while wildflowers on the lower slopes are the attraction in this spring season.

Grand Canyon National Park

Superlatives pop up continually when speaking of the Grand Canyon. I wonder what Don Lopez de Cardenas—a Captain in Coronado's expedition—felt when he discovered the Grand Canyon in 1540? Perhaps the same feelings that people still experience today when they see this vast gash in earth slowly, yet violently, incised into rock by the Colorado River. Through periods of geologic uplift, the river has often met opposition as revealed by its twisting, turning, 277-mile (446-km) journey through the park. The Colorado is no smooth-bottomed, easy-flowing stream; raft expeditions on the river encounter 95 sets of rapids that attest to changing passageways between cliffs, rock-studded whitewater, and river as rain sink from upstream and overhead. Layers of exposed rock reveal geologic stories that reach back 2 billion years and can be read like pages in a book. The wild and exhilarating river—along with rain, snow, frost, gravity, and wind—has performed a stupendous act of erosion.

EXPLORING THE SOUTH RIM

The highway brings you into the park at Grand Canyon Village on the South Rim, where tent and trailer campgrounds, a store, a post office, a bank, a ranger station, and a visitor center are located. From here you can set out on foot or by vehicle to explore. Also available are motor coach tours along the rim.

The easy South Rim Trail on the brink of the twisting canyon connects Hermit's Rest—where a unique cliff house with an observation deck is available at the termi-nus of the West Rim Drive—to Mather Point in a little over 18 miles (29 km). If you have enough time in the park, this is obviously an excellent way to continuously view the canyon from varying perspectives, perhaps doing one section at a time.

A great way to visit the sites in the village area and see the canyon is to walk the short section between Lookout Studio and Mather Point, stopping along the way. Lookout Studio—with free telescope services—is constructed of rough-cut limestone and designed to blend in with the rim. The fireplace in Bright Angel Lodge is composed of all the types of rock in the canyon placed in proper chronological sequence. Hopi House is modeled after a Hopi Indian pueblo of Old Oraibi; an historic railroad station is just across the road. Grandeur, Yavapai, and Mather points offer superb vistas of the canyon.

The West Rim Drive to Hermit's Rest delights with viewpoints and many places from which to access the Rim Trail, with the Colorado River visible far below at Hopi, Mohave, and Pima points. Near the end of this drive you can see trails zigzagging far below in the canyon. At this eleva-

Lone sunset watcher at Grand Canyon, AZ.

tion of approximately 7,000 feet (2,134 m), the river is about a vertical mile below.

The Bright Angel Trail is the famed trail into the canyon and to the river, and some visitors even hike down to the river and back up to the North Rim—a difficult although outstanding way to see Grand Canyon (permits are required). Several other long hikes penetrate the canyon area. John Muir and John Burroughs descended this trail by mule in the snow, and mule trips still can be taken into the canyon, either overnight or one-day trips. Advance reservations are required for the mule trips and for overnight stays at Phantom Ranch and Bright Canyon Campground. Rafting the river with commercial operators elicits intimacy with the canyon and is the best perspective for some, but this requires reservations long in advance for a trip of up to three weeks. Horse tours also are offered on the rim.

It takes no advance plans, however, to sample the Bright Angel Trail on a day hike, and many take advantage of the opportunity to place their feet on this path, some traveling a short distance, others hiking to the 3-mile (4.8-km) Resthouse or 4.6 miles (7.4 km) to Indian Gardens. The first three miles are the most difficult as the trail switchbacks down to the Tonto Plateau. The return trip is a steep climb in warm weather, but it's fun if you're in shape; you might even see some wildlife along the way (perhaps an Albert squirrel) and certainly some geology. I have good memories of doing this while someone down below played a flute, sending mystical, sweet sounds to accompany the visual high.

Sightseeing along the East Rim Drive can be part of the route east out of the park. Along this drive is the trailhead to the more difficult descent into the canyon, the South Kaibab Trail, and a side road to Yaki Point. At Grandview Point there is a connecting trail to the long, east-west Tonto Trail. Tusayan Ruins and Museum tells the story of people who made the Colorado Plateau and this canyon their home. Surprisingly,

Mule trip into Grand Canyon, AZ.

hundreds of small ruins of ancient Indian pueblos are found in the canyon and on the rim. Lipan Point offers a river view. An excellent stopping point is Desert View and the Watchtower, with unsurpassed views of Marble Canyon, the Colorado River, and the Painted Desert.

It's of interest that Lieutenant Joseph Ives led an expedition into the canyon area in the 1850s and admired its beauty but said, "The region is, of course, altogether valueless. . . . Ours has been the first, and will doubtless be the last, party of whites to visit this profitless locality."

How would Ives react to the notion that beauty is sufficient to attract vast numbers to the Grand Canyon today? And although millions of years have produced the present canyon scene, it continues to change and enchant everyone who visits. This dazzling, swirling, perforated, and striated landscape woven with such kaleidoscopic earthy hues is a marvel of nature's endless versatility and power.

CHAPTER 2

Oklahoma's Cherokee Strip: *History Tour with Wildlife*

MILEAGE

Approximately 500 miles (800 km)

RESOURCES

- Oklahoma Tourism and Recreation Department, P.O. Box 60789, Oklahoma City, Oklahoma 73146-0789; (800) 651-OKLA.
- Bartlesville Chamber of Commerce, 201 S.W. Keeler, Box 2366, Bartlesville, OK 74005; (918) 336-8708, (800) 364-8708.
- Prairie Song, Rt. 1, Box 286, Dewey, OK 74029; (918) 534-2662.
- Tallgrass Prairie Reserve, P.O. Box 458, Pawhuska, OK 74056; (918) 286-4803.
- Kaw City KawFest: (405) 363-1260.
- Ponca City Tourism Bureau, 5th & Grand, Box 1109, Ponca City, OK 74602; (405) 767-8888; (800) 475-4400.
- Enid Chamber of Commerce, 210 Kenwood Building, Box 907, Enid, OK 73702; (405) 237-2494.

- Salt Plains National Wildlife Refuge, Refuge Manager, Route 1, Box 76, Jet, OK 73749; (405) 626-4794.
- Cherokee Chamber of Commerce, 111 S. Grand, Cherokee, OK 73728; (405) 596-3053.
- Fairview Chamber of Commerce, 105 S. Main, Box 180, Fairview, OK 73737; (405) 227-2527.

CAMPGROUNDS

OSAGE COVE CAMPGROUND ON KAW LAKE: Several campground loops along the water with hookups, restrooms with showers, and dump station; (405) 762-5611.

GREAT SALT PLAINS STATE PARK: Three miles (5 km) north of Jet off OK 38; tent and hookup campsites, restrooms with showers, dump station; (405) 626-4731.

ALABASTER CAVERNS STATE PARK: Seven miles (11 km) south of Freedom; tent and hookup sites; restrooms with showers; (405) 621-3381.

BOILING SPRINGS STATE PARK: Six miles (10 km) east of Woodward on OK 34C; tent and hookup campsites, restrooms with showers, dump station; (405) 256-7664.

ROMAN NOSE STATE PARK: Eight miles (13 km) north of Watonga on OK 8A; tent and hookup campsites, restrooms with showers, dump station; (405) 623-7281.

Do you remember the words of that grand musical, *Oklahoma*? They told of the joys of a beautiful morning in a brand new state that was going to treat people great.

It was in 1907 that Oklahoma became the 46th state, not long after the Cherokee Strip—also called the Cherokee Outlet—was opened to settlers on September 16, 1893, in the greatest land rush in the history of the West. Imagine what happened on a long strip of land just south of Kansas—226 miles (364 km) wide by 58 miles (93 km) long—when a pistol shot allowed some 100,000 settlers to race by buggy, horse, bicycle, or foot to stake out a homestead on 7 million acres of free land. It was a time of pandemonium and instant towns.

Directly west of the Cherokee Nation in what was then called Indian Territory, the Cherokee Strip was originally set aside for the Cherokee as a passageway west to the great buffalo hunting grounds. The land rush changed all that. It was an event urged by "boomers"—bankers, merchants, railroad builders, and business and political leaders—to allow settlement and development. Statehood joined the Indian and Oklahoma territories.

Today, less than a hundred years after statehood, it's exciting to visit this historical acreage and see the changes. But, as the song says, the flowers still bloom on the prairie, there is still plenty of room to swing a rope, plenty of air, and plenty of heart.

Spring is a delightful time to visit, before the heat of summer. The eastern redbud trees (Oklahoma's official state tree) are in blossom and wildlife refuges are vibrant with migrating birds. April temperatures are in the low seventies; in May, they climb toward eighty degrees. Spring also heralds the beginning of the unique selenite crystal digging season in the Great Salt Plains. (Autumn is also a good time to visit, when the rich crops of the strip are harvested and the tall grass of the prairie is high.) To travel west across the Cherokee Strip is to move from the "green country" of northeast Oklahoma to a more arid landscape where cowboys and cattle furnish strong clues that this is where that vast landscape called "the West" begins.

Bartlesville

The eastern gateway to the Cherokee Strip, Bartlesville is a good place to begin your tour in slow fashion west across the state for a peaceful, yet exciting trip. The terrain is easy to negotiate, the traffic is light, the roads are pleasant, and no really large cities are en route.

Many of Bartlesville's buildings are historic, built during the oil boom that occurred between 1900 and 1920. The home of Frank Phillips—the barber-turned-banker-turned-oil tycoon who founded Phillips Petroleum Company—is one of these. This Greek revival-style building is now open to the public. You can also tour the Dewey Hotel, a building constructed in 1900 that drew early ranchers and oil developers to its gaming room in the tower. A structure of distinction of more recent origin is the award-winning, nineteen-story Price Tower, which was designed by Frank Lloyd Wright and constructed in 1956. The town even offers a Tom Mix Museum. In addition to oil, the Cherokee tribe, based in nearby Tahlequah, is a strong influence on the character of northeastern Oklahoma. Today, more Native Americans live in Oklahoma than in any other state.

To the north of Bartlesville, near Dewey, is Prairie Song, one family's way of honoring the heritage of the cowboy culture that dates back to the original era of

Special Events:

Planes, Trains, and Sunfest Thangs is an event held the first weekend in June that includes the National Biplane Expo, the Sunfest Festival (entertainment, art, international cuisine), and Sunfest Express Rail Excursions. The OK Mozart International Festival, a tribute to Wolfgang Amadeus Mozart that includes parades, outdoor markets, art exhibits, garden cafes, and concerts, is held the second weekend in June. (If you're near Bartlesville in mid-September, the Indian Summer Festival features an Indian powwow, food, storytelling, crafts, and other tours and activities.)

Woolaroc Museum near Bartlesville, OK.

homesteading in the 1890s. Although it can be seen only via group appointments or during the Cowboy Rendezvous, Prairie Song is a quaint village of several authentically decorated buildings that were added on to a working cattle ranch to host group affairs.

Woolaroc

Enter the magic of the Cherokee Strip by taking OK 123 twelve miles southwest of Bartlesville to Woolaroc. Keep a lookout along both sides of the highway for wild horses—mustangs moved here by the Bureau of Land Management that now graze the grasslands of the Prairie National Wild Horse Refuge. Don't approach them; they are wild.

The discovery of oil on these plains brought a new era and riches to some of its people. Frank Phillips, oil man and adopted White Chief of the Osage tribe, diverted some money to start Woolaroc, a 3,600-acre area that began as his ranch retreat and was expanded to include a museum, a wildlife preserve, nature trails, and a Y-Indian Guide Center, which is affiliated with the National YMCA. Artists and craftpersons

give insights into how tools and ornaments were made hundreds of years ago.

The first room of the Woolaroc Museum—and the reason for its founding—was a sandstone "hangar" built to house and display the monoplane that won the 1927 Trans-Pacific Dole Flight. It now hangs in the lower level. Visitors enter the museum through an impressive doorway that features an artistic display of dancing Indians; the museum showcases original paintings, sculptures, artifacts, and has an extensive accumulation of Native American crafts that chronicle human history in the West. Works by Remington, Russell, Leigh, and others are magnificent. Such art makes it easier to visualize wagons and horses on the "Trail of Tears," a Navajo Fire Dance, and the Great Temple Mound Village. Indian beadwork of various tribes, an Osage cradle board, a blanket used by Geronimo, Hopi pottery, and a fine collection of Colt firearms are some of the museum pieces.

The exterior of the museum is enhanced by stained-glass windows, colorful flower gardens, and sculptures. The tulips blooming in the spring are spectacular.

The adjacent Phillips Lodge, where Frank Phillips entertained such guests as Will Rogers, Herbert Hoover, and Harry Truman, is also open to the public and, on the guided tour, you will hear anecdotes about the bark-covered piano, the "million dollar" chandeliers, and Blackstone's magic card. An excellent assortment of Indian rugs and blankets decorate the lodge. Although not a hunter himself, Phillips acquired a collection of animal heads and horns that was highly rated by Lloyds of London. Many are game trophies from friends; others, such as the zebra, camel, and wildebeest, are from an unsuccessful attempt by Phillips to breed and raise wild animals from foreign lands at Woolaroc.

From the lodge porch you can view Clyde Lake—built to power oil wells—and Indian teepees. Live native animals such as deer, elk, longhorn cattle, and bison, can be seen along the 2-mile drive through the wildlife preserve. Buffalo barbecue sandwiches and other refreshments may be purchased and eaten in the picnic area. You'll

Special Event:
Prairie Song Cowboy Rendezvous, a weekend of food, entertainment, workshops, and demonstrations, is held in late spring.

soon learn that tea in Oklahoma is served iced unless otherwise specified.

The Tallgrass Prairie Preserve

Pawhuska, the capitol of the Osage Indian Nation, is another town replete with historic buildings and the Osage Tribal Museum. It is also a place where cattle culture is evident and the barbecue served at restaurants is superb. To visit the country's largest Tallgrass Prairie Preserve, turn north on Kihekah Street. Big bluestem, switchgrass, and Indiangrass once covered much of this prairie land, part of the 142 million acres of tallgrass prairie in the heart of the United States. Today, nearly all the original tallgrass prairie is gone.

Frontier homestead of Prairie Song, OK.

The Nature Conservancy purchased a 30,000-acre parcel from the Chapman Bernard Ranch in late 1989 to create this preserve. Fire and grazing bison (along with some initial cattle grazing) are used to replenish the tallgrass ecosystem and maintain its natural ecological processes. In the spring of 1993, 22,000 acres were burned. By late summer, grasses up to 10 feet high waved and rippled in the wind across the open prairie. Three hundred head of bison arrived in October.

The tallgrass ecosystem is more than grasses and bison. In addition to some 300 species of birds and 80 species of mammals, more than 250 species of plants find niches, with wildflowers providing splashes of color from mid-May into summer. Prairie

chickens "boom" in the mating season of spring. Hawks survey the land for prey.

Osage writer John Joseph Matthews described this prairie best: "The impression was one of space . . . wild space but never silent. In summer the grasses whispered and laughed and sang, changing to mournful whispers during the autumn, then screaming like a demented woman when winter turned the emerald to copper."

The historic bunkhouse on the preserve resounds with memories of when John Wayne came to visit Ben Johnson. Two scenic turnouts and two self-guided walking tours are reached along the 50-mile (80-km) drive, where vistas change throughout the seasons. The mostly level road is gravel and can be dusty in dry weather or soft in wet conditions.

Kaw Lake

As the tour continues west on US 60, it passes the southern tip of Kaw Lake, a 17,000-acre impoundment on the Arkansas River. Otoe-Missourian Chief Francis Pipestem offered the groundbreaking dedication prayer in 1966, in which he asked, "that men will come to see more clearly not that which divides them, but that which unites them." Named after the Kaw Indians, this winding lake spreads from the dam north and into Kansas. It is a popular outdoor recreation spot with camping, hiking, fishing, boating, swimming, and picnicking. Osage Cove, a U.S. Army Corps of Engineers facility, offers the most accessible campground on the tour. A great way to start the day is with a breakfast cruise on the lake, or you might prefer some angling. This campground provides access to the Eagle View Hiking Trail, which edges the lake for a few miles north.

Special Event:
Kaw City sponsors the KawFest the first weekend of June, a celebration featuring a car show, jet-ski races, and sailboat regatta.

Ponca City

The site of Ponca City was chosen by B. S. Barnes before the land run. Unusual among Cherokee Strip towns, it was a planned town settled by a lottery drawing, founded by individuals rather than the typical government-designated townsites. It developed into a gracious community, but there is little doubt that the Marland Estate and Mansion is an outstanding highlight.

Between 1925 and 1928, former governor and oil baron E. W. Marland spent 5.5 million dollars to construct a 55-room, Italian Renaissance "Palace on the Prairie" that was modeled after the Davanzatti Palace in Florence, Italy. Open to the public, the Marland Mansion on Monument Road is three floors and 30,000 square feet of splendor. This work of art has hand-carved wood paneling, Florentine grillwork, polished stone staircases, stained-glass windows, sparkling crystal chandeliers, arches, and vaulted ceilings embellished with intricate designs. The family history is fascinating, and you may come away wanting to know more about Marland's second wife, Lyde.

Philanthropist Marland was responsible for a wonderful addition to Ponca City that is a tribute to the thousands of women who suffered hardships to create homes in new lands. He commissioned a $300,000 sculpture by Bryant Baker—voted the winner based on models submitted by twelve sculptors nationwide—titled "Confident." This famous Pioneer Woman Statue can be viewed at 14th and Lake Road. The 17-foot-tall (5 m) bronze figure of a woman striding hand-in-hand with her son embodies the courageous spirit of the pioneers who came to settle the Cherokee Strip. Admission to the adjacent Pioneer Woman Museum is free.

Marland's first home is now Ponca City's Cultural Center and Indian Museum, an outstanding facility honoring Oklahoma's pioneer spirit and Native American culture; it also houses Bryant Baker's studio, which was moved there after the sculptor's death.

Government Springs Park in Enid

A jog southwest on US 60 will take you to another city spawned by the land run, Enid. Although this is the largest city of the Cherokee Strip, it has a population of only 45,000 and is still easily traversed. This is one area where the famed Chisholm Trail crossed the Cherokee Strip as it headed north from Texas to railheads farther north. After the Civil War, Texas had some six million head of longhorn cattle, but little market for them until they began driving their cattle across the Outlet to railroad markets in Kansas and Missouri. Before

Special Event:
Ponca City celebrates its Iris Festival in early May, which is an assortment of activities including a juried fine art and craft show, bicycle tour, chocolate festival, and flower and garden tours.

Native American art on entryway to Woolaroc Museum, OK.

Special Event:
Enid celebrates the Cherokee Strip Days Celebration in early September, an annual commemoration of the original land run that includes a parade, luncheons, an arts and crafts show, entertainment, a 5K fun run, and Professional Rodeo and Cattleman's Association rodeo.

long, the locals realized it was more profitable to raise cattle on the lush grasses of the Outlet than to drive herds from Texas.

Enid was one of the four designated land offices for the land run in 1893 and the only one surviving today. Complete with huge old books mapping the land parcels, you can visit the land office in the Humphrey Heritage Village, restored for the Cherokee Strip Centennial celebration and located east from US 60 on US 412. It is adjacent to the Museum of the Cherokee Strip and to Government Springs Park. Of particular interest in the park is a statue unveiled at the centennial. To honor those who staked claims and spent a lonely night waiting for their families to catch up with them, a life-sized bronze sculpture, "Holding the Claim," was created by Harold T. Holden. It was fitting that Dr. Charles Ogle, who had a grandfather who participated in the land run, unveiled this artwork in 1993 at its permanent site in Enid's Government Springs Park. I was lucky enough to see this symbolic sculpture unveiled. A 29-cent postage stamp of the land run was also released.

Homesteaders Original Sod House Museum

From Enid, head west on US 60-412. Here the wind blows across the prairie grasses and across the fields of wheat, and it's not difficult to sense the pioneer spirit still so vibrant in this region. This county, Garfield, is one of the largest wheat-producing counties in the country. If you turn north

on OK 8 and travel toward Aline, you will be able to sample a little of that pioneer spirit at the Sod House Museum.

The first homes for the new settlers were usually "soddies," homes that were hastily constructed of blocks of grass-covered sod (using what the land offered) that dried in the sun. Of the thousands of these soddies originally built on the Oklahoma plains, only one, built by homesteader Marshal McCully in 1894, survives. You can walk inside it and view its furnishings and photographs at the Sod House Museum.

Ponder what happened after the wild land run when 50,000 settlers had staked claims. Most of the pioneers came back in the spring of 1894 to build these sod houses; it was too late to plant crops. In 1894, there was an abundance of two crops: watermelons and turnips. In the years that followed, sweet potatoes and cornmeal were staples, with meat furnished by hunting squirrel, jackrabbit, prairie chicken, and quail. Cow chips (dried manure) were used to fuel cooking fires. The first good wheat crop was harvested in 1897, when times were easier for the pioneers. They then were able to raise turkeys.

Great Salt Plains

Not many miles to the north of the Sod House Museum—a jog east on US 64 and then north on OK 38—is a unique natural area: the Great Salt Plains. If you think salt plains are boring, think again. This vast recreation area includes a state park, the Great Salt Plains Reservoir, the Salt Fork of the Arkansas River, and Sand Creek, all mostly encompassed by the Salt Plains National Wildlife Refuge.

GREAT SALT PLAINS STATE PARK

Great Salt Plains State Park is a wonderful place to stay for a few days and enjoy digging for crystals, swimming, boating, hiking, water skiing, fishing, and viewing the wildlife in this huge recreational complex. You can choose riverfront camping or sites along the reservoir, where there is a sandy beach. The riverfront campground has great views of the fluid perfection of the water rolling over the dam and white pelicans skimming across the river. A handicapped-accessible fishing dock on the reservoir is a short drive away. Channel catfish and bass are abundant in the lake and fishing lines are often seen strung out along the river. Located near the river in the RV camping area is the 0.25-mile (0.4-km) wheelchair-accessible Tonkawa Interpretative Trail, which provides a good introduction to the flora of the area. Allow some camp time for visiting the Selenite Crystal Area and the Salt Plains National Wildlife Refuge.

SALT PLAINS NATIONAL WILDLIFE REFUGE

Named "Salt Plains" because of the thin layer of salt that covers the flats, the area consists of a deltaic river deposit of varied and mixed layers of clay, sand, and gravel. Although the salt plains were once in the midst of Cherokee Indian Territory, the treaty with the United States provided that the salt plains were for the use of other Indian tribes as well, since the salt obtained there was needed by all. The area also had great value to the Indians for its rich hunting, as vast herds of animals were attracted to the salt supply and the various habitats.

Today, this area is a 32,000-acre national wildlife refuge, with 12,000 acres of salt flats, 10,000 acres of impoundment, and 10,000 acres of upland. The refuge is an island that supports many special habitats surrounded by a sea of agricultural lands. During the spring and fall migrations, some 24,000 geese and 25,000 ducks are attracted to these wetlands; more than 100,000 waterfowl are tallied in some winters. The

wildlife refuge is a designated National Natural Landmark; the headquarters are located 1 mile west of OK 38 and 2 miles south of OK 11.

A combination of pondweed, cattails, wild millet, smartweed, and other wild plants and some 1,300 acres of planted wheat, maize, peas, and rye feed the waterfowl. Cottonwood, red cedar, willow, and sandhill plum trees are found in certain habitat areas. Forbs and grasses provide food for the wildlife. Mulberry, hackberry, walnut, elm, and soapberry proliferate in the woodland habitat, which provides cover for deer and wild turkeys.

The 2.5-mile (4-km) Harold F. Miller Auto Tour and the 1.25-mile (2-km) Eagle Roost Trail, both of which are accessible near the refuge headquarters, are excellent ways to observe the flora and fauna of the refuge among marshes, woods, ponds, tree nesting sites (high nesting boxes are provided for wood ducks), and planted feeding fields. A tower lets visitors watch wildlife without disturbing them.

Look for the state bird—the scissor-tailed flycatcher—which nests in the refuge. Mallards, pintails, green-winged teals, and 16 other species of ducks are frequently sighted. Sandhill cranes and the endangered whooping cranes stop during migrations. Other large birds include herons and egrets. Waterbirds include Franklin's gulls, avocets, yellowlegs, sandpipers, dowitches, white-faced ibises, and godwits. Mississippi kites nest in the refuge yearly. Bobwhite quail and ring-necked pheasants are common. In all, 296 species of birds are enough to thrill birders.

White-tailed deer are sighted frequently in the spring. Other mammals found in the refuge are raccoons, badgers, opossums, squirrels, coyotes, muskrats, beavers, and bobcats.

SELENITE CRYSTAL AREA

Stretching out an openness that is dazzling white in the sunlight, the salt flat on the western edge of the reservoir has become a magnet for those who enjoy "selenite crystal digging." Adults are just as uninhibited as children as they become absorbed in this

Selenite crystal digging at Great Salt Plains, OK.

unusual activity. During the season in which it is permitted—daylight hours from April 1 through October 15—human figures dot this expanse, which is devoid of vegetation, intently concentrating on the delicate search for interesting crystal formations. You might note the similarity of the scene to that of beach walkers collecting agates by the ocean. The area for digging, which is rotated yearly, can be reached by traveling 6 miles (9.6 km) west of Jet on US 64, continuing north on a dirt road for 3 miles (4.8 km), and going 1 mile (1.6 km) east to the gate.

Insider's Tips:

No permits are required. Ten pounds of crystals plus one large cluster for personal use per day are allowed. Drive only on prescribed routes in the salt plains, as quicksand is found in some areas, and dig only in the posted area. Please do not disturb nesting birds.

Selenite is a crystalline form of the common mineral gypsum (which is hydrous calcium sulfate and is used to make plaster casts for broken bones). In these salt flats, gypsum forms selenite crystals just below the salt-encrusted surface in the wet, salty soil. The chocolate brown color is caused by the presence of iron oxide. The finer the soil, the clearer the crystal. Sand and clay particles are incorporated within the crystals, often resulting in an "hourglass" shape only found here. Crystals can occur as singles, penetration twins, and clusters. Individual crystals have measured up to seven inches, with complex combinations that weigh as much as 38 pounds. For selenite to crystallize, the minerals in the soil must be present in a certain concentration. If rain dilutes the minerals too much, the crystals will dissolve.

A little rain, however, is no problem, and does not produce the expected usual muddy affair because the salt flats do not have the sticky consistency of ordinary mud. Although it isn't difficult to find crystals, you'll pick up some good techniques if you read the brochure on the selenite crystal

area available at the campground. With a shovel or some sort of scooping tool, dig a hole about two feet deep and allow some water to seep into it (the water table is near the surface). Then use your hand (this tactile tool is best) or a container to splash around and gently explore for crystals. Remember that the crystals are fragile, so handle them gently. Some diggers like to use a flat, rectangular wooden strainer to wash off the crystals. Let them dry in the sun and wind.

An observation tower with a 20-power spotting scope has been placed at the entrance to the digging area. An array of mounds accumulate where people have been digging, but these just provide a more intriguing habitat for threatened snowy plovers, American avocets, and the endangered interior least terns that nest in this area.

Special Event:

In late April, Cherokee sponsors the Crystal Festival with a selenite digging contest that includes instructions for beginners, citywide garage sales, crystal bingo, and a barbecue dinner (advance tickets needed).

Alabaster Caverns State Park

West along the Cimarron River and a jog south on OK 50 is the small town of Freedom, where you drive through "Cowtown Main Street." Size doesn't keep the people of Freedom from sponsoring an annual rodeo billed as "The Biggest Open Rodeo in the West" the third weekend in August.

Another outstanding natural attraction is just a few miles south of Freedom: Alabaster Caverns State Park. The underground centerpiece of this 200-acre park is billed as the world's largest gypsum cave open to the public. This cave has three surveyed levels for a total of 6,146 feet (1,873 m) of passageways, with the central layer of 2,300 feet (701 m) open for tours; it is a comfortable walk-through. The other levels are not walkable and are often just a jumble of rocks. Twelve openings are discernible in the main cavern, although only half of these are accessible.

In addition to the hydrous calcium sulfate (gypsum) formations in the cave, there are formations of alabaster (anhydrous calcium sulfate) and selenite (the crystalline form of gypsum). It is believed that this black alabaster deposit is the only one in North America. A sample from here is displayed at the Smithsonian Institution; only three caves worldwide have this type of rock formation. With the energy of moving water continuously at work, change is constant in the cave. Formations are different here from those found in limestone caves because of the solubility of gypsum.

Wear good walking shoes and a light jacket for the fifty-degree temperature during the one-hour guided tour down the 330 steps of the cave. After entering the large natural opening, you will descend about 40 feet (12 m) on a stairway to the lowest point of the tour. The Nescatunga gypsum ceiling in this first area, called the collapsed section, looms 50 feet (15 m) overhead. The tour then passes the selenite mouse and sandwich rock, followed by black alabaster, and then the stream that formed the cave. After viewing the encampment room, the selenite boulder (680 tons of gypsum), and the total darkness room, the tour enters the hand-carved walkway to the second, or dome, section of the cave, where there are nine major domes, including the Cathedral, Sweetheart, and Keyhole domes. The third, or channel, section is the best place to observe the abrasive action of water. A small waterfall is found here along with the only stalactite included in the tour, although it is only 0.75 inch in length since gypsum stalactites are extremely slow in forming. This one is probably 30,000 years old. A shuttle returns people to the entrance area after a walk of approximately 0.75 mile (1.2 km).

Bats are the most distinctive animal residents of the park, particularly in the caves. Five species use the cave on and off during the year: cave myotis, western big-eared, eastern pipistrelle, Mexican free-

RV exploring backroads near Glass Mountains, OK.

tailed, and western big brown bats. In addition to their unusual proficiency in natural sonar, they "swim" through the air, rather than actually flying. Tiger salamanders and a cave-dwelling crayfish are also found in the caverns.

The 0.5-mile (0.8-km) Cedar Canyon Interpretative Trail offers some insights into the vegetation of the park on this more arid side of the Cherokee Strip. The path leads down into Cedar Canyon and up the other side, where a natural bridge of gypsum rock once stood; it crumbled in 1992. The gypsum rock, a soft, easily scratched rock, in this landscape was once covered with water. A small stream flows in the canyon bottom. Lizards (the collared lizard is the state lizard) are seen among the rocky outcrops, where they can abscond into cracks if spooked or if they become too hot in the sun. These reptiles also do "push-ups" to cool off, raising their bodies away from the hot rock surface.

 Insider's Tips:
The cave tour is not recommended for those who are claustrophobic or have respiratory or heart problems. Watch for poison ivy along the trails.

Boiling Springs State Park

Thirty miles (48 km) southwest of Alabaster Caverns State Park is a major river, the North Canadian, and Boiling Springs State Park, so named for the cool springs that "boil up" at some 200 gallons per minute through white sand at the edge of the river. Containing the last stand of "big timber" in western Oklahoma, the park is a pleasant overnight choice, with hiking trails, a swimming pool, and adjacent golf course. Even in spring the paths are thick with leaves; morels often are found by observant hikers. Near the campsites, slender trees immersed in the waters of a pretty lake create enchanting morning reflections reminiscent of a bayou.

Special Event:
In early September, Fairview hosts the Old Time Threshing Bee, with living history demonstrations of early Oklahoma that include threshing, baling and milling, an antique car show, a tractor pull, music, and food and fashion shows.

Woodward and the Glass Mountains

Just to the west of the Boiling Springs State Park is Woodward, a city forged by the iron wheels of the Santa Fe Railroad and home of the interesting Plains Indians and Pioneers Museum. The next stop is Fairview—southeast on US 412—but the drive there is part of the fun. Although there are some good views along the highway, the gravel roads south of the highway are easily traveled in dry weather and offer good vistas of the Glass Mountains. These mountains rise as photogenic rust-hued ridges, spires, and buttes of eroded shale and sandstone layered and capped with harder gypsum and alabaster rock. This countryside is awash with red soil and green grasses among the scattered farms that are interspersed with richly colored arroyos and badlands-type hills—a pretty place to wander slowly. Rockhounds hunt for jasper, quartz, agate, alabaster, petrified wood, fossils, hematite pyrite, and dolomite pyramids in these mountains. Indian artifacts and prehistoric animal bones are found throughout the county.

Fairview

Another town founded in 1894, Fairview is home to one of the state's largest Mennonite communities and the Mennonite Brethren Church, where tours are offered. This is a peaceful, friendly agricultural town where activities include quilt-making and threshing bees. The Major County Historical Society Museum features antique tractors, steam engines, and historic buildings; the refurbished railroad depot is a recent addition.

Roman Nose State Park

Although Fairview is the last stop on our tour in the Cherokee Strip, travelers heading south might want to stop at Roman Nose State Park, a theme resort that highlights the rich heritage of the Cheyenne and Plains Indians. Named after a Cheyenne Chief, this recreational complex has an intriguing assortment of attractions including the Spring of Everlasting Waters, a campground, rent-a-Tepee, trails, golf, and fishing. *Vacations* Magazine named this place one of the top ten best family vacations in the nation in 1991.

Traveling Oklahoma's Cherokee Strip will probably surprise you with its spectrum of surprisingly refreshing attractions and landscapes. I must admit I would never have thought of touring the area if I had not been invited on a writer's tour. I came home thinking: do RVers have any idea what they're missing? So I'm passing along my recommendation.

The people of Oklahoma are friendly and known for their quality beef and barbecued meat. They've built a good life here and they judge people fairly. If you hear the expression "all hat and no cattle," you'll know they're referring to someone pretending to be something he or she isn't. After touring the Cherokee Strip, you might feel like singing, "Yeeow! a-yip-i-o-ee-ay! You're doin' fine, Oklahoma!"

CHAPTER 3

Northern California Coast:
Redwood Cathedrals along a Wild Shore

MILEAGE

Approximately 300 miles

RESOURCES

- Redwood National Park: (707) 464-6101.
- Eureka Chamber of Commerce: (800) 346-3482; (707) 442-3738.
- Skunk Railroad: (800) 77-SKUNK; (707) 964-6371.
- Victorian Village of Ferndale: (707) 786-4477.
- Fort Bragg–Mendocino Coast Chamber of Commerce: (800)-726-2780; (707) 961-6300.

CAMPGROUNDS

REDWOOD NATIONAL PARK: South from the Oregon border; Jedediah Smith Redwoods State Park, Prairie Creek Redwoods State Park, Elk Prairie Campground, and Gold Bluff all have campsites, restrooms with showers; reservations by calling MISTIX: (800) 444-7275 (May through September).

PATRICK POINT STATE PARK: Ten miles (16 km) north of Trinidad; campsites and restrooms with showers; call MISTIX at (800) 444-7275 for reservations.

HUMBOLDT REDWOODS STATE PARK: Forty-five miles (72 km) south of Eureka via US 101; two park campgrounds located along Avenue of the Giants: Burlington near park headquarters on CA 254 has campsites, restrooms with showers; Hidden Springs Campground is five miles (8 km) south of headquarters with campsites, restrooms with showers; reservations by calling MISTIX at (800) 444-7275.

WESTPORT-UNION LANDING STATE PARK: Two miles (3.2 km) north of Westport; several entry roads to primitive campsites with pit toilets.

MACKERRICHER STATE PARK: Three miles (4.8 km) north of Fort Bragg; campsites and restrooms with showers, some hookups; reservations: MISTIX (800) 444-7275.

RUSSIAN GULCH STATE PARK: Two miles (3.2 km) north of Mendocino; campsites and restrooms with showers; phone MISTIX at (800) 444-7275 for reservations.

Any time of year works for viewing the temperate rain forests of northern California. In rain or sun, in slanting sunbeams or summer fog, in spring or autumn, even in winter storms, you can witness how year-round factors influence the dominance of the magnificent redwood trees. And you will certainly be impressed.

The world's tallest living things, these conifer trees and their surrounding forest are a national treasure. Mind-boggling sights greet travelers who get out of their cars and walk among them; you can almost feel the pulse of natural forces that produced these wondrous green cathedrals. Consider that this redwood tree species has been around since the time of dinosaurs. This lengthy period of successful natural architectural construction should surely evoke our reverence. There is no better place to feel at peace and connect with the spirit of all life than in this forest. Walk softly, but do walk there!

One season stands out as particularly enchanting for a visit to the redwood forest: spring. In late April or early May, graceful rhododendron shrubs burst into a profusion of pink-purple flowers beneath the towering red-barked trees. Spring is a time of exuberance in this rich, wild ecosystem. Sweet-smelling azaleas and dogwood trees also blossom and add to the ambiance. And in the shade of the forest floor, wildflowers contribute to the mystique. Trilliums are a favorite for naturalists in the forested Pacific Northwest looking for the first signs of spring. Spotting tiny, delightful fairy lanterns along a forest trail requires a sharp

eye, and redwood sorrel blooms as a ground cover. Lucky hikers might even find a calypso flower—the delicate redwood orchid—and a variety of birds. Mushrooms pop out to join the wild growth; berry bushes put out flowers as nature gears up for summer and new growth.

Spring has other enticements along this wild and lonely rocky coastline. Gray whales are migrating north with their newborn calves and a hike in the redwoods can lead to a rocky headland with good viewing. Cormorants fish in the surf, while willets and sanderlings work the beach. And the surf is always exciting for wave watchers.

The climate is never very cold here, but spring still has its share of rain (as it does in most places) which is essential to the natural happenings, so enclosed vehicles are better than tents. Victorian architecture, excellent museums, and shops with local arts and crafts are featured at several villages along this tour, but don't miss the chance for a walk beneath sheltering trees in a mild rain; it's a rewarding experience.

This tour begins near the Oregon-California border and heads south, but it also works well going the opposite direction as long as you plan to be in the northern area in late April or May if you want to catch the rhododendrons flowering.

Redwood National Park

Redwood National Park—a World Heritage Site and International Biosphere Reserve—is under the cooperative management of both the National Park Service and the California Department of Parks and Recreation. Most of the campgrounds are part of the state park system, so Golden Age passes are not applicable for camping.

JEDEDIAH SMITH REDWOODS STATE PARK

From US 101, head for the most northern section of Redwood National Park, the Hiouchi Area, by following the Smith River along CA 197 or via US 199. At the confluence of Mill Creek and the Smith River, Jedediah Smith Redwoods State Park is the popular spot in this area and contains 36

The Stout Memorial Grove in Jedediah Smith Redwoods, CA.

memorial groves, with nature trails through several of these, including the 0.5-mile (0.8-km) wheelchair-accessible path in the Frank D. Stout Memorial Grove (with the state park's largest redwood). Because it is farther inland than much of the national park, this area is often sunnier and warmer than those areas along the coast. Otters are frequently spotted in the river, where the fishing is good. The park was named after the intrepid explorer, Jedediah Smith, the first American to see this area, in 1831.

Insider's Tip:

All of the state parks publish brochures with trail maps, which are a great help for hikers. If you want longer hikes than the short, nature variety, you will find many opportunities. Be aware, however, that footbridges over waterways are in place only in summer.

CRESCENT CITY TO KLAMATH

Most of Redwood National Park is south of Crescent City, strung along the coast like inviting jewels to be inspected and enjoyed. You might want to check out the Battery Point Lighthouse in Crescent City, tide permitting, with its museum, artifacts, and tours. Birders often take a side trip on Lake Earl Drive to the Lake Earl State Wildlife Area, which is a hot spot for observing birds.

US 101 becomes hilly and curvy south of Crescent City and into Del Norte Coast Redwoods State Park. Four miles south of this park's two campgrounds, at Henry Solon Graves Memorial Grove, consider a hike on Damnation Creek Trail. The trail winds downhill through dense forest to a beach with tide pools; the trail originally was used by the Yurok Indians to gather shellfish and seaweed.

Lagoon Creek is a fine wetland with a pond and is worth a stop for picnicking, photography, fishing, and walking the 1-mile (1.6 km) Yurok Loop Nature Trail. Along this walk, look for spring wildflowers and climb to panoramic ocean views where you can scan for sea mammals. I've enjoyed the section of the Coastal Trail that continues south from this loop.

Sculptures of bears guard the tiny community of Klamath and the Klamath River, just a short distance before it enters the sea. This river is famous for fishing and river rafting.

PRAIRIE CREEK REDWOODS STATE PARK

After curving inland through private land, US 101 soon enters Prairie Creek Redwoods State Park, but the traveling here is best via the alternate Newton B. Drury Scenic Parkway. Turnouts are many and you'll want to allow time for frequent stops such as the short trail at Big Tree (over 300 feet [91 m] high and 21 feet [6.4 m] in diameter). Just past this is the state park visitor center and the picnicking and camping areas. Roosevelt Elk have frequented the meadows near the road in this area for many years, stopping traffic (there is parking for this). Indians called these animals "wapiti," meaning white rump. I've camped here in early spring when only the cow elks shared the campground with me. As I drove out in the morning, dew glistened on the grass and the elk as they munched breakfast across the road in the sunlight—beautiful!

A special treat for visually impaired

Damnation Trail, Redwoods National Park, CA.

A buck and his harem of Roosevelt elk cows, Prairie Creek area in Redwoods National Park, CA.

people is near the visitor center, the 0.2-mile (0.3-km) Revelation Trail. Walkways that are edged with rope handrails guide hikers and encourage them to discover the redwood forest through their other senses—touching redwood and tan oak bark, listening for the creek, and smelling the leaves of California bay.

The 260 species of birds in this state park include the spotted owl and marbled murrelet that are involved in logging controversies elsewhere; they're pretty safe here. Steller's jays are more obvious, and the eerie, whistled notes of the varied thrush can be heard in the forest. Osprey, belted kingfishers, and the rarer pileated woodpecker are also sometimes sighted. Discover some of these by hiking any of Prairie Creek Redwoods State Park's 70 miles (113 km) of trails. Bicyclers, equestrians, and even joggers are allowed on some trails. The terrain is easy in this park, with few changes in elevation.

A highlight of the national park is the 7-mile (11-km) stretch of dunes and sandy beach in the Gold Bluffs area. Gold mining lured the first settlers, and remains of this activity still exist. The vehicle access is via Davison Road, a narrow, rough, gravel road (four-wheel drive is not required) where ve-

hicles over 24 feet (7 m) in length or 8 feet (2.4 m) in width are prohibited. It is 4 miles (6.4 km) to Gold Bluffs Beach and another 4 miles to Fern Canyon, where a 0.6-mile (1-km) trail loops past a lush canyon walled with ferns and complete with a creek and old-growth forest.

Don't despair if your vehicle isn't allowed. A bicycle route gets you there from the Prairie Creek Campground, and there is also a hiking trail. By combining the James Irvine Trail, the Fern Canyon Loop, a jaunt along the beach cliffs, and a return on the Miners Ridge Trail (11 easy miles [18 km]), you'll begin to appreciate this landscape. Lush, boggy carpets of tiny mushrooms, wildflowers, mosses, old-growth trees, creeks, a variety of ferns, starbursts of sunlight, and elk along the bluffs hold your attention and invigorate your walk. This is a favorite hike of mine; I highly recommend it. Both the Prairie Creek and Gold Bluff campgrounds make excellent bases for exploring. Among the varied wildlife are infrequent sightings of black bears and the more secretive mountain lions; never leave food out when you are not around.

The Bald Hills Road provides access to some spectacular redwood groves. However, because of the 17 percent grade, motorhomes and trailers are not advised on this road to the 1-mile (1.6-km) interpretive trail looping through the Lady Bird Johnson Grove. Farther along this road is the strenuous 3-mile (4.8-km) round-trip hike to the Tall Trees Grove, where the world's tallest tree, 367.8 feet (112 m) tall, can be seen. Growing from a seed the size of a tomato seed, a mature redwood tree may weigh 500 tons and is impenetrable to fire and insects. Road access is by permit (these can only be obtained at Redwood Information Center near Orick early in the day) for vehicles 18 feet (5.5 m) or under in length. Inquire about the availability of the shuttle to this trailhead, which also stops at the grove dedicated by Lady Bird Johnson, who said, "People who seek tranquillity—a chance for reflection—will find and love this place."

Wild Coastal Parks

The scenery changes dramatically to the south as the park ends and the highway swings near the ocean, edging wide coastal views at Stone Lagoon and Big Lagoon. Primitive campsites front the lagoons, and windsurfers find this a great place for moving across the water. The openness is perfect for spotting some of the 200 species of birds that frequent this sandy marshland along the Pacific flyway. Spring also promises sun-loving wildflowers. Anglers might find cutthroat trout, starry flounder, and steelhead in the lagoons.

From wide, shimmering waters, the coastal terrain magically changes to wooded cliffs overlooking beaches with agate and jade rocks at Patrick Point State Park. Consider the developed campground here and take time to visit the outdoor museum and the sea lion overlook. Enjoy the walk past ferns, wildflowers, and forest along the Rim Loop Trail and take some of the side trails to sensational destinations such as Mussel Rocks, Wedding Rock, Agate Beach, Lookout Rock, Abalone Point, and Palmer's Point. A wheelchair-accessible section of the trail, with Braille plaques along the way, heads from Wedding Rock to Patrick Point.

As a photographer, I've always thought the small fishing village of Trinidad possesses a good measure of charm and scenic ambiance. Trinidad Head is an enormous rock formation that seems to act as a sentinel positioned to protect the tiny harbor. It is also a nesting place for tufted puffins, which arrive in April at the southern extreme of their coastal range. The views from the Tsurai Loop Trail on Trinidad Head reveal some of the great scenery here. Humboldt State University Marine Laboratory and Aquarium have self-guiding tours on weekdays. And, check out the state beaches; you might see some puffins.

Arcata and Eureka

Northern California is so quiet and the roads so meandering that the Humboldt Bay area may seem large and busy, especially if you happen to pass through during the noontime traffic. But there is a wealth of outdoor activities linked to the busy communities of Arcata and Eureka.

Although much changed from the days of the gold rush and now quite the college town, Arcata is where Bret Harte worked as a miner and journalist; he used the location as a model for some of his mining stories. Arcata has been written about more recently for the success of its low-cost, low-tech wastewater reclamation methodology. Witness this system and judge for yourself how well this wetland project works to attract wildlife and outdoor recreation as you walk some of the 4.5 miles of trails of the Arcata Marsh and Wildlife Sanctuary, which is accessible from South I, South H, and South G streets. The experience belies its origins. More than 200 species of birds use the

Special Events:
Held during the last week in April, the Rhododendron Festival in Eureka includes a parade and flower show. The annual Wildflower Show is held at Humboldt County's Office of Education in Eureka on the first weekend in May.

Victorian home in Ferndale, CA.

strolls or horse-and-buggy tours through "old towns" will find historic Eureka quite special, particularly "the 1885 Queen of Victorians," the Carson Mansion. Other fun activities include a waterfront walkway, a bay cruise, kayaking, windsurfing, sailing, a sport fishing charter boat, or one of several railroad excursions. This city has been a major lumber, shipping, and fishing center since the 1850s, and the museums, mill tours, and Fort Humboldt Historic Park reflect some of this history.

The rich ecosystem bordering vast Humboldt Bay includes the Humboldt Bay National Wildlife Refuge at the south edge of Eureka. Take Hookton Road west from US 101 to this staging area for waterfowl and shorebirds during the spring migration. Two interpretive trails, Hookton Slough and Shorebird Loop, are open to visitors. This road also accesses the South Jetty Road along the bay going north and the Eel River Wildlife Area to the south.

Victorian Ferndale

A few miles south of Eureka, drive across the Eel River via the arched span at Fernbridge to the lovely small town of Ferndale. A State Historic Landmark, this village, replete with well-preserved Victorian buildings, offers an excellent walk along its Main Street. Ask for a Walking Tour Guide at one of the artifact-packed stores, candy shops, old-fashioned mercantiles, or the saddlery. Don't miss the Gingerbread Mansion, the Gum Drop Tree House, or the intricate architectural details of Main Street shops.

Founded in the mid-1800s, Ferndale soon became noted for its successful dairy farming. In fact, some of the town's houses are called "butterfat palaces." Drive west on Port, Dillon, or Centerville roads for the pastoral scenery of historic farmhouses, tiny schoolhouses, and dairy farms. Bicyclists will find excellent exploring near the Eel River Delta, an ecosystem that illustrates the richness of this landscape. Beach strollers can head 5 miles (8 km) west on the Centerville Road. Those with smaller rigs might drive the slow and twisting Mattole Road to Cape Mendocino and the light-

refuge, including the rare Arctic loon.

While in Arcata, consider taking the walking tour of murals and checking out the nearly 2,000 fossils at the Humboldt State University Natural History Museum. Historic Jacoby's Storehouse has a railroad museum, galleries, shops, and restaurants. "The Plaza" is worth checking out if you're sightseeing in the city.

Humboldt Bay sprawls west of both Arcata and Eureka. The Samoa Bridge exit off US 101 crosses the water between the two cities and takes you to the Woodley Island Marina. In addition to the spectacular location of the moorage for pleasure and commercial craft, view the 25-foot copper sculpture titled the "Fisherman," the 1890 Bluff Lighthouse, and the egret rookery on Indian Island. This route also accesses the Samoa Peninsula, location of the Samoa Cookhouse and Museum and the Samoa Dunes Recreation Area—300 acres of public land that offers hiking, surfing, bird watching, picnicking, fishing, and terrain for off-road vehicles at the south end of the peninsula.

Those of you who are invigorated by

house, where raptors frequently soar the open slopes descending to the Pacific.

Humboldt Redwoods State Park and the Avenue of the Giants

US 101 southeast of Ferndale follows the Eel River through timber towns for a short distance, but soon offers travelers the scenic option of the 33-mile-long (53-km) Avenue of the Giants north of Pepperwood. This good paved road is a slot right through majestic redwood forests, with trees so close to the road that your driving requires careful attention. You'll want to go slow anyway and stop frequently to wander among the frequent memorial groves and hiking trails.

This vast forested ecosystem is preserved in Humboldt Redwoods State Park, 51,143 acres in the Eel River Basin offering two campgrounds—Burlington and Hidden Springs—that are accessible along the scenic road. Fifty-one miles (82 km) of hiking and riding trails will get explorers off vehicular roads and into solitude and discovery, whether it's along a forest creek, through redwood groves, or even climbing to the 3,381-foot (1,030-m) Fire Lookout on Grasshopper Peak. Consider dropping off hikers or bikers along the route and picking them up down the way.

The Burlington and Bull Creek trails closely follow the Avenue of the Giants and Flats Road near Bull Creek, connecting to other trails occasionally. A park map is most helpful. Park headquarters is near the Burlington Campground just south of Weott.

> **Special Event:**
> Usually the second weekend in May, the "Bicycle Tour of the Unknown Coast" is Humboldt County's largest annual sporting event and draws over 2,000 participants. Supported tours of varying lengths, skill clinics, and pasta feeds are part of the fun. Check in Ferndale for information.

> **Special Event:**
> The Avenue of the Giants Marathon is held the first Sunday in May.

One of first points of interest heading south is the Founder's Grove Nature Trail. Soon, a park road heads west of the Eel River to the outstanding Rockefeller Forest and longer trails in the Bull Creek area. The California Federation of Women's Clubs Grove along the Avenue of the Giants features the beautiful outdoor Hearthstone Fireplace and vast, long picnic tables. A concentration of recreation choices exists between Weott and Myers Flat, with the southern terminus of the Avenue of the Giants just below Phillipsville.

Overhead circle of redwood trees, Redwood National Park, CA.

Although scatterings of redwood forest continue south to the San Francisco Bay area, the historic holdings began to dwindle as civilization encroached. This region was the home of the Sinkyone Indians for thousands of years, and they had little impact on the redwood forests. It was only when settlers began clearing the forest for pastureland, and lumbering followed, that concern arose about the survival of these trees and their necessary natural associations. Once you have wandered among the redwood forests, would you want them to become extinct?

Farther south along the Eel River is the elegant English-style Benbow Inn and the adjacent RV resort and golf course. The inn offers daily tea and scones as well as

Sunday brunch. There is also camping at the Benbow Lake State Recreation Area, a seasonal lake that resulted from the damming of the Eel River, and guided horseback trail rides (except in winter). Camping choices abound, with Richardson Grove State Park a few miles south and Standish-Hickey State Recreation Area just north of Leggett. Both of these are in the midst of redwood forest.

Mendocino County's Rugged Coast

At Leggett, it's time to make route choices to reach the trip's final destinations along the Mendocino coast. CA 1 heads for this wild and lovely coast via a very slow and winding downhill section through the forest to Westport. Long motorhomes and trailers will have a rough time, although I encountered some big rigs managing the 20 miles (34 km) of this route.

An alternate route is CA 20 west from Willits, although this too is a rather slow, curvaceous downhill road through demonstration forest, hiking trails, and conservation camps. The most common southerly approach, if starting from that direction on this tour, is via CA 128 from Cloverdale to Albion; you might choose to exit that way. I wouldn't recommend taking CA 1 north from San Francisco unless your rig is small and compact; it's much more difficult than Oregon's coast road. Alternatively, you can continue along US 101, park your rig in Willits, and head to Fort Bragg and the coast on the "Skunk Train." (You'll miss the rest of this wonderful rugged coast, however.)

Those who choose to pass through Westport and continue south to the Fort Bragg-Mendocino area will be surprised to find the lovely quiet spectacular scenery of this farthest reach of the CA 1 highway. It is reminiscent of Big Sur, but mostly undiscovered, with gorgeous seascapes. The most northerly of the seven primitive camping areas of Westport-Union Landing State Beach is just north of Westport, with fantastic sites at the edge of the cliff. (Smart RVers have discovered this place.) Beach access in the park is at several points (don't freelance

Masonic Temple in Mendocino, CA.

a trail down from your campsite), and tide pools, whale watching, and simply walking on the beach are enjoyable activities here. One private campground along this stretch features camping on the beach itself.

Campers who want a more developed site need to travel only a few more miles to MacKerricher State Park, although the sites do not overlook the Pacific. At this park, a wheelchair-accessible boardwalk trail heads for Laguna Point and a seal-watching station, where gray whales can be spotted in spring. A skeleton of a gray whale is on exhibit near the park entry station. Hikers can circle freshwater Lake Cleone (stocked with trout and visited by ducks) or walk the 8-mile (13-km) abandoned logging road (Haul Road) to the southern end of the park.

Fort Bragg

Fort Bragg is known for its active fishing port along the Noyo River and the western terminus train depot for the Skunk Trains, which is adjacent to a museum-marketplace decorated with a great train mural. Originally a logging railroad that dates back to 1885, the California Western Railroad now offers relaxing excursions on three different trains along the famous "Redwood Route." The favorite travel choice is the original No. 45 Steam Engine, which reminds passengers of the old days as it puffs up a good head of steam. The name "Skunk," however, arises from the gasoline-powered 1925 and 1935 motorcars: "You can smell 'em before you see 'em!" Only one of these, the 1925 M-100, survives. The "Super-Skunk" diesel-powered locomotives painted fire-engine red with gold accents are popular for the 40-mile trip along the Noyo River to Willits (wheelchair accessible). It's an exciting trip through redwood forest, rocky cliffs, placid meadows, and two tunnels. Half-day and full-day trips are available.

For a chance to feel the rhythms of being afloat on the Pacific, Fort Bragg offers charter boats for whale watching and deep-sea fishing, as well as scuba classes and ocean kayak rentals. There is more to the sea than just looking at it.

Lots of restaurants will keep you well nourished in this coastal town. I was delighted with my lunch at Headland Coffeehouse (near the marketplace), an informal gathering place with a full espresso bar and myriad choices of other hot and cold beverages. This is the kind of place frequented by the locals, with nightly entertainment of music, art, and poetry.

Mendocino

The route south to Mendocino passes the Mendocino Coast Botanical Gardens and then follows the coast more closely by heading to Point Cabrillo Lighthouse. This ocean-skirting route will eventually get you to the Mendocino Headlands State Park, a wonderful place for exploring clifftop paths above the many rocky coves at the enchanting village of Mendocino. Springtime is great for discovering wildflowers, but the sights and sounds of wild surf, logs heaving in and out of the sea, and a beautiful rocky coastline make this a very special place.

The amenities and visual charm of Mendocino invite strolls through streets rich in gingerbread architecture, filigree moldings, steep gables, and white picket fences. What began as a logging settlement to furnish redwood timber to growing San Francisco is now a sophisticated artists' colony and popular vacation spot—it's also a National Historic Preservation District. You can't miss the rustic water towers of the town or the ornate Masonic Temple topped by sculpted figures, but there's also the 1855 Chinese Joss House Temple, the 1861 Kelley House Museum, the Mendocino Art Center, and the 1854 Ford House Museum. The latter is the interpretive center for Mendocino Headlands State Park. An array of specialty stores and galleries offer shells, artwork, books, Irish goods, antiques, and the world-class varietals and sparkling wines of Mendocino wine country.

Spring on the Mendocino coast is most dramatically a time for nature and adventure activities. Hikers and bikers—and campers—can head for Russian Gulch State Park and the pretty and easy day hike through lush forest to a 35-foot (11-m) waterfall along the Falls Loop Trail. Mountain bikers can travel part way on a paved trail along a creek. Jughandle State Reserve has wave-cut terraces, an underwater park with skin diving, and walking tours. Local adventure companies suggest joining them on guided ocean kayak trips to explore the hidden coves and sea caves of Mendocino Bay and coastal estuaries. Big River offers easy access to a canoeing trip upstream, with nearby rentals. Or, you might consider traveling a few miles south to Point Arena to see the lighthouse and Manchester State Park before returning to US 101 via CA 128 or CA 20.

It's refreshing to realize that the California coast has this diverse assortment of quiet outdoor activities on its northern reaches. You will find a rare ecosystem of redwood forests, beaches, and rocky headlands that are not yet overpopulated, and charming towns where you can park the car easily and walk about, perhaps savoring the freshest of seafood in restaurants, and certainly the freshest air possible. Travel is meant to rejuvenate the human spirit; that happens easily along this tour.

Special Events:
The Annual Rhododendron Show and Run is held the last weekend of April in Fort Bragg. The Wildflower Festival and Headlands Walks is held the second weekend in May at Mendocino. The Skunk Train Barbecues are scheduled during much of May.

CHAPTER 4

A Wyoming-Northern Utah Trip: River Canyons, Geysers, and Glaciers

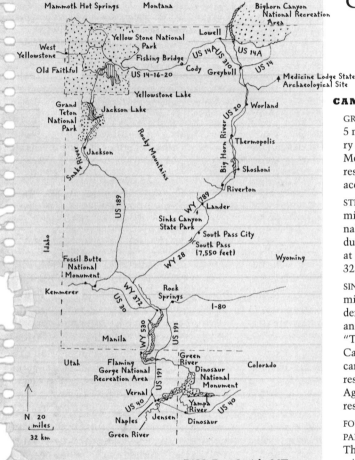

MILEAGE

Approximately 1,100 miles (1,770 km).

RESOURCES

- Dinosaur National Monument, Superintendent, Box 210, Dinosaur, CO 81610; (970) 374-2215.
- Flaming Gorge National Recreation Area, P.O. Box 279, Manila, UT 84046; (435) 784-3445.
- Bighorn Canyon National Recreation Area, PO Box

7458, Fort Smith, MT 59035; (406) 666-2412.
- Cody Chamber of Commerce, P.O. Box 2777, Cody, WY 82414; (307) 587-2297.
- Yellowstone National Park, Superintendent, WY 82190-0168; (307) 344-7381.
- Grand Tetons National Park, Superintendent, P.O. Drawer 170, Moose, WY 83012.
- Jackson Information Center, 532 N. Cache, Jackson, WY 83001; (307) 733-3316.

CAMPGROUNDS

GREEN RIVER CAMPGROUND: 5 miles (8 km) east of Quarry in Dinosaur National Monument; campsites with restrooms, reservations not accepted.

STEINAKER STATE PARK: 7 miles (11 km) north of Vernal; campsites, restrooms, dump station; reservations at (801) 322-3770 or (800) 322-3770.

SINKS CANYON STATE PARK: 6 miles (9.7 km) south of Lander on WY 131; campsites and restrooms below "The Sinks" at Sawmill Campground (no water); campsites, water, with restrooms at larger Popo Agie Campground upriver, reservations not accepted.

FOUNTAIN OF YOUTH R.V. PARK: On the north side of Thermopolis; campsites with hookups, restrooms with showers, large mineral pool; (307) 864-3265.

MEDICINE LODGE STATE ARCHEOLOGICAL SITE: 6 miles (9.7 km) northeast of Hyattville; campsites, restrooms, reservations not accepted.

YELLOWSTONE NATIONAL PARK: Counterclockwise following route; Fishing Bridge RV (opens May 19, reservations: [307] 344-7311) has hookups and nearby showers and laundry; Canyon (opens June 9, reservations) has restrooms and nearby showers and laundry, dump station; Mammoth (open all year, reservations) has restrooms, dump station; Madison (opens May 1; reservations) has restrooms, dump station; opening dates are approximate.

GRAND TETONS NATIONAL PARK: Obtain a campsite early in the day if possible; Colter Bay Campground has sites, restrooms, dump station, and nearby showers and laundry (opens May 20, reservations not accepted); Colter Bay RV park has hookups, reservations at (307) 543-2811.

Our first national park, Yellowstone, and its neighbor, Grand Tetons, embrace remarkable and beautiful landscapes inhabited by some of this country's most easily viewed wildlife. So popular are these parks, however, that you need to plan a visit on the edge of the summer season, when the crowds have not yet filled the campgrounds and parking lots. Otherwise, some of the magic is lost. Yet you'll want weather warm enough to hike some trails edging the glacial lakes and perhaps see some wildflowers. Arriving in early June is usually the best compromise. If you want to spend time in the high country, though, late summer is better (the snow will have had a chance to melt by then). Early June is also the season for sighting young animals such as bison calves, goslings, and newborn elk.

So why not start south, visit some other fascinating geologic areas, and finish your trip with the climactic Yellowstone region? It's intriguing to begin with dinosaur fossils in the nice spring weather of Utah, continue north along several deep and stunning

A buck Rocky Mountain elk in Yellowstone, CO.

river canyons, cross the Rockies where the Oregon Trail pioneers did, and camp along some mountain streams roaring with spring snow melt.

Dinosaur National Monument

When Andrew Carnegie needed something "as big as a barn" to fill the new wing of a museum, paleontologist Earl Douglass headed for the Split Mountain area near the Green River of Utah. North of Jensen, in the northeastern part of the state, Douglass was looking for dinosaur fossils and speculated that this place was his best bet. Several months later he wrote in his diary: ". . . I saw eight of the tail bones of a brontosaurus in exact position. It was a beautiful sight." Within a few years, thousands of such bones were found on a single ridge. Designated a national monument in 1915, this quarry site now occupies one wall in the park's visitor center, a working laboratory with fossil bones still being exposed in high relief by quarry paleontologists. The fulfillment of Douglass's dream, the Dinosaur Quarry building, sits high above the river.

Why were so many fossils found in this location? It's a wonderful example of conditions being just right for preservation. Obviously, many dinosaurs inhabited this area, and the bones of a certain percentage were buried and preserved in the sands of an ancient river. Time passed and more layers of sediments were added as the sea moved in and out. The strata became hard sandstone as dissolved silica percolated through the sediments; the bones became mineralized. Eventually, erosion and weathering revealed these intriguing fossils atop a jagged ridge, and Douglass discovered them in the 145-million-year-old Morrison Formation. Today, rangers talk about the time when the dinosaurs roamed a green, lush, semitropical area where ferns and tall conifers grew in the wet climate.

Although the monument is now mostly semiarid basin-and-plateau land that is rugged and remote, the Green River sashays through the landscape in a general southwest direction and creates a linear oasis often enveloped by sheer canyon walls. The most intimate way to see swatches of the monument's backcountry is to float down either the Green River or the Yampa River with a commercial guide (brochures available from concessionaires).

TOUR OF THE TILTED ROCKS

Most people, however, tour Dinosaur National Monument via the scenic drives. Pick up the park brochure for the auto tour introduction to the park, The Tour of the Tilted Rocks, at the Dinosaur Quarry building.

The 2-mile (3.2-km) Desert Voices Trail begins at the Split Mountain boat ramp area. Notice the nearby badlands that are richly pigmented with iron. This moderately difficult trail begins near a cave with an ant lion exhibit and continues through sweeping views of colorful desert and rock formations streaked with purple, mauve, red, and gray. The route includes some provocative interpretive displays that were done by and for kids.

Continuing on the tour route, a road soon leads off to Green River Campground, where campsites are shaded by enormous cottonwood trees along the river. Monarch butterflies are attracted to the golden clumps of flowering arrowleaf balsamroot. Stars are brilliant at night, and birds sing you awake in the morning.

Insider's Tip:

If you fish, be aware that four native fishes are endangered: the Colorado squawfish, the razorback suck, the humpback chub, and the bonytail chub. Anglers who catch any of these species are responsible for identifying them and returning them unharmed to the water.

The auto tour continues east on Cub Creek Road and leads to the Josie Bassett Morris homestead (see below), a part of the monument since her death in 1964. Although the road is gravel the last couple of miles, that isn't a problem unless heavy rain has flooded the creek. Several tour markers are along the route, but "must" stops are the petroglyphs at markers number 13 and 14. Fremont Indians carved elaborate diagrams

into the cliffs approximately 1,000 years ago. Look for lizards, a flute player, and the "three princesses," with their trapezoidal bodies, necklaces, and headdresses.

The terminus of the drive at Josie's place is a wonderful level spot that served her needs. Although she had been married several times and counted Butch Cassidy among her admirers, Josie chose to live here alone in her roomy log cabin complete with a cook stove and red brick fireplace. Outside were shade trees, grape vines, spring wildflowers, a water supply, fertile fields of crops, and a couple of shaded box canyons that served as corrals. A photo at the homestead shows Josie with her gun. She died after a fall from a horse, but she must have been around 90 years old at that time. Eat a picnic lunch at the outdoor table, stroll about the paths and into the canyons, and contemplate her life here. I can understand her affection for this place, lonely as it was.

HARPERS CORNER SCENIC DRIVE

For the ultimate in canyon viewing, drive the Harpers Corner Self-guiding Scenic Drive, which is accessible just over the Colorado border near the headquarters visitor center of the monument. This 31-mile (50-km) tour (a brochure is available) begins with smashing displays of geology at the intersection of the Colorado Plateau and the Rocky Mountains. Red buttes, mesas, buckled and tilted rock layers, and rock textures that include swirls, geometric shapes, domes, scallops, squiggles, and colorful stripes are visible in every direction. After passing a section of pastureland where sage grouse live, mule deer cross the road, and ravens circle overhead, a high point of aspen trees is reached and the road drops downhill to canyon country.

At the end of the road is an easy but wonderful 1-mile (1.6-km) trail that meanders on a high finger of land past spring wildflowers and other interesting discoveries to an outstanding point from which to view the canyons of Echo Park, at the merging of the Green and Yampa rivers. Listen for echoes off nearby Steamboat Rock as you view the Canyon of Lodore, Mitten Park Fault, and Whirlpool Canyon—named

Tyrannosaurus in front of Utah Field House of Natural History, UT.

by John Wesley Powell on his trip down the Green River in 1869. Evidence of geologic events is everywhere in the surrounding rocks, including the ones on which you are standing.

For more about dinosaurs, head west to Vernal.

Utah Field House of Natural History

Because many of the area fossil discoveries were ending up back East, the local community wanted some of the area's prehistoric wealth to be preserved in a local museum. As a result, the Utah Legislature established the Utah Field House of Natural History in Vernal, with dinosaurs and their history the star attraction. In addition to various fossils and displays on geologic history, there are Indian and historical exhibits, a natural history room, a mineral room, and a replica of a dinosaur (one of Douglass's first finds in the area), the *Diplodocus*.

Outside the building, however, is the most exciting attraction, a dinosaur garden—one of the finest collections of dinosaur replicas in the world. When you walk through this natural setting of ponds and vegetation amid seventeen replicas, it is as if you've journeyed a time machine—ex-cept the dinosaurs don't move. Along the paths are a life-size *Tyrannosaurus*, a six-ton *Stegosaurus*, a huge, flying *Pteranodon*, a fin-backed *Edaphosaurus*, and a large, bird-like *Ornithomimus*.

Flaming Gorge–Uintas Scenic Byway

Also known as the "Wildlife Through the Ages" tour, the Flaming Gorge–Uintas Scenic Byway heads north from Vernal on US 191 and climbs gradually from 5,200 feet (1,585 m) to 9,500 feet (2,896 m) through pine- and juniper-covered foothills to Flaming Gorge. From Vernal to Manila the byway covers 67 miles and a billion years of geologic time; names of various formations and fossil information are posted on highway signs.

Steinaker State Park is the first inviting stop, with both high viewpoints and cottonwood-shaded campsites by a reservoir. Although surface waters are warm, the deep portions of the lake have fine cold-water fishing. The quiet waters are great for practicing kayaking skills. Varied vegetation and wetlands offer hiding places for wildlife and interesting walks. Look for great blue herons in unusual places. Spring wildflowers include squirrel-tail barley and the beautiful sego lily, the state flower of Utah. Ask the park ranger for trail directions to the relatively unknown Moonshine Arch.

With rock formations resembling the prows of ships edging the reservoir, Red Fleet State Park is a few miles north in picturesque red slickrock country. A fun activity is boating or swimming the narrow channel to a slanted rock shelf sloping into the water, where dinosaur footprints have been found preserved in rock. Paleontologists have identified the tracks as those of three-toed (tridactyl) dinosaurs that walked on two legs (bipedal), and they left these footprints some 200 million years ago. Wanderers can also explore rocky coves along the lake and look for wildlife in the sagebrush terrain. Camping consists of marked-off spots on a parking lot, where mountain bluebirds are your neighbors.

The byway soon enters Ashley National Forest on the eastern flank of the Uinta Mountains and nine long, signed switchbacks with grades of 5 to 8 percent—no problem for most RVers, but it's always wise to have your rig in good condition. Scenery is pretty here with high country stands of aspens alternating with meadows on the approach to Limber Flag summit.

Flaming Gorge National Recreation Area

To view the Flaming Gorge Dam on the Green River and its visitor center, head east on US 191 at the entrance to Flaming Gorge National Recreation Area. Otherwise, continue the byway west on UT 44. The side road to Red Canyon Visitor Center (opens Memorial Day) and Overlook is 4 miles (6.4 km) west, and is a highlight of a park. The spur road was full of potholes when I traveled it but, even so, it pays to go slow here—the views of this stunning gorge carved by the river are spectacular from the walkways, especially when the sunlight

View of Green River in Flaming Gorge National Monument, UT

blazes on the canyon rock, creating rich warm colors against the deep blue of the twisting lake far below. Small mountain lakes and three campgrounds are along this spur road.

The byway next traverses a high forested landscape, a side road that provides access to the Sheep Creek Canyon Geological Area, primitive campgrounds, grand overlooks of the lake, and water access and a

boat ramp at Sheep Creek. Navajo Cliffs Picnic Area is just off the road, where the geological tour loop rejoins it.

Past Manila (where there is nothing much in the way of services), the park is again accessible at Lucerne Valley, where there is a campground near the water—a marina and boating are the main attractions. As travelers head toward the town of Green River, Wyoming, they leave the high wild country and see, instead, flat sagebrush desert complete with open-range cattle.

Fossil Butte National Monument

For a look at some engaging fossils of plants and animals that lived after the dinosaurs perished, consider a side trip to Fossil Butte National Monument, just west of Kemmerer. Wonderfully preserved in freshwater lake sediments of the 50-million-year-old formation are more than 20 species of fish, 100 insect varieties, and an uncounted number of plants—evidence of a much more vibrant wildlife scene than suggested by the semiarid landscape of the tan-buff-colored, layered sedimentary Green River Formation and the red, pink, and purple Wasatch Formation seen today. Many of the fossils are huge, mounted specimens, often preserved in stone. The details in these fossils are extraordinary. Especially impressive are the crocodile and palm frond, the stingray, the soft-shell turtle, a school of herring, and a paddlefish with a smaller fish. The stories told by some of these fossils require expert sleuthing skills. A couple of trails let you climb to the quarry site and view the high desert flora and fauna of today, which includes an aspen grove and a beaver pond.

From Fossil Butte National Monument head northeast and pick up WY 28, where you'll begin following the route of the Oregon Trail.

South Pass Historic Site

Crossing the Rocky Mountains was not something the pioneers heading west on the Oregon Trail looked forward to. When faced with negotiating the Continental Divide, they found that the "easiest" place to do so was at the 7,550-foot (2,300-m) South Pass, now a national historic landmark. In 1867, after gold was discovered in the area, South Pass City popped up not far from there. Although this town boomed as the busy, dynamic community reached a population of some 2,000 residents, it soon followed a cycle of booms and busts. Eventually, it was restored as a state historic site. Primarily a half-mile main street of buildings along Willow Creek, you might spot an old covered wagon abandoned on a green meadow in this peaceful landscape. The thirty-two attractions listed in the town brochure include the old livery stable, the Sherlock Hotel and adjacent restaurant, the recorder's office, a bank, a dance hall, the Carissa Saloon, a one-room schoolhouse, gold miners' cabins, a visitor center, a picnic area by the creek, a nature trail, and more fascinating reminders of the past. And although gold mining is not booming now, it has not died. Notice the mining structures on the drive east.

Sinks Canyon State Park

South of Lander on WY 131, Sinks Canyon State Park is a treasure, a place I camp when I'm in the area because it's so special, yet relatively undiscovered. On the northeastern slopes of the Wind River Mountains at 6,000 feet (1,829 m), the raging Popo Agie River slices through the park. A geologic phenomenon occurs in the process: the river plunges into a cavern at the base of a cliff and reappears in a large trout-filled pool a short distance downhill. You can stop at the visitor center and walk the nature trails, but best of all, you can camp alongside the wide river next to the swinging bridge or where the stream roars like a lion after being diverted. I watched rock climbers and bighorn sheep as I relaxed, and golden wildflowers were abundant among the vegetation. Wildlife abounds, and many species of fish inhabit the stream. The park is also a gateway to exploring the backcountry of the Wind River Mountains.

Popo Agie River in Sinks Canyon State Park, WY.

Wind River Canyon

Heading north out of Lander on WY 789, pick up the Wind River at Riverton and follow it past the dam at Boysen Reservoir, where the wild emergence of the river is quickly narrowed by the 2,500-foot-high (762-m) canyon walls of Wind River Canyon. The several miles through this canyon reflect a billion years of engrossing geology; highway signs help to decipher the story. Although the canyon is part of the Wind River Indian Reservation, commercial guides lead whitewater trips through here.

When you exit the canyon you'll be following the Big Horn River. Wait a minute! What happened to the Wind River? It turns out that this is still the same river. Perhaps that fact wasn't so obvious in the past and the canyon hid the secret. Locals call this merging the "Wedding of the Waters." The Big Horn River from here to the Montana border beckons anglers with superb trout fishing, particularly in late spring and fall.

Thermopolis Hot Springs

The third most visited tourist site in Wyoming—after Grand Tetons National Park and Yellowstone National Park—is the river city of Thermopolis. The reason is its hot springs. The Shoshone and Arapahoe Indians deeded 10 square miles including the hot springs to the U.S. government in 1896 with the stipulation that there be free use of these soothing mineral waters in the future. This promise has been kept—visitors today can enjoy both inside and outside pools at the Bath House of Hot Springs State Park. Concessions at the park include an assortment of giant waterslides, pools, and other entertainment facilities, some of which were used in the past by such personalities as Buffalo Bill Cody and Butch Cassidy.

Trails lead to Big Horn Spring, flower gardens, the cooling pools, and Rainbow Terrace, where cascades of water flow into the river and leave behind glittering salt deposits of calcite and gypsum that are colored by algae. A swinging bridge lets you walk over the river. A driving tour leads to a small herd of bison and young calves in the Buffalo Pasture.

RVers might head just north of Thermopolis to the Fountain of Youth Recreation Vehicle Park, where soaking in the huge mineral pool is included in the fee. The campground borders the Big Horn River and offers lovely views of sunlight on the striated ochre shades of the Owl Creek Mountains at sunset. Rain falling on these mountains and percolating underground through volcanic rocks is believed to be the source of the hot springs in the park. Water analysis shows at least 27 different minerals in these smoking waters that smell of sulfur.

Dinosaur aficionados can check out the Wyoming Dinosaur Center in Thermopolis, which includes a museum complex, dinosaur displays, fossil beds, and tours of excavations.

Medicine Lodge State Archeological Site

As I travel, I search for campgrounds in unusual settings, where more than just a night's sleep is on the agenda. In the foothills of the Big Horn Mountains northeast of Hyattville, Medicine Lodge State Archeological Site is one of Wyoming's best kept secrets, although the locals certainly visit frequently.

A dig begun at this archeological site in 1969 by the state archeologist, Dr. George Frison, revealed continuous occupation here for over 10,000 years. Although this dig has been filled in for preservation purposes, interpretive signs provide information about how scientists reconstructed the past history of the early inhabitants. Stone artifacts, stone tool flaking debris, seeds, bones, pollen, and charcoal from this site have been used to trace over 60 different cultural levels during this span of human occupation. Petroglyphs and pictographs, although fading, are numerous on the red sandstone cliffs.

It's the beauty of the landscape today, however, that's so inviting. Medicine Lodge Creek rushes through the park and campers can pull up next to it in several different areas. It's easy to explore cross-country and the meadows are lush with wildflowers. Old roads wind uphill through waving grasses and follow the creek past rock formations punctuating the open terrain—one is aptly named Ship Rock. This land is permeated with a feeling of agelessness. If you try, you can visualize the early Americans in the mind's eye. Part of the Medicine Lodge Wildlife Habitat Management Unit, it is home for elk, deer, sage grouse, chukar partridge, wild turkey, black bear, and mountain lion. Several species of trout in the creek support a trout fishery.

Scenic Byways into the Big Horn Mountains

After a visit to Medicine Lodge State Archeological Site, return to WY 789 along the Bighorn River. An interesting side trip loops east into the Big Horn Mountains via US 14, the Big Horn Scenic Byway. You might want to check on road conditions at the summit early in the season. This route takes you through Shell Canyon and past dynamic Shell Falls before climbing into the mountains.

After reaching Granite Pass at 8,950-foot (2,728-m) elevation, US 14A, the Medicine Wheel Passage Scenic Byway, heads back west, with a side road leading to the mysterious 245-foot (75-m) circular Medicine Wheel, a sacred structure in the religious life of the ancient Indians. (Visitors are requested to walk this 1.5-mile [2.4-km] road.) The descent from these mountains is quick and steep from this high elevation, so be careful. The views of the Big Horn Basin,

Devil Canyon Overlook in Bighorn Canyon National Recreation Area, MT.

however, are incredible. You can gaze for miles and miles across Wyoming and admire the mountain ranges that surround the basin.

Bighorn Canyon National Recreation Area

The descent from the scenic road brings you near the Bighorn Canyon National Recreation Area where you can boat, fish, swim, water ski, and camp in a spectacular setting of cliffs rising almost a half mile above Bighorn Lake. As you drive the park road (WY 37) north past the Horseshoe Bend Campground to Barry's Landing, carefully scan the countryside for wild mustangs in the Pryor Mountain Wild Horse Range. Established as a sanctuary in 1968, the range is home for 120 to 140 horses that are either descended from Indian ponies or escaped from ranches and reverting to wild horses.

Stop at Devil Canyon Overlook to view some stunning geology and perhaps see a boat whizzing through the curving canyon far below. This side canyon was carved by Porcupine Creek and cuts across a 1,000-foot-high (305-m) segment of the fault

blocks that make up the Pryor Mountains. It is a place to get out the camera. Camping and picnic sites are at the end of the paved road at Barry's Landing. The north end of the recreation area is in Montana; there's no direct road connecting to the south end in Wyoming. Surrounding Bighorn Canyon is the Crow Indian Reservation, land of the renowned hunting people described by a member of the Lewis and Clark Expedition as "the finest horsemen in the world."

Cody and Shoeshine Canyon

It's time to head west to Yellowstone National Park. You'll pass through Cody, the town founded by Buffalo Bill, where the flavor of the wild west is preserved in nightly rodeos and the complex of four museums that make up the Buffalo Bill Historical Center: the Buffalo Bill Museum, the Firearms Museum, the Plains Indian Museum, and the Whitney Gallery of Western Art.

Called the "most scenic 52 miles in America" by President Theodore Roosevelt, Bill Cody Scenic Byway, US 14/16/20 heading into Yellowstone, edges Buffalo Bill Reservoir and State Park, traverses the Shoeshine Canyon through the Shoeshine National Forest, and climbs into the Absaroka Range. You'll pass several campgrounds along the Shoshone River just before the park entrance.

Yellowstone National Park

Our first national park, Yellowstone is also an International Biosphere Reserve and World Heritage Site. Yellowstone is like no other place on Earth, a landscape shaped by

Special Events:

June is a busy festival month in Cody. The Frontier Festival is held on the second weekend, and the Old West Show and Auction, Antique Gun Show, and Plains Indian Powwow are all held on the last weekend.

several catastrophic volcanic eruptions that occurred from 2 million to 600,000 years ago. The last event was 1,000 times as powerful as the recent one of Mount St. Helens. In this violent upheaval the central portion of the volcano collapsed, leaving a 28- by 47-mile (45- by 76-km) caldera, or basin, in the center of today's park. Even after all this time this core marks a hot spot deep in the Earth's mantle that produces thirty times more heat than is normal for North America. The result is a landscape bubbling and boiling with geysers, hot springs, mud pots, fumaroles, and paint pots. Magmatic heat continues to power some 10,000 thermal features, including 200 to 250 geysers.

Surrounding this center of deep heat are rugged mountains, an enormous lake, waterfalls, trout-filled rivers, and an astounding array of wildlife that walks, flies, and swims in this strange land. Enough time has passed to allow trees, grasses, and wildflowers to take root and flourish.

The road from the east entrance climbs over 8,530-foot (2,600-m) Sylvan Pass and descends to Yellowstone Lake at the outer edge of the caldera; Yellowstone Lake is this continent's largest mountain lake. You'll pass a hot spring remnant along a fault at Steamboat Springs and wetlands along Pelican Creek as you approach Fishing Bridge over the Yellowstone River. Although now closed to fishing, the river is a superb place to view wild trout spawnings and white pelicans that feed on the native cutthroat trout. Because of bear activity in the area, only hard-sided RV units can use the campground at Fishing Bridge.

Although there are many ways to do the looping figure-eight roadway in the park, our tour now heads north to Canyon Village on a route designed to cover most of the Grand Loop while still aiming for the Grand Tetons.

 Insider's Tip:
Since road construction is a perennial event somewhere in Yellowstone, it's best to ascertain affected areas before you enter the park. Ask locally or call (307) 344-7381.

HAYDEN VALLEY

Wildlife is abundant in the Hayden Valley. The Yellowstone River wiggles through the landscape near the road, but Yellowstone Lake once covered this area and left behind soil that nourished rich shrubland that attracts large numbers of animals. The openness makes for easy viewing of bison, moose, and occasionally grizzly bears. Waterfowl are numerous in the marshy areas. Cutthroat trout are the attraction at Le Hardy Rapids.

Become initiated to the weirdness of the landscape along the Mud Volcano Trail. Bubbly mud seems pretty funky, but do stay on the trail because it's also dangerous terrain. You'll see the Mud Caldron, Dragon's Mouth Spring, Sour Lake, and Mud Geyser. Don't get disoriented, this is still Planet Earth you are visiting. Volcanic gases, hot springs, and decomposed volcanic rock produce strange brews.

GRAND CANYON OF THE YELLOWSTONE RIVER

Flowing out of Yellowstone Lake, the Yellowstone River zigzags through an awesome canyon birthed from a thermal basin and then scoured and deepened by glaciers and the river. Rhyolite lavas have been boiled and baked for millennia, changing the original brown and gray rhyolite rocks physically and chemically into the soft yellow, pink, fiery rose, and reddish-brown hues of the canyon walls. Less altered, more resistant rhyolite rocks form the brinks of the waterfalls that are so famous for their powerful beauty.

Called the Grand Canyon of the Yellowstone River, a painting of this magnificent gash in a volcanic plateau by Thomas Moran and photographs by William H. Jackson were visual messages to Congress that influenced the vote to preserve this park in 1872.

The North Rim Drive provides access to Inspiration Point, Grandview Point, and Lookout Point, with short trails to closer views of the canyon and Lower Falls, Upper Falls, and Crystal Falls. For more continuous observations, try the longer North Rim Trail from Chittenden Bridge to Inspiration Point.

The South Rim Drive provides access to the steep Uncle Tom's Trail and to Artist Point—the quintessential view of the canyon and 308-foot (94-m) Lower Falls. It is never boring, however, to walk the South Rim Trail to Artist Point—or farther to Sublime Point—as the canyon unfolds its panorama of geology and colors. A sharp eye will spot steam in the canyon.

A different way to arrive at Artist Point is via a loop trail that begins across the road from Uncle Tom's parking lot, traverses meadows and forests (and perhaps wildlife, so be alert and cautious) to Clear Lake, and continues to Lily Pad Lake, where you can head north to Artist Point. The South Rim Trail will lead you back to your vehicle. This loop is approximately 3.5 miles (5.6 km), a nice day hike.

Horseback riders can rent mounts in Canyon Village. Check the guide brochure to the canyon area for longer hikes that are also good riding trails. Bicycles are not allowed on most trails.

Insider's Tip:

Never forget that this is the home of grizzly bears. In addition to being especially alert, you might want to wear a bell or whistle, or you might want to sing while hiking. You don't want to surprise a bear. Do not run if you encounter a bear; if threatened, play dead! In campgrounds, never leave out food—including pet food—or anything else that might be edible. Bison are also very dangerous and unpredictable; never approach them.

MOUNT WASHBURN AND TOWER FALLS

The road north of Canyon Village is the highest and most difficult road in the park as it winds along the slopes of Mount Washburn and heads over 8,859-foot (2,700-m) Dunraven Pass. But it is a scenic route with wildflowers in June and July and panoramic views of the Absaroka Range, the Yellowstone caldera, and sometimes the Teton Mountains to the south. This area is prime grizzly country. To the north, 132-foot (40-m) Tower Falls—named for the adjacent volcanic pinnacles—pours into the Yellowstone River.

MAMMOTH HOT SPRINGS

Headquarters for the park, the Mammoth Hot Springs area is a landscape of sparkling hot spring terraces. Pick up a brochure with a map and walk up and down the walkways of the Lower Terraces near Minerva Spring, Jupiter Spring, and Liberty Cap. A one-way drive—a narrow road with sharp curves on which vehicles longer than 25 feet (7.6 m) are prohibited—provides access to the Upper Terraces.

The travertine terraces at Mammoth Hot Springs were formed when acidic hot water (from dissolved carbon dioxide) dissolved underlying limestone and this hot mix gushed to the surface. When the carbon dioxide gas escaped, calcium carbonate (from limestone) was deposited as these crystalline cascades. Although travertine is a white mineral, the terraces are sculptures of color contributed by the oranges, pinks, yellows, greens, and browns of living bacteria and algae. You'll see a lot of these colors in the thermal areas of the park.

NORRIS GEYSER BASIN

The world's largest geyser, Steamboat Geyser—more than 300 feet (91 m)—is at Norris, although it is irregular in its erupting, which ranges from days to years. Echinus Geyser is a more predictable hourly event. Norris is thought to be the hottest and most active geyser basin in the park. Also along the walkway in the Back Basin are the beautiful Emerald Spring, Cistern Spring, and Vixen Geyser.

In the same area, the Porcelain Basin is delicately colored and has walkways where you will find several more geysers, a view of 10,336-foot (3,150-m) Mount Holmes, and perhaps see a mountain bluebird fly from its perch on a bleached snag.

MADISON AND FIREHOLE RIVERS

One of my favorite camping spots is the Madison Campground along the river of the same name, not far from the west entrance. Bison usually wander the green meadows along the river, often crossing the river and

Black Sand Basin, Yellowstone National Park, WY.

rolling afterward in the dirt. I awoke one night when a bison grazed right under my cabover bed, and I also found that you need to be alert going to the restroom. Elk often are seen nearby but are not so unwary of people (although on one trip I noticed they didn't object to a lone Canada goose that joined one group).

Large mammals wander in the park protected and easily seen. Bison soak in warm pools and frequently cross in front of vehicles and stop traffic. Coyote, mule deer, moose, black bear, pronghorn antelope, and even the frightening grizzly are at home in the park. And, it's not impossible that you might spot a wolf. (If you do, park personnel ask that you report such sightings.) Bighorn sheep can be seen at high elevations. Uinta squirrels and yellow-bellied marmots are numerous.

The drive south to Old Faithful is thick with evidence of thermal activity. For a look at a steaming river, travel the Firehole Canyon Drive. Stops at the Fountain Paint Pot Nature Trail in the Lower Geyser Basin and the Great Prismatic Spring in Midway Geyser Basin are worthwhile.

UPPER GEYSER BASIN

As you approach Old Faithful in the Upper Geyser Basin, visit Biscuit Basin and Black Sand Basin with their colorful pools, springs, and walkways. Stop at the Old Faithful Visitor Center for orientation and maps. The geyser display at Old Faithful varies with earthquake activity but recently has been occurring every 75 minutes. This is a centerpiece of the park and is

treated as such. A walkway (bicycles allowed) from Old Faithful along Firehole River edges a vast area of thermal surprises. It also connects to trails to both Biscuit Basin and Black Sand Basin.

Geysers are the visible results of a mostly underground and complicated process of plumbing and the heating of water under pressure until the lid of cemented gravels on the surface is violently opened, releasing some water and steam. The cycle repeats when enough pressure is regenerated to reopen the lid. In hot springs, bubbles flow up through the water to the surface without this pressure buildup. Fumaroles, lacking enough moisture to flow, vent steam. When acidic gases decompose rocks into mud and clay above fumaroles, mud pots are formed.

As you head south to the Grand Tetons past Lewis Lake you'll cross the Continental Divide three times.

Grand Tetons National Park

Rising some nine million years ago, the Teton Range is the youngest of the Rocky Mountain systems. With no foothills to obscure vistas, these jagged peaks rise abruptly above a series of glacial lakes. The Tetons are one of this country's most beautiful and rugged arrays of mountains. The highest peak is 13,770-foot (4,197-m) Grand Teton, but twelve peaks soar above 12,000 feet (3,658 m). Numerous small glaciers did the final awesome carving of this range and gouged U-shaped canyons between peaks. More recently, the Snake River cut through glacial moraines, flowed south out of Jackson Lake, and now curves seductively through the park.

Although much different in appearance from Yellowstone, the Grand Tetons are similar in their richness of habitat for large animals. Look for them where there is natural food. Moose and beaver eat willows in wetlands; the country's largest elk herd grazes in high elevations in summer; and an array of fascinating birds can be seen in the forest, near water, or flying overhead. Black and grizzly bears find refuge and food here but are not seen frequently. Mule deer, pronghorn antelope, bison, and bighorn sheep are other possible sightings. The wide expanses of meadows between the lakes are particularly appealing when they are ablaze with color in early summer. Look for yellow columbine, bluebells, red paintbrush, pink daisies, and lavender asters. Dazzling flower displays edge canyon streams.

JACKSON LAKE AND COLTER BAY

Scoured out by an enormous glacier on the valley floor and dammed by glacial debris, Jackson Lake is the largest of the park's lakes and an excellent area to select as a base camp for exploring. The waterfront near the Colter Bay Campground is special in early morning as the cirque walls and peaks of the Teton Range shimmer reflections on the water while a profusion of golden balsamroot flowers edge the beach in the foreground. Watch for a V-formation of white pelicans overhead at dusk.

The Hermitage Point Trailhead provides access to a system of interconnecting short trails that begin a short distance southeast of the Colter Bay Visitor Center and Indian Arts Museum, where you can obtain a trail map and make your own choices. Paths weave among small lakes and ponds and along the waterfront of the bay and lake. I found a family of beaver at Heron Pond one year that was great fun to watch as the father carried lily pads to the lodge and the mother vocally communicated with her young inside the lodge. Look for swans and moose; I almost bumped into an immature moose on a trail here. Another nearby complex of trails is across the

road from Jackson Lake Lodge. For several years, I found a pair of trumpeter swans nesting on the vegetation of Christian Pond in this location.

Jackson Lake is the only lake where sailboats, water skis, windsurfers, and jet skis are allowed, and boating permits for all craft are required. Boats and canoes can be rented. An interpretive lake cruise is also available. A couple of commercial corrals schedule breakfast and dinner horseback rides.

South of Jackson Lake, you can choose between two roads. Teton Park Road—with wide shoulders for bicycle touring—runs nearer the lakes and mountains; the faster John D. Rockefeller Jr. Memorial Highway skirts the Snake River. Don't miss either drive, which is easy if you return to the Colter Bay Campground on the highway.

JENNY AND STRING LAKES

The North Jenny Junction is a one-way route to String and Jenny Lakes. String Lake is tiny and a fine place for canoeing or kayaking. It is also the trailhead for an interesting hike that begins at the picnic area and heads north along the shoreline to a water crossing near Leigh Lake. From here you can head west to the intersection of the Paintbrush Canyon Trail. (Take this trail for a longer hike to this flower-edged canyon.) Head south and left and climb just above String Lake; the high elevation and open countryside offers lake views and the feeling of backcountry exploring. The trail soon dips down to connect to String Lake, ending a 3.3-mile (5.3-km) loop.

Boating on Jenny Lake is restricted to canoes, kayaks, and motorboats with a maximum 7.5 horsepower. This small but often busy area is one of the park's special places; ranger-led activities are diverse and full of fun, wildlife sightings, and information. Jenny Lake is a popular base for climbers and it's very difficult to find a campsite; only tents are allowed.

The scenic Cascade Canyon Trail can be done two ways to Hidden Falls and on to 7,200-foot (2,195-m) Inspiration Point, which is a good area for viewing wildlife such as golden-mantled squirrels, pikas, yellow-bellied marmots, and for hearing

Swans on Christian Pond, Grand Tetons.

the sounds of songbirds. Both the trailhead and a boat shuttle begin from the dock at South Jenny Lake. If you walk the scenic trail around the lake, the round-trip is 5.8 miles (9.3 km). By taking the boat across the lake, you'll hike only 2.2 miles (3.5 km) round-trip. Via the lake trail, you can take a path to Moose Ponds where there is a good chance of finding these large mammals.

BRADLEY, TAGGART, AND PHELPS LAKES

Another complex of trails weaves through the landscape south of Jenny Lake. The Lupine Meadows Trailhead connects to backcountry trails and to trails heading to Bradley and Taggart lakes. You can also reach these southern trails from the Taggart Lake Trailhead and traverse the Beaver Creek Fire area, where wildflowers are numerous.

Moose Visitor Center is park headquarters and a raft launch. Other attractions are the Chapel of the Transfiguration—with its stained glass windows and cross within a framed mountain view—and the Menor's Ferry Historic Site.

Southwest of Moose Visitor Center, a road leads to the Death Canyon Trailhead. It's an easy hike to views of Phelps Lake, but continue a little farther to the canyon for a scenic hike full of discovery and mountain vibes. When I hiked this trail, I turned around when I hit snow, but a couple of horseback riders kept going ahead.

JOHN D. ROCKEFELLER JR. MEMORIAL PARKWAY

Wide-open views are part of the scenic drive along the John D. Rockefeller Jr. Memorial Parkway. Several launching sites

Jenny Lake in the Grand Tetons.

for rafts are located along the river for river trips of various lengths. Stops at the Snake River Overlook and the Cunningham Cabin Historic Site are rewarding.

The Oxbow Bend Turnout is another inviting view of the Snake River; Mount Moran dominates the background. Take time here to scout for wildlife, particularly in early morning or at dusk when beaver and muskrats might be swimming. Plentiful fish lure river otters, osprey, bald eagles, white pelicans, and mergansers.

Nearby grassy meadows are good possibilities for sighting elk and moose. Across the road, trails lead to the Emma Matilda and Two Ocean lakes through varied terrain.

When you head out of Grand Tetons and toward home, it will seem as if you've seen wildlife and nature through a time slot that stretches back to the age of dinosaurs and volcanic eruptions, and that you have glimpsed the continued richness of life. You don't need to go to the moon, outer space, or even foreign countries to visit wondrous environments and view spectacles of wild animals. The West is rich in landscapes, history, and open spaces that nourish the spirit.

Special Event:
The Annual Old West Days celebration is held Memorial Weekend in Jackson, Wyoming, with a parade, rodeo, cowboy poetry gathering, Native American dancers, cutting horse competition, barn dance, country music, and a reenactment of a mountain-man rendezvous.

Summer Trips

Summer in the West is a special time. The warm sun melts the snow in the mountains and nourishes a short season of wildflowers that splash color against an awesome background of rocky peaks and glacial lakes. It is really the only time for those not inclined to winter sports to visit and explore this often secret terrain, and it is certainly the best time for hiking and RV travel in this high country. Rivers roar with the added snowmelt as rafters and kayakers test their courage and expertise in the exuberance of the season, while canoeists and windsurfers enjoy other waterways. It's also a time to see firsthand how volcanic upheavals rearrange landscapes.

Desert monkeyflower (Mimulus fremontii)

Western bleeding heart
(Dicentra formosa)

CHAPTER 5

Cascade Mountain Magic:
Columbia Gorge Waterfalls to Newberry National Volcano Monument

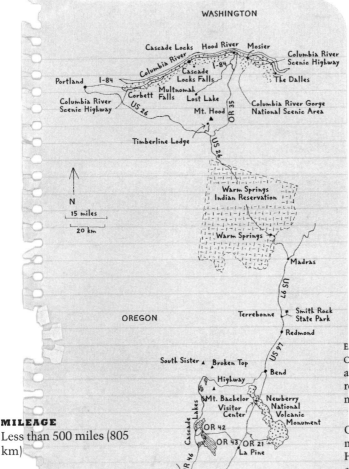

MILEAGE
Less than 500 miles (805 km).

RESOURCES
- Columbia River Gorge National Scenic Area: 902 Wasco Avenue, Hood River, OR 97031; (541) 386-2333.
- Mount Hood Scenic Railroad: Phone for reservations at (800) 872-4661.
- Sternwheeler *Columbia Gorge*: Cascade Locks; (541) 374-8427.
- Lava Lands Visitor Center: 58201 S. Highway 97, Bend, OR 97707; (541) 593-2421.

CAMPGROUNDS

AINSWORTH STATE PARK: Off Interstate 84, 21 miles (34 km) east of exit 18, 1.2 miles west off exit 35; campsites with full hook-ups, restrooms with showers; reservations not accepted.

EAGLE CREEK FOREST CAMP: Off Interstate 84 at exit 41; campsites and restrooms; reservations not accepted.

VIENTO STATE PARK: Off Interstate 84, 8 miles (13 km) west of Hood River; tent sites and RV sites with electrical sites, restrooms with showers; reservations not accepted.

LOST LAKE FOREST CAMP: Thirty miles (48 km) southwest of Hood River; campsites, vault toilets; reservations not accepted.

SHERWOOD FOREST CAMP: Off OR 35, 24 miles (39 km) south of Hood River; campsites, vault toilets; reservations not accepted.

ROBIN HOOD FOREST CAMP: Off OR 35, 28 miles (45 km) south of Hood River; campsites, vault toilets; reservations not accepted.

TRILLIUM FOREST CAMP: One mile (1.6 km) west of US 26 and OR 35 junction, then south on FR 2656 for 1.3 miles; campsites, vault toilets; reservations not accepted.

ELK LAKE FOREST CAMP: Off Cascade Lakes Highway, 33 miles (53 km) west and south of Bend; campsites, vault toilets (10 more sites at adjacent Point Campground); reservations not accepted.

LAVA LAKE FOREST CAMP AND LAVA LAKE LODGE: Off Cascade Lakes Highway, 38 miles (61 km) west and south from Bend; campsites, vault toilets, reservations not accepted; adjacent Little Lava campsites, vault toilets, reservations not accepted; lodge has RV park with hookups, reservations at (541) 382-9443.

CRANE PRAIRIE FOREST CAMP AND CRANE PRAIRIE RESORT: Off Cascade Lakes Highway at junction with Road 42, go east 3 miles (4.8 km) and then north on Road 4270 for 4.2 miles (6.8 km); campsites, vault toilets, reservations at (541) 383-9443; resort has RV park with hookups, reservations at (541) 383-3939.

SOUTH TWIN AND WEST SOUTH TWIN LAKES FOREST CAMPS AND TWIN LAKE RESORT: Off Cascade Lakes Highway, 44 miles (71 km) southwest of Bend; South Twin and West South Twin have campsites, vault and flush toilets, with showers available nearby; resort has RV park with hookups, reservations at (541) 593-6526.

NEWBERRY NATIONAL VOLCANIC MONUMENT: Off US 97, 18 miles (29 km) east on Road 21; Paulina Lake Campground has campsite, restrooms; Little Crater has campsites, vault toilets; East Lake has campsites, restrooms; Hot Springs has campsites, vault toilets; Cinder Hill has campsites, restrooms; Chief Paulina Horse Camp has horse campsites; reservations for all at (800) 280-2267.

Several years ago, as I drove through the Columbia River Gorge in early morning, I was greeted with one of those rare, seductive sunrises when the mist was breaking up as the sun pierced and warmed it. Such a transforming mist has a way of defining individual subjects, and a stunning succession of rocky pinnacles, tall conifers, sheer rock walls, and waterfalls were highlighted on this natural stage. Ridges appeared to slide into the river, daring it to devour them; waterfalls seemed suspended in midair. In my mind, I visualized a Chinook Indian poised on a rock near the river, a spear over his head, waiting for a salmon to swim by. I have returned often to hike the rich forest trails to the top of waterfalls and see what splendors the day will bring in the Columbia River Gorge National Scenic Area. It is never the same, but it is always wonderful.

How was this spectacular gorge formed? Imagine the scene some 12,000 years ago when melting glaciers precipitated catastrophic floods and landslides. Ten times the combined flow of all the rivers of the world sluiced into a slot carved by the Columbia River through the Cascade Mountains. According to geologist John Eliot Allen, this widening of the river valley "cut away the lower courses of the tributary streams and left high on the valley walls the hanging notches from which the falls depend." The result was the greatest concentration of high waterfalls in North America towering above the Columbia River.

Columbia River Gorge National Scenic Area

Begin this tour by heading east out of Portland, Oregon, on Interstate 84, preferably during midweek to avoid crowds in the gorge. By traveling eastward you will follow the sweep of weather moving in from the Pacific Ocean, letting you see how mountains influence the rainfall and vegetation of the western side of the Cascades.

Two options are available at exit 18 past Troutdale: continue on Interstate 84 or take the historic Columbia River Scenic Highway. Promoted by the vision of Sam Hill and designed by Sam Lancaster, this engineering marvel of a road was dedicated in 1916 and received an enthusiastic international response. The first 22-mile (35.4 km) section climbs from farmland to rain forest and twists like a sidewinder at the edge of lichen-encrusted cliffs past a succession of super stopping points. Since a few accesses

The Columbia River Scenic Highway, OR.

to viewpoints and waterfalls do exist along Interstate 84, consider whether you wish to take a long motorhome or trailer unit on the scenic route. The historic highway merges with the interstate again near Ainsworth State Park, where the tour continues east. The tour presented here follows the historic highway, with comments on where connections from the interstate are found.

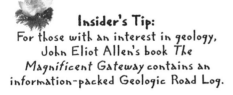

Insider's Tip:
For those with an interest in geology, John Eliot Allen's book *The Magnificent Gateway* contains an information-packed Geologic Road Log.

Two quiet day-use parks—Lewis and Clark, and Dabney—are along the historic highway before Corbett, exit 22 on Interstate 84, where a short road climbs to the scenic route near Portland Women's Forum State Park. This park offers the best high viewpoint of the gorge area; it is spectacular. For an even higher viewpoint, a 13-mile

(20.8 km) side trip is possible just past this park via the Larch Mountain Road. The road ends at a picnic spot at the top of the mountain, the terminus of the 7-mile Larch Mountain Trail from the Multnomah Falls Lodge, and is a great place from which to view the sunset on five major Cascade peaks at Sherrard Point.

The Vista House viewed from Women's Forum is another mile along the historic highway at Crown Point State Park. In addition to more awesome views of gorge geology, the intriguing Vista House structure contains a gift shop and many exhibits, among them an informative three-dimensional table map of the gorge.

 Insider's Tip:
I was in this elevated area on the historic highway one evening when the sun had just set. Looking west, the river was a soft purple color, with a ripe orange layer above the horizon; green dots of many lights accented the scene. A super find for a photographer.

Vehicles travel the "figure eight loops" a mile east of Crown Point before reaching Guy W. Talbot State Park, where the first of the famous gorge waterfalls are located. At 249 feet (76 m), Latourell Falls is the second highest in the gorge. Trails and picnic sites invite spending time here.

Some of the appeal of the historic highway is in its bridges, rock barriers, and moss-covered stone guardrails, which are examples of dry masonry construction by Italian stonemasons. Lancaster wanted the highway to be a work of art that blended with the beauty of the gorge, and a testament to his success is shown splendidly by the slow pace of driving.

Bridal Veil Falls State Park is a rewarding stop for several reasons. In addition to the hike down to see the falls, this is a nice spot for picnicking (watch out for falling pears from the trees overhead). Of special interest is the barrier-free interpretive trail adjacent to wildflower meadows and camas fields on a level walk to a view of the gorge. Another picturesque stop is at Wahkeena Falls, where the trails get serious and interconnecting. One of my favorite hikes in the gorge is the 3.3-mile (5.3-km) Wahkeena-Perdition Loop. It starts at the Wahkeena Falls Picnic Grounds below the falls on Wahkeena Trail No. 420, crosses Wahkeena Creek, and meets Perdition Trail No. 421 in 0.4 mile (0.6 km). This trail is somewhat unusual in that it has many stairsteps along the way. In 1.2 miles (1.9 km) you'll come to Larch Mountain Trail No. 441; take this trail for 1.1 miles (1.8 km). This last trail takes you to the top of Multnomah Falls and is a great place for solitude or a wilderness picnic along the stream that feeds the falls. Continue down the trail past the double falls to the highway. To return to Wahkeena Picnic Grounds, follow Return Trail No. 442 on the west side of the lodge for another 0.6 mile (1 km). It's only a mile via the highway to Multnomah Falls.

Multnomah Falls is a highlight of the Columbia Gorge. In fact, it's the most visited tourist attraction in Oregon. A spectacular 620-foot (189 m) double falls, the Multnomah Falls area is a busy place and includes an interpretive center, gift shop, and lodge. Meriwether Lewis didn't miss this attraction, and he commented that it was "the most remarkable of these cascade falls." He was right.

A short distance past Multnomah Falls is Oneonta Gorge, where a creek flows through a gash in basalt rock. In addition to considerable botanical and geologic interest at this stop, the unusual attraction is a side trip upstream to view a waterfall. You simply wade 900 feet (274 m) up the creek.

More waterfalls are yet to be seen along the highway, with Horsetail Falls a short distance farther. Another fine loop trail (2.7 miles or 4.3 km) worth taking here imbues you with the essence of the gorge. Begin by climbing a trail alongside this high falls (Horsetail Falls Trail No. 438) for 0.4 mile (0.6 km) to Upper Horsetail Falls. From here you can simply turn around to return or continue by walking along a ledge behind this falls that has been nicknamed "Ponytail Falls," the site of many photographs. This trail continues across a bridge over Oneonta Creek and reaches a junction with Oneonta Trail No. 424 at 1.3 (2.1 km) miles. From here it's 0.9 mile (1.3 km) to the scenic highway, where a 0.5-mile (0.8-km) stroll on this road returns you to Horsetail Falls. The historic highway ends just past Ainsworth State Park, which offers an easy walk to Horsetail Falls, and this is one possible campground in the gorge.

In mid-July, spots of color are found by waterfalls and in the forest: golden monkeyflowers, columbine, bleeding hearts, pearly everlasting, penstemon, and thimbleberries, turning ripe red and edible. The wealth of both short and long trails here offer a great way to get some needed exercise after RV traveling. The forest is lovely—even some old growth survives—and the wild mountain streams and vegetation are fine accompaniments to hikes. While hiking I've surprised several ospreys flying to their nests with fish in their talons; they always alert me with their frenzied "cheereek!" It's wonderfully peaceful away from the main road.

If you have elected to stay on Interstate 84—and you will see the distant waterfalls and the river from this highway—Rooster Rock State Park at exit 25 offers a boat basin, some trails, a view of Vista House, and a sandy beach with "clothing optional" sunbathing on Sand Island. Lewis and Clark passed this area after riding the "great chute," a wild place on the Columbia River now drowned by the Bonneville Dam. Travelers on Interstate 84 can use exit 27 for Bridal Veil State Park and follow the exit instructions for parking at the Multnomah Falls area.

Dam construction on the Columbia River greatly tamed its once wild nature and affected the numbers of salmon. The informative stop at Bonneville Dam (exit 40) features a fish hatchery, lock, fish ladder, and visitor center on Bradford Island. Particularly fascinating is viewing the fish at the center's underwater windows. In addition to seeing a close-up view of salmon and steelhead swimming upriver (steelhead and summer Chinook in early summer, fall Chinook in late summer), other fish species—shad, sturgeon, lamprey—sometimes swim past the window. Official counters tally individual species.

Another excellent camping base is Eagle Creek Forest Camp, the nation's oldest such camp (which is accessible directly only by those eastbound from exit 41; westbound travelers can loop back east from the Bonneville Dam exit). This camp provides access to several trails that offer wonderful recreation, including the very popular Eagle Creek Trail, which comprises 13.2 miles (21 km) carved into basaltic cliffs above forested Eagle Creek; the trail sometimes descends to the creek. Several scenic destinations are along the way: Punch Bowl Falls is only 2.1 miles (3.4 km), where you

Windsurfers in Columbia River Gorge, OR.

might see someone flyfishing between the maidenhair fern-splashed walls of the rock canyon, or you can continue on to High Bridge and Tunnel Falls. This is not a difficult hike, but those phobic about hiking near a steep drop-off should not do this trail. Again, though, you'd be wise to do this hike midweek. The day use and campground areas have some fine examples of rustic stone construction, which were built by the Civilian Conservation Corps.

> Special Event:
> The Sternwheeler Days Festival is held the third weekend in June at Cascade Locks.

Cascade Locks was named for the navigation locks that were built in 1896 so ships could avoid the dangerous river cascades. The locks are unnecessary now because the Bonneville Dam flooded the cascades, which were problems for both Lewis and Clark and pioneers on the Oregon Trail. In 1890, the sternwheeler *Harvest Queen* caused some excitement when she shot the cascade rapids.

Camping is available in Marine Park. Consider boarding the sternwheeler *Columbia Gorge* there for an excursion downriver (historical narration included). This cruise passes under the "Bridge of the Gods," offers views of Indian fishing platforms, and stops at Bonneville Dam and Stevenson, Washington. Brunch and dinner cruises are available. At the rest stop at Starvation Creek State Park, a short trail leads to another waterfall, and serious mountain climbers take the 7-mile (11 km) trail to the summit of Mount Defiance to get in shape for climbing Mount Hood.

Insider's Tip:
Exit 58, eastbound only, directs travelers to the Mitchell Point Overlook, the site of Sam Hill's five-window Mitchell Point Tunnel along the old highway, with a trail now under construction. It also provides access to three primitive state park areas. The primary attraction is the Wygant Trail, a little-used trail that I found had a sensational spot for a lunch stop at the second gorge viewpoint. Use caution at this sheer drop-off—but what a view!

The strong summer winds that develop on this stretch of river along Interstate 84 lure amateur and international hot-shot windsurfers. Viento State Park is the first place you'll come to where you can camp and get out onto the water. Even if you're not a windsurfer, you'll probably enjoy watching this fun spectator sport. Wind-surfing races are featured throughout the summer at the Waterfront Event Site in

ablaze with wildflower color in spring. This site vividly shows the contrast of the wetter western face of the gorge with the dry eastern terrain.

Mount Hood Loop

For a switch to mountain vistas and moods, return to the town of Hood River and head south on OR 35 following the East Fork of the Hood River, with 11,240-foot Mount Hood looming upstream. Would you enjoy camping by a lake with that mountain dominating the scene? If so, take a side trip to a place where paddlers take to the water in canoes and hikers easily circle the lake, all feeling the overpowering presence of Oregon's highest mountain. It's a lovely 30-mile (48-km) drive southwest of Hood River past fruit orchards to Lost Lake.

The main tour continues south on OR 35, with camping options at either Sherwood or Robin Hood forest camps, which are near the highway but immersed in the

Bunchberry flowers at Trillium Lake Campground, Mount Hood Loop, OR.

> **Special Events:**
> The Columbia Gorge Pro-Am windsurfing competition is held at the Hood River Event Site in late June. Hood River also hosts the Gorge Games—featuring wind-surfing, paragliding, kayaking, mountain biking, and more—in mid-July. The Cross Channel Swim is on Labor Day; anyone willing to stroke across the river from the Washington side may participate.

Hood River, a town permeated with board-sailing enthusiasm and businesses. For any-one interested in learning the sport, this is the place. Experts on the subject abound. Historical Memaloose State Park (west-bound access only), east of Hood River, is another popular campground for wind-surfers, while Mayer State park is a day-use access spot for them. Bring your board and sails and join the fun.

Although our tour heads south on OR 35, a pretty side trip is the 9-mile section of the highway that climbs from Mosier to the Rowena Crest Overlook and to the Tom McCall Nature Preserve, where hawks whirl overhead and trails meander through a species-rich Nature Conservancy area

> **Special Event:**
> In mid-July and mid-August, the Mount Hood Scenic Railroad features a staged train robbery on their scenic four-hour round-trip ride from Hood River to Parkdale through fruit orchard country complete with Mount Hood vistas.

green forest. A 3-mile (4.8 km) river trail connects the two campgrounds. Sherwood is near a day hike to Tamanawas Falls and Robin Hood offers a switchback trail to the Gumajuwac Saddle across the highway. Anglers enjoy fishing the stream.

Hiking possibilities are numerous in the Mount Hood National Forest and Mount Hood Wilderness. The most famous trail is the 37.6-mile (60.5-km) Timberline Trail through the alpine country, where weather swirls around the summit of Mount Hood. Although 21 trails connect

Mount Hood View and East Fork of the Hood River, OR.

Many campers choose to stay overnight at nearby Trillium Lake Campground among the blossoming rhododendrons and bunchberries. This is a jewel of a lake where canoes glint in the first light of day under the magic of Mount Hood. Accessed by a road just before the intersection of OR 35 and US 26; this is just west of the spine of the Cascades and vegetation is lush.

Many of the Oregon Trail pioneers circled Mount Hood to the south rather than via the Columbia River, although this route probably was no easier. It was a boggy trail of roots, snags, and forest. Men and women strained muscles as they pitched down the mountain side, using ropes tied to trees to lower their wagons on the old Barlow Road. Ribs of roads now connect support points of civilization, and traveling by RV is easy.

So far, the tour has followed what is called the Mount Hood Loop, which continues on US 26 back to Portland, but unless you wish to spend time hiking, fishing, and exploring the Mount Hood area—certainly not a bad choice—why not see more Cascade peaks? To do so, continue southeast on US 26 through Warm Springs Indian Reservation to US 97 at Madras.

An exciting stop along the route to Bend is just east of Terrebonne at Smith Rock State Park. The Crooked River flows through a spectacular canyon of multicolored rock pinnacles and crags, geologic features that lured a movie company to shoot the film *Rooster Cogburn,* starring John Wayne, here. Because the main attractions are hiking the trails and watching expert

with this high-country loop around the mountain, the easiest way to sample a bit of this trail is to drive to Timberline Lodge and walk right out on it among the summer bloom of wildflowers. To do this, follow OR 35 to US 26 west, where a short, steep road branches off to Timberline Lodge. Chair lifts take people up the mountain for sightseeing or year-round skiing on the Palmer Glacier Snowfield.

It is worth the trip to Timberline Lodge just to see this project of the Works Progress Administration. The Lodge is an impressive example of conservation and creativity by Oregon craftspeople. Andirons for the great fireplace were handwrought from old railroad tracks; scraps of uniforms became handwoven rugs; telephone poles became carved staircase posts; huge wooden beams anchor the openness of high walls. A sculpted bear head adorns the exterior stone structure.

An excellent family hike is just a few miles farther west on US 26, where a trail leads south off the highway to Mirror Lake.

Columbia Gorge Sternwheeler at Cascade Locks, OR.

rock climbers negotiate the sheer vertical rock surfaces, hot summer days are not the best time to stop here. In spring and fall, creeping humans scaling the walls seem to be everywhere. This place is beautiful with the cool waters curving between red rock cliffs. No camping is allowed except at the off-road bivouac area. I enjoyed doing that one evening in my backpacking tent. It's a great place to wake up to the sounds of birds and watch the rising sun light the canyon. If it's early or late in a not-too-hot day, do stop.

Cascade Lakes Scenic Byway

Close your eyes and try to envision an ancient scene when molten rock was belched from the bowels of Earth into a period of glaciation. Can you imagine the intervening years, as nature softened and added to this fire-and-ice scene and gave us today's spectacular Cascade Range? The spine of these mountains sashays north from northern California across Oregon, through Washington to the Canadian border, and one of best roads for getting close to several volcanic peaks, an abundance of lakes, and the Three Sisters Wilderness is the Cascade Lakes Highway, a National Forest Scenic Byway.

In Bend, be alert for signs directing you southwest to the Cascade Lakes Highway, the Mount Bachelor Ski Area, or Century Drive, or look for small mountain-peak signs labeled "Tour Route"—all will aim you toward the correct route. The initial jogging tour route takes you through downtown Bend, past Drake Lake, and a flurry of condos. A detour around construction might also be thrown in before you're out onto the open road. Maps designate this road OR 372, but on a recent trip I uncovered no such highway signs along the road. You will, however, soon see some signs for OR 46. It is possible to access this byway south of Bend from a couple of other entry roads, but going in this direction will definitely result in a few scenic "Wows!"

Near mile 17, as the road climbs slowly toward the mountains, you'll catch the first dazzling appearance of Mount Bachelor—

centerpiece of the largest ski resort in the northwest. This peak booms across your vision for an incredible three miles. The dazzle has barely faded when both South Sister and Broken Top span the horizon; these overwhelming images in a sunlit sky definitely merit another "Wow!" Continue past the turnoff for the mountain lodge unless you want to see it or take a ski lift to the summit for a scheduled talk by the rangers on the natural history of the Cascades.

Smith Rock State Park, OR.

Soda Creek and a turnoff on your left for Sparks Lake soon appear at an elevation of 5,428 feet. The Sparks Lake area offers camping possibilities and includes a boat launch, wildflowers, and a chance to see a variety of birds, deer, and perhaps elk. At the foot of Bachelor Mountain, shallow Sparks Lake is becoming marshland that spreads out sinuously over a large area.

A short distance west, on the north side of the highway, is the Fall Creek Trail (No. 17) to Green Lakes. Popular long before an article appeared in *Outside* magazine list-

Backpacker at Green Lakes; Broken Top Mountain in the background; Cascades Lakes Highway, OR.

ing it as Oregon's contribution to America's top fifty hikes, it is a wonderful hike, but because of concerns about overuse hikers are urged to go gently and treat the land kindly. It is only 4.5 miles (7.2 km) to the lakes, an easy 1,100-foot gain in elevation into the Three Sisters Wilderness, so it can be done as a day hike. The path follows a mountain creek past a vibrant waterfall and a massive obsidian flow that created the basin containing these three stunning and appropriately named lakes. What contributes to the overall beauty is the juxtaposition of Three Sisters and Broken Top as a backdrop, with meadows of subalpine flowers blooming in summer. It's a perfect overnight backpacking trip for those who want a day away from the RV and into wildness (I went after Labor Day during midweek). The only way to appreciate mountain peaks reflecting on the placid water in early morning, and a sunset painting Broken Top a burnt orange, is to camp overnight. A horse trail is also available. Overnight permits and site reservations are required.

The scenic road continues past the soft green beauty of Devils Lake, where ca-noeists frequently paddle the calm water. Roadside scenery now includes lava chunks piled high; then there are 4 miles (6.4 km) of access roads to attractions along Elk Lake—forest service information, a resort, two campgrounds, and a couple of picnic areas. Windsurfers take off from Sunset Cove, on the east side of the lake. On the easily reached west side, the campsites are not overly long, but they are popular. Early arrivals pull right up to the shallow edge of the water and children float on inflatables in the warm sunshine, perhaps startling a great blue heron into flight. Daytime temperatures are comfortable in summer at these elevations, although nights are cool. Bringing layers of clothes is the best approach. An easy hike into the wilderness, the trail to Horse Lake, is just across the highway. The trail intersects the long-distance Pacific Crest Trail. The trailhead for another popular day hike—Sisters Mirror Lake—is a few miles north along the highway.

At Lava Lake and Little Lava Lake, a resort caters to anglers and rents boats for some of the area's superb fishing; a campground with hookups and another one with spaces for tents are found here. The location is pretty, with mountain views and wetlands bordering the lake. The headwaters for the Deschutes River is at Little Lava Lake, where the newborn stream curves through meadows before its wild flow is impounded first by Crane Prairie Reservoir and then Wickiup Reservoir. After that it continues in a wild frenzy of zigzagging bends and curves on its way to the Columbia River. Kayaks are sometimes seen on the young Deschutes River near Deschutes Bridge.

As the highway jogs around Crane Prairie, a spur road near mile marker 48 leads to Osprey Point. Anglers take the short trails to stream fishing; bird-watchers choose the longer trail (only 0.25 mile or 440 yards) to Osprey Point. Along the undulating shoreline are platforms for osprey nests on old snags, which is their preference, and other appropriate nesting sites for Canada geese and wood ducks. More mountain views are a backdrop for the wetlands in this place of wild solitude. Be alert for ospreys overhead and their fish-catching dives into the lake.

Cultus Lake, on the west side of the highway, offers more trails into the wilderness area and shallow sandy beaches. Equestrians might consider a base camp at Cultus Corral Horse Camp.

Just north of Wickiup Reservoir are a couple of small but deep lakes, North and South Twin lakes, which are classic examples of volcanic maars (craters). A resort at South Twin Lake offers hookups and a campground with a rare tenter access to shower facilities. The campground is a great place for watching the interplay of sunlight and morning mist rising from a warming lake while canoeists and anglers take to the water against a forest backdrop.

To visit the developed area at Crane Prairie, where services are available, head east on OR 42. Our tour also heads that way at first, and continues to the intersection with OR 43 and takes this to US 97. This latter route passes through the Pringle Falls area, which is a lovely natural area where camping is available along the Deschutes River.

Insider's Tip:
An excellent birding and flyfishing lake is Davis Lake, which is a few miles south of this tour. Both the East and West Davis camps are off the beaten track.

Newberry National Volcanic Monument

Three miles (4.8 km) north of the junction of OR 43 with US 97, journey toward this country's newest national volcanic monument, Newberry, on paved County Road 21 (winter route for snowmobiles). The central feature of the monument is a 500-square-mile caldera, Newberry Crater, that has two high-elevation lakes inside it—Paulina Lake and East Lake. Paulina Mountain (7,985 feet), was left sitting on the crater rim overlooking the lakes when Newberry Volcano lost its summit.

Ten thousand years ago, Native Americans lived near the active volcano, hunted for obsidian for arrowheads, and traded this valuable commodity with faraway tribes. It seems appropriate that Paulina Lake was named for Paiute Indian Chief Paulina. Forest Service archaeologists continue to compile data concerning the human history of Newberry Crater. If you find an arrowhead, pick it up to look at it, but return it to the same spot.

On the 18-mile (28.8 km) road into the monument, Paulina Creek Falls is a scenic picnic stop. Numerous campgrounds are accessible past the entrance station, and it's a good idea to choose one that's located near your favorite activities. Two of the camps—North Cove and Warm Springs— are accessible only by boat or the 7.5-mile (12-km) trail circling Paulina Lake, Paulina Lake and Little Crater campgrounds also edge Paulina Lake. Hot Springs, East Lake, and Cinder Hill campgrounds are near East Lake, where you can sail or boat over hot springs that feed this lake. All the campgrounds are near one of the many trails lacing the crater area, so you can get in great shape here given enough time. The elevation of these lakes is over 6,000 feet, considerably higher than those on the Cascade Lakes Tour; therefore, the temperatures are cooler.

Newberry Crater is a landscape with visible volcanic features: ash and obsidian flows, cinder cones, pumice rings, and rhyolitic domes. Rumblings of geothermal activity and temperatures of up to 500°F are evidence that future volcanic eruption is not unlikely.

Various hikes offer excellent reasons for staying to explore. The 21-mile (34-km) Crater Rim Trail, which passes scores of great views of the surrounding area in central Oregon, is accessed at several points along its loop; another trail slashes through the center of the crater in 8.5 miles (14 km); other trails make connections. Many of the trails allow equestrians.

The most unusual hike, however, is the 1-mile (1.6 km) Obsidian Flow Trail, complete with interpretive signs. This 1,300-year-old flow is the youngest known lava flow in Oregon. And this was the place where Astronaut R. Walter Cunningham, accompanied by scientists and engineers, came in 1964 to test the mobility of moon-suited workers on the shattered black volcanic glass and stark pumice surfaces. Just taking a walk on this slippery black obsidian in regular clothes requires caution.

Be on the lookout for unusual plants and wildlife throughout the monument. In August, thousands of frogs migrate up the flow from nearby Lost Lake, so keep an eye out for them. The entire crater area is within the Newberry Caldera Wildlife Refuge, with bald eagles nesting near East Lake, and migrating ducks, geese, and tundra swans seen around the high lakes. Bats in the

Misty morning paddlers on Twin Lakes, Cascade Lakes Highway, OR.

caldera busy themselves catching mosquitoes (up to 600 per hour). Here, you can learn about the interconnectedness of life's events. For example, ash deposited in the monument from the eruption of Mount Mazama 7,700 years ago (now Crater Lake) nourishes a rare and sensitive plant called the pumice grape fern.

The monument includes considerably more than the crater area. North along US 97, watch for signs to the Lava Cast Forest and follow gravel Forest Road 9720 10 miles (16 km) east to see the 1-mile (1.6 km) interpretive trail of tree molds and smooth-textured pahoehoe lava. If you like caves—and are prepared to explore one—the Lava River Cave is farther north along US 97.

Although I have taken you through the back door and most significant part of the monument first, a stop at the monument visitor center, just north of the cave area, is adjacent to interesting Lava Butte and has a couple of short self-guiding trails. Northwest of the center, Benham Falls, Dillon Falls, and Lava Island Falls are easily viewed from trails along the Deschutes River. Kayakers and canoeists often run the river below and above these turbulent chutes of water. Eagles, ospreys, otters, beaver, and dozens of species of birds inhabit the river corridor.

After visiting Newberry, the Cascade Lakes, and the Columbia Gorge in Oregon, you'll no doubt agree that volcanic areas provide an intriguing backdrop for recreation, especially when lakes, wetlands, and rivers add zest to the choices of activities.

Special Event:
Informative evening stargazing is scheduled throughout the summer. It's usually held at Lava Butte, but sometimes takes place at Lava Lake Campground. Check with a ranger for details.

CHAPTER 6

Northwest Mountains and Historic Trails: *Wallowa Mountains to Glacier National Park*

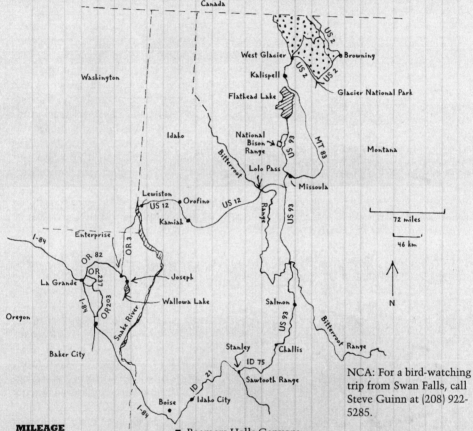

MILEAGE

Under 2,000 miles (3,220 km)

RESOURCES

- National Historic Oregon Trail Interpretive Center, Bureau of Land Management, Box 987, Baker City, OR 97814; phone (541) 523-1843.
- Joseph Chamber of Commerce: (541) 432-1015.
- River Quest Excursions: Full and half-day trips to Hells Canyon; (208) 746-8060; (800) 589-1129.

- Beamers Hells Canyon: Day, dinner, and overnight trips to Hells Canyon; (509) 758-4800; (800) 522-6966.
- Nez Perce National Historic Park, P.O. Box 93, Spalding, ID 83551.
- Kamiah Chamber of Commerce: (208) 935-2290.
- Polson Chamber of Commerce: (406) 883-5969.
- Salmon Valley Chamber of Commerce: (208) 756-2100.
- Stanley-Sawtooth Chamber of Commerce: (800) 878-7950.
- Snake River Birds of Prey

NCA: For a bird-watching trip from Swan Falls, call Steve Guinn at (208) 922-5285.

CAMPGROUNDS

WALLOWA LAKE STATE PARK: Off OR 82, 6 miles (10 km) south of Joseph; year-round camping with full hookup and tent sites, restrooms with showers; yurt with heat, lights, and beds and couch that sleeps 5; Reservations: (800) 452-5687.

PACIFIC PARK CAMPGROUND: Off OR 82, 6 miles (10 km) south of Joseph; free sites (PP & L) at Wallowa Lake; Reservations: PP & L in Portland (503) 464-5035.

FIELDS SPRING STATE PARK: Off WA 129, 3.9 miles (6.3 km) south of Anatone; tent campsites; reservations not accepted.

HELLS GATE STATE PARK: Four miles (6.4 km) south of Lewiston on Snake River Avenue; marina and store, campsites (many with electric and water hookups), restrooms with showers; reservations: (208) 799-5015.

WILDERNESS GATEWAY FOREST CAMP: Located 48 miles (77 km) east of Kooskia on US 12; campsites in several loops, small RVs and tents in loop C along the river and up to 40-foot RVs in loop B (flush toilets here only); horse camping loop; reservations not accepted.

GLACIER NATIONAL PARK CAMPGROUNDS (WEST TO EAST): Apgar near the west entrance; Fish Creek; Avalanche; Sprague allows no towed units; Rising Sun; St. Mary; Many Glacier; all have restrooms; showers are only available at Rising Sun and Swiftcurrent motor inns for a fee; reservations not accepted.

ROCKY MOUNTAINS LAKE CAMPGROUNDS ALONG MT 83 (NORTH TO SOUTH): Swan Lake (1 mile [1.6 km] northwest of Swan Lake); Seeley Lake (just south of Seeley Lake); Salmon Lake (5 miles [8 km] south of Seeley Lake); reservations not accepted.

BITTERROOT VALLEY CAMPGROUNDS: Spring Gulch Forest Camp (5 miles [8 km] northwest of Sula on US 93); Lake Como (5 miles [8 km] north of Darby off US 93, follow signs west to park); reservations not accepted.

REDFISH LAKE CAMPGROUNDS, SAWTOOTH NATIONAL RECREATION AREA: Five miles (8 km) south of Stanley on ID 75; first-come, first-served sites at Sunny Gulch, Chinook Bay, Mountain View, Mount Heyburn, and Sockeye; reservations at Glacier View, Outlet, and Point: (800) 280-2267.

FAREWELL BEND STATE PARK: Off Interstate 84, 4 miles (6.4 km) southeast of Huntington; electrical and tent sites, covered wagons sleep four and different size Tepees sleep up to 12 people, restrooms with showers; reservations: (800) 452-5687.

W hen explorers and pioneer settlers first came to the Pacific Northwest, they encountered majestic mountains that tested their courage and endurance. Finding the best route for travel was often a necessity for survival and for reaching their destination.

The wild and frequent waterways offered swift passage for daring spirits, yet overland journeys were often required. The local Indians were familiar with these landscapes and mountain passes and often helped in finding routes to ease the trekking of early explorers. As an intrepid wanderer of landscapes, I can't resist imagining what those other travelers encountered, can you?

This tour lets RVers easily travel some of the route of the Lewis and Clark Expedition of 1805 to 1806, the path of covered wagons on the Oregon Trail, and the passages of the Nez Perce Indians. Rivers are a vital part of this tour and offer recreation and escape from the summer heat. And since today's highways permit some travel through the high country, a trip through Glacier National Park will illuminate the significance of time, geologic uplift, and glacier movements in producing the magnificent vistas of the northwest that have historically challenged travelers. You'll see awesome landscapes.

National Historic Oregon Trail Interpretive Center

To put travelers into an historical and reflective mood, this tour begins five miles east of Baker City, Oregon, at the Bureau of Land Management's National Historic Oregon Trail Visitor Center on Flagstaff Hill. The view from the center is a stunning panorama. Imagine what it was like for the pioneers who were seeing for the first time the promise of the Oregon Territory in the Powder River Valley to the west, which was so different from the sagebrush plain they had just crossed. Honoring the nearly 400,000 emigrants who made the 2,000-mile journey between 1841 and 1869, the

Special Event:
Joseph celebrates Chief Joseph Days annually during the last weekend in July, when a major attraction is a top-notch rodeo, with riders on the Wrangler circuit.

center's exhibits explore six major themes: the Oregon Trail experience, mining in the West, explorers and fur traders, natural history of Northeast Oregon, Native American history, and the General Land Office. Period costumes, stage productions, and outdoor programs enhance your visit. Outside, follow in the footsteps of early pioneers by walking some of the 4.2 miles (6.8 km) of the interpretive trail system as it passes an encampment of covered wagons, drops into the valley to a rutted campsite, and passes a lode mining operation. I hope you will experience some of the emotional impact I felt when considering these brave pioneers.

Travel continues in this rural mood by taking OR 203 a few miles north of Baker City as it skirts national forest and passes camping possibilities at quiet Catherine Creek State Park. At the quaint town of Union, head north on OR 237 and pass Cove Hot Springs before connecting with OR 82 at Island City.

Aiming toward the Wallowa Mountains, pass through Imbler with its old wooden church and then through valley views of checkerboard fields fringed by mountains. With little traffic, the road climbs gradually past the Grande Ronde River and wildflower-flecked meadows as you experience the sensation that a camping trip is underway. At 3,538-foot (1,078 m) Minam Summit, a road heads north two miles to Minam State Recreation Area, with fishing and primitive campsites along the Minam River. Keep an eye out for bald eagles and other raptors. This is the edge of Wallowa County, "land of many winding waters," with four rivers that are popular for fishing and float trips: the Snake, the Imnaha, the Wallowa, and the Grande Ronde.

The magnificent rustic log building in Enterprise, the Wallowa Mountains Visitor Center, beckons a stop for all sorts of

national forest information. An impressive 383-year-old Ponderosa pine stretches tall inside the building. For a bird's-eye view of the Elk Cap Wilderness, Wallowa Lake, the Lostine River, and the route later on OR 3, scan the three-dimensional map of the surrounding area to see where you're heading.

Joseph is a small town full of summer happenings amid the always present fine arts and crafts shops. Art festivals, antique car shows, air shows, summer stock theater, and a weekly reenactment of the 1896 Joseph Bank robbery are a few of the fun attractions.

Wallowa Mountains—Little Switzerland of America

After passing the burial site of Chief Joseph of the Nez Perce Indians, much of the 6-mile (9.7 km) drive south to camping and picnicking at Wallowa Lake State Park follows Wallowa Lake, a spectacular glacial lake edged by high mountains of the same name. Because of its great location, the park was picked by *National Geographic* as one of six outstanding state parks in the far West. Camp there and you'll have wonderful territory to explore.

Amid the glorious scenery that was the cherished summer home of the Nez Perce Indians, fishing, boating, and canoeing are obvious activities, but consider hiking one of the many trails into the mountains. This is horse country and nearby facilities rent mounts.

My best experience here was taking the tramway, which is a short walk from the park, to the top of 8,200-foot (2500 m) Mount Howard. It is exciting enough to ride the steepest vertical lift for a four-passenger gondola in North America, but during that fifteen minutes the panorama of the Wallowa Mountains, mountain streams, and the countryside surrounding Wallowa Lake unfolds. At the summit, two miles of alpine trails and wildflowers beckon hikers to make discoveries in the crisp mountain air as views stretch into four states past a row of peaks. Some visitors just relax at the Summit Deli and Alpine Patio.

The Wallowa Mountains comprise

Insider's Tip:

Trailhead passes are required in the Wallowa-Whitman Forest and must be purchased for the day or year at National Forest offices—not at trailheads—and displayed on your windshield.

twenty-eight peaks over 8,000 feet and six-teen peaks over 9,000 feet. The Matterhorn is the highest at 9,845 feet. The fact that this grouping of peaks contains tropical coral fossils, mollusks, and sponges lends support to the theory that these mountains are displaced or suspect terrains transported by continental drift—and a considerable amount of geologic upheaval—from tropical islands in the middle of the Pacific Ocean.

From Wallowa Lake, retrace the route back to Enterprise and head north on OR 3, which is a good road that gradually climbs past rolling hills into national forest and over a 4,693-foot (1,430-m) summit along the Nez Perce Trail. About thirty miles along OR 3, watch carefully for the Joseph Canyon Viewpoint, from which you can peer into the Joseph Creek Valley, once a winter home of the Nez Perce. It is said that Chief Joseph was born in a cave along the creek.

The road is downhill now and soon be-comes curvy and steep as it descends, so go slow and enjoy the beauty of the green hills rolling downward into the valley and clouds painting a pattern of light and dark ripples on the rounded shapes. It helps that traffic usually is sparse, so travel is not stressful. Crossing the border into Washington, the route is now WA 129 and soon meets the zigzagging Grande Ronde River. About 14 miles into Washington, a change of scenery at forest-enveloped Fields Spring State Park invites a pleasant picnic or camp stop among the tall conifers, wildlife, and wild-flowers. For exercise, the park offers a trail with a steady mile climb to Puffer Butte.

After my picnic lunch, I chose to con-tinue 30 miles to camp overnight at Hells Gate State Park in Idaho. The highway de-scends very slowly toward its meeting with the Snake River. The openness of the mead-

View of the Clearwater River from the road to Weippe Prairie.

ows seemed a perfect accompaniment for the recording of Camille Saint-Saëns' "Organ Concerto" that was playing on my radio. Down in the valley, the town of Asotin was visible long before I arrived.

Hells Gate State Park, Idaho

From Asotin, Hells Gate State Park is visi-ble across the river, but you must continue north and then east onto US 12 to cross the Snake River into the Gem State of Idaho. A turn south on Snake River Avenue leads to the state park; there is no need to go through Lewiston now if you camp in the park. The park has some charm, being along the Snake River, but it is a busy place with grassy lawns (good for tents), not the expected wildness of a river in a canyon. Anglers can fish, and the park includes a swimming beach, bicycle path, hiking path, and horse trail. The Canada geese flying by the river at dusk and early morning are welcome sights and sounds. A plus is that the park offers an easy way to visit Hells Canyon National Recreation Area, as boat tours embark here at the marina (be sure to make reservations; I missed out on this great trip).

To continue along the Clearwater River Scenic Byway, return to US 12 and go

Special Events:

Wallowa Lake State Park holds its annual Jazz at the Lake festival in mid-July. In September, Alpenfest is held at the lake.

through Lewiston. This follows the Lewis and Clark Trail past patches of Palouse country picturesque and colorful with variegated yellow, green, and brown hills that remind me of the nap of velveteen or the soft-looking texture of peach fuzz. Be on the lookout for two historic Nez Perce sites, "Coyote's Fishnet" and "Ant and Yellowjacket," which involve legends about Coyote.

Insider's Tip:
At an information center, be sure to pick up a brochure called "Lewis and Clark Across the Lolo Trail." It tells about the explorers' route in Idaho and includes a map with campground locations along the Lochsa River.

This is the treasured land of the Nez Perce, and a short detour south onto US 95 takes you to the Spalding Visitor Center, headquarters of the Nez Perce National Historical Park, which is "as much an idea as it is actual physical property." The exhibits offer insights into the culture and lives of these Indians, who inhabited the valleys of the Clearwater and Snake rivers where they fished, hunted, and dug bulbs of edible camas lily on high plateaus. The intricate bead-weaving designs are fascinating but even more so is the lovely cornhusk weaving, which is very difficult and slow handwork, a craft passed down through generations.

It was from this homeland that, in 1877, the Nez Perce were chased 1,170 miles (1,884 km) on the Nez Perce Trail (Nee-Me-Poo Trail) from Wallowa Lake to Bear Paws, Montana, near the Canadian border. At the time, when a peaceful move to the reservation was underway by Chief Joseph, an unfortunate revenge attack by a few Nez Perce Indians resulted in the flight of some 750 Nez Perce. They fought twenty defensive battles with the Army before their final defeat, just short of refuge in Canada. The irony was that the Nez Perce had been loyal friends and allies of the whites for almost three-quarters of a century.

Insider's Tip:
To visit more of the Nez Perce historic sites than on this tour, follow the directions in the Nez Perce brochure from the center.

The next Nez Perce historic site on US 12 is the Lenore Archeological Site. A stop at Canoe Camp provides a short loop trail, picnic tables, benches, and the exhibit of a canoe that illustrates how Lewis and Clark fashioned five travel canoes out of hollowed logs at this location. Across the river is the Dworshak Dam.

Until Orofino, this tour has followed both the Nez Perce and the Lewis and Clark trails, but the Lewis and Clark Trail now diverts from the Nez Perce Trail and climbs up to Fraser Park Picnic Area and the Weippe Prairie. I wanted to see what this landscape looked like and how it differed from the river canyon I was following, so I took a side trip on ID 11 to see the prairie. Following this drive up a good but winding paved road for about 8 miles (13 km), I marveled at the remarkable change in landscape. For miles—as far as I could see—was prairie, complete with cows and farms; easy travel compared with the river canyon below. It was at Weippe Prairie, the site of several villages and where the Nez Perce dug camas roots, that Lewis and Clark first met the Nez Perce Indians on September 20, 1805, as they traveled west. The expedition was weak after eleven grueling days crossing the Bitterroot Mountains on the Lolo Trail, their severest test, but the Nez Perce gave them dried salmon, camas roots, supplies, and information. On the expedition's return trip, the Nez Perce met them in June 1806, and guided them back across the Bitterroots, and were remembered most fondly by members of the expedition for their food and help. What befell the Nez Perce in 1877 certainly seemed poor reward.

Back on the Clearwater River, the Lewis and Clark Long Camp—where the expedition waited for the snow to melt in 1806— is just over the bridge at Kamiah, followed by the Heart of the Monster site, an excellent place for a rest stop or picnic near the river. Walk the short path and listen to the audio that tells the legend that this is the place of creation in Nez Perce mythology.

Insider's Tip:

The good road on ID 11 continues to the town of Weippe, and then the Lolo Motorway follows the Historic Lolo Trail, Lewis and Clark's route, through the Bitterroot Mountains until it intersects with US 12 just before Lolo Pass. Built by the Civilian Conservation Corps, the motorway is a primitive dirt road—four-wheel drive only—that provides access to some of the original Lolo Trail, where you can only hike or ride horses. Snow covers the high eastern end until late June.

Wild and Scenic Lochsa River Corridor

At Lowell, US 12 leaves the Clearwater Canyons Scenic Byway and proceeds east along the Wild and Scenic Corridor of the Lochsa River, which is a fine-traveling road in the beautiful Lochsa Valley. On summer weekends, river runners are out in colorful rafts and kayaks. Some white water is encountered, but nothing too wild, even though the river's name means "rough water." You might choose to spend several days in the area, participating in this sport on your own or with one of the commercial vendors, and camping at one of the several forest camps. The Colgate Licks National Recreation Trail, to the east near the Jerry Johnson Forest Camp, might interest some hikers. I spent a delightful overnight at the Wilderness Gateway Forest Camp—where equestrians also have facilities and paths—

Special Event:

Kamiah is the location for Chief Lookingglass Days in mid-August with a traditional Powwow by descendants of Chief Lookingglass of the Nez Perce Indian tribe.

Wilderness Gateway Forest Camp along the Lochsa River, Idaho.

with my tent pitched next to the roaring Lochsa, where it was people quiet, although the ground squirrels were curious. I woke to a mood-invoking layer of morning fog that quickly dispersed as it flirted with sunlight.

History buffs—or anyone who likes log buildings in wild settings and appreciates seeing the efforts of ingenuity and craftsmanship in a roadless environment—will enjoy a stop at the Lochsa Historic Ranger Station, 2 miles (3.2 km) west of Wilderness Gateway Campground. After stopping at the visitor center for information, walk the short loop past several log buildings (handicapped parking is available). Imagine living in the ranger's dwelling, a comfortable, well-equipped two-story house built in 1933. It took men and horses three days to bring a bathtub on a sled-like contraption to the site and maneuver it into the upstairs bathroom. Although overgrown now, a garden behind the house still produces grapes and berries. Naturally, there's a woodshed and root cellar. A path leads past Zion Creek to the barn and corral, where horses and mules are still kept to assist present-day workers.

It is surprising to find a lodge, cafe, motel, and gas station grouping, with a campground nearby, on this wild and rural drive, all near the Powell Ranger Station. This patch of development is quickly countered by a walk among tall cedars on the wheelchair-accessible trail at the De Voto Memorial Grove. A stone memorial honors historian and Lewis and Clark scholar

Bernard De Voto, who often camped among the cedar trees while working on his writings. Picnic tables invite a lunch break by the river.

Lolo Trail

Climbing to Lolo Pass via the highway is easy—it's only at 5,233 feet (1,595 m)—and the pass marks the beginning of the Lolo Trail west. Indians aimed Lewis and Clark to this trail after the intrepid explorers did a bit of wandering near the Montana-Idaho border. Native Americans from all directions used this route historically as a hunting and trade path through the Bitterroot Mountains. With rough mountain and forest terrain ahead, however, Lewis and Clark became disoriented and traveled as far as Wendover before climbing to the ridge trail.

Today's summer travelers find a hospitable visitor center and rest area at the pass. Drivers change to downhill tactics as they coast into Montana, where it's only a few miles to Lolo Hot Springs, complete with restaurant, motel, hot springs pool, and a campground. Clark found these springs "nearly boiling hot."

Montana quickly tries to live up to its "big sky" moniker and opens up; you're no longer in a canyon. Relaxed driving changes pretty quickly too, as the tour passes through Lolo on US 93 and then north through Missoula. I made some hectic turns off the highway in Missoula to stock up on fresh meats and deli and bakery items at Rosauers supermarket, and was somewhat disoriented by so much traffic. The traffic continued to be quite busy and fast for many miles north. Is everyone going in my direction?

National Bison Range

For a less hectic side trip, go west on MT 200 and follow signs for the National Bison Range near Moiese. In late August and early September, you might see the bison in the noisy, exciting, short-tempered, and dangerous rutting season. With a population maintained at around 370 head, bison roam the 18,541 acres of this national wildlife refuge in a landscape of steeply rolling hills and riparian areas along the Jocko River and Mission Creek, an area reminiscent of their habitat more than a hundred years ago. You can see considerable numbers of other animals along the 19-mile (30.6 km) Red Sleep Mountain Scenic Drive (a one-way dirt road) on a summer tour: mountain goat, black bear, bighorn sheep, white-tailed and mule deer, Rocky Mountain elk, blue grouse, pronghorn antelope, coyote, and an intriguing assortment of other native western wildlife. Visitors are required to remain at their vehicles and on the road at all times on the drive. (This is for your safety. Rattlesnakes are part of the range, and bison can weigh up to 2,500 pounds.) Allow plenty of time to enjoy the wildlife and do bring binoculars. No trailers or large motorhomes are allowed on this drive, but a couple of short drives are possibilities if you have such a rig. Rangers at the visitor center have a handout with a map for campgrounds in the area.

Traveling northeast along MT 212 from the refuge will return you to US 93. You'll skirt Ninepine National Wildlife Refuge, a vast wetland expanse with ducks and wading birds and backed by mountains; backtrack south on US 93 to find the information pullover. A few miles north you'll arrive at immense Flathead Lake. You have the option of traveling around either side of this lake. Both sides are more developed than I prefer, but you'll find sweet cherries, raspberries, and even jam for sale in mid-July on the east side of the lake (MT 35). Several state parks here are rather primitive.

Special Events:
During the last week in July, the Flathead Lake Hoopfest brings some 300 basketball teams to compete on the streets of Polson, with celebrity players contributing their expertise.

Glacier National Park

You can't miss the signs going north, via MT 206 and then US 2, to Glacier National Park, called the "Crown of the Continent" by early conservationist George Bird Grinnell, who helped establish the park. Soon you're in West Glacier, where you'll find a crush of last-minute services before entering the park, and where you'll receive a helpful map and a newspaper. Make sure you read the sheet with warnings about the bears and, be prepared—this is grizzly country.

Campgrounds are often full before noon, so plan your time accordingly. On the major route, Apgar and Fish Creek are near the west entrance fronting on Lake McDonald; Avalanche Creek is 16.2 miles (26.1 km) from West Glacier; and Rising Sun, St. Mary, and Many Glacier are at the other end of the Going-to-the-Sun Road and will be full when you get there, unless you are traveling quite early in the day—which is a good idea. I noticed a considerable increase in traffic between my visits here in 1990 and 1997.

 Insider's Tip:
Be prepared for mosquitoes in midsummer; they come and go with the wind.

Other travel considerations for RVers are mandated by the sharp curves, sheer drop-offs, and narrow highway between Avalanche campground and the Sun Point parking area. Vehicles and towed units are restricted to a maximum of 21 feet (6.4 m) in length or 8 feet (2.4 m) in width. Consequently, many RVs will have to be left at campgrounds. Although you'll see some pickup campers on this stretch of highway, passenger cars are dominant, so be prepared. Another option—and this works for those who are just sightseeing—is to take the red, stretched touring cars. These stop at the major viewpoints and allow time for a few snapshots. Some visitors prefer to leave the driving to someone else here.

GOING-TO-THE-SUN ROAD

Glacier National Park is beautiful. You'll marvel at the waterfalls plunging down the mountains and the swift streams that complement the glacier-chiseled peaks, lush forest, and crystal-clear lakes. Notice the rocky horns, pyramid shapes, and jagged, knife-edged ridges along with the red strata, gray-green rock, and pink quartzite of the mountains. Peer into the clear streams with their bottoms of bloodred, plum, and mauve cobbles. All the wildlife species present 1,000 years ago still inhabit the more than one million acres of the park.

Summer brings lots of white-cloud, blue-sky days in the upper 70s that are delightful here near the Canadian border. At Lake McDonald Historic District, a Swiss chalet-style lodge offers all services, including a store that sells film. If you ride horses, consider renting one and joining a group for a ride. I watched a column of horses and riders enjoying the opposite and wilder side of McDonald Creek.

At 12.8 miles (20.6 km), you can take a short 0.5-mile (0.8 km) walk through red cedar and hemlock forest to look for moose and waterfowl at boggy Johns Lake. Another even shorter forest walk is adjacent to Avalanche campground, the wheelchair-accessible Trail of the Cedars, with its wild gorge. This trail has an extension—the 2-mile (3.2 km) Avalanche Lake Trail—that makes a great day hike. (This might influence your camping choice.) More than half the park's visitors do take a hike, independently or with a ranger, for a closer look at this wild and wonderful area. The choices are many, so check with a ranger for up-to-date information on the trails.

You'll want to stop at almost every pullover to see another vista, raging river, or mountain peak along the 52-mile (83.7 km) Going-to-the-Sun Road, which can usually be traveled from mid-June to mid-October. At "the Loop," where the road does just that, Heaven's Peak is an attraction; some visitors set out on the strenuous 4-mile (6.4 km) hike to Granite Park Chalet (reservations only). At Bird Woman Falls Overlook, a waterfall plunges down from a valley on the slopes of Mount Oberlin, while Haystack Creek flows below the road. In another 2 miles, you'll pass the Weeping Wall, where a waterfall cascades onto the road.

Rising Sun Campground in Glacier Mountain National Park, MT.

At 32 miles (51.5 km), the high point of the road is 6,680-foot (2,036 m) Logan Pass. Just east of the pass, an excellent activity at the Logan Pass Visitor Center is the self-guided, 1.5-mile (2.4-km) Hidden Lake Trail. It takes a bit of stair climbing (there are also ramps) to the trail's beginning just behind the visitor center, but you'll find a glorious landscape, with glacier lilies carpeting the subalpine meadows and mountains circling you. The trail begins on a boardwalk and then climbs over the Continental Divide at 7,100 feet (2,164 m) and then to the Hidden Lake Overlook. (It's possible to encounter snow on this section early in the season.) What a feeling to walk on the backbone of North America!

When I was there once on July 15, I overheard a visitor comment, "Joe's going to ski and David's going bicycling, isn't that a hoot?" That's possible here during the narrow window of summer at Logan Pass. A few miles east, past Siyeh Bend and Going-to-the-Sun Mountain, is the best view of a glacier from the road, the Jackson Glacier.

Look for one of those underwater foraging birds, the dipper or water ouzel, in the rushing water at Sunrift Gorge. At the next stop, Sun Point along St. Mary Lake, RVers can approach and park from East Glacier. The lovely 0.7-mile (1.1-km) Sun Point Nature Trail that follows the lake offers a splendid view of this ice-sculptured valley and leads to Baring Falls, a torrent of water pouring over rock formations. Another 1.6 miles of easy trail leads to St. Mary Falls.

You might want to stop at 40 miles and camp at Rising Sun, where one edge of the campground has views of the mountains beyond St. Mary Lake. Sunrise colors these peaks a blazing orange-red. The curious Columbia ground squirrels tried to make friends with my cat (on a leash). There is a store here, and 1.5-hour scenic boat tours are available across the road at St. Mary Lake, with an optional guided walk to St. Mary Falls. Check for departure times. Or you may just want to fish along the shore.

Insider's Tip:
With roads edging the major glacial lakes of the park, consider accessing some of the wild areas, which often have hiking trails, by boating across the water. If you don't bring your own boat, consider renting a canoe at Apgar, Two Medicine, or Many Glacier; a kayak at Apgar or Many Glacier; or a rowboat at Apgar, Lake McDonald, Many Glacier, or Two Medicine.

MANY GLACIER AREA
The short trip out of the park past Lower St. Mary Lake and then back into the park from Babb takes you to the Many Glacier area, one of my favorite parts of Glacier. Along the entry road is a 1-mile (1.6-km) trail to Appekunny Falls (the Indian spelling is Apikuni), and although the initial path is through a wildflower meadow, the trail gets steep and has slippery scree near the end. Several popular longer trails lead to Redrock Falls, Iceberg Lake, and Grinnell Glacier. A nature trail circles Swiftcurrent Lake and can be reached from the picnic area at the Grinnell Glacier trailhead. Sprawling Many Glacier Hotel sits across the lake backed by

an exquisite grouping of mountain peaks. Boat motors are prohibited on the lake, but lake tours are available from the hotel, with guided walks on to Grinnell Lake from the touring boat.

Once out of the park, you can opt to enter Canada (see chapter 7 for entry tips) and see the Waterton Lakes section of this international peace park, or head south on US 89, which is what I did. To the east, "big sky" country of meadows alternates with rumpled hills. It is startling to come to a place where the Great Plains roll right up to the Rocky Mountains.

I had planned to visit the Two Medicine Area of Glacier National Park, but the weather chased me off. Heavy rain moved in and blanketed the scene as I approached and it lost its appeal. I was almost at the park entrance, having traveled winding, sharply banked MT 49 when I changed my destination. You might want to try this area on a sunny day, as several of the trails and the terrain sound promising. Be warned, however, that the same vehicle restrictions as for Going-to-the-Sun Road apply on MT 49. I backtracked to US 89 and went through the Blackfoot town of Browning, where I picked up US 2 to East Glacier.

East Glacier

The small community of East Glacier includes a few motels, a gas station, and a couple of restaurants—all the necessities. Glacier Village Restaurant is worth a visit, even if it's just for coffee, to view the rare black-and-white photos of many historic events in the lives of the Blackfeet Indians in this countryside. One photo shows Clark Gable being inducted into the Blackfeet tribe by a chief in 1938; another shows a Blackfeet chief receiving a hand-delivered copy of the *Saturday Evening Post*. I heard that the food was commendable, but I only had a coffee to go at the Espresso Bar, a beverage bar where buses are welcomed and you can get lattes, imported teas, and other beverages to go.

The drive back to West Glacier on US 2 was wonderful even in the rain, and I was sorry the sun wasn't out so I could stop,

take photos, and hike on one of the many trails. Ribbons of clouds lay low on the mountains and forest, with easy, rolling curves on the road. I stopped to see the historic Izaak Walton Inn in Essex, where a multitracked train yard is visible from the lounge windows. The Great Northern Railway needed "helper engines" for the steep west-side grade of Marias Pass and accommodations for the crews. Today, both crews and travelers stay at the inn. Several milky green rivers flow down from the Lewis Range along this route, and although it was raining when I passed by, many rafters were on the canyoned Flathead River.

Rocky Mountain Lakes

A relaxed route south is via MT 83, a picturesque natural environment replete with campgrounds by the many lakes at the edge of the Bob Marshall Wilderness Area. The first major waterway is Swan Lake, where you'll find camping and the Swan Lake National Wildlife Refuge. Allow time for some quiet activities. Near Seeley Lake are both the 3.5-mile (5.6-km) Clearwater Canoe Trail and the easy 2.5-mile (4-km) Morrell Falls National Recreation Trail.

Bitterroot Valley

To get the most varied fun on this tour, stay on US 93 south of Missoula through the U-shaped glacial Bitterroot Valley, with the Bitterroot Mountains to the west and the Sapphire Mountains to the east. Named by Lewis and Clark, the bitterroot plant has showy rose and white flowers and roots that nourished the Indians.

Fort Owen State Park is a pleasant short stop at Stevensville, the site of the first permanent white settlement in Montana. Walk the small grounds that include a homestead cabin, grist mill equipment, a rock-lined well, a root cellar, and a furnished 1860s barracks unit.

I opted to investigate the 4-mile side trip to Lake Como (southwest of Hamilton), which edged up close to the mountains and featured picnic tables at a fine gravel beach beside the swimming area—

not a bad place to enjoy a sandwich, chips, and fruit. The newly paved campground with nice sites was a surprise (and was full at 2 P.M. on the Friday I was there). The trailhead for the 7-mile (11.3-km) Lake Como National Recreation Loop Trail (mountain bikes allowed) that circles the lake is located near the campground. Later I found a nice forest camp—Spring Gulch Forest Camp—along the Bitterroot River just north of the Sula store; it even has a wheelchair-accessible fishing pier. Spring Gulch was a stopover for Lewis and Clark and has an exhibit with information.

Following the route of Lewis and Clark, the tour continues over 7,014-foot (2,138-m) Lost Trail Pass, where this expedition had a bit of trouble (as the name implies). They connected after some time with the Salmon River, which proved to be a mistake. The Indians sent them back to take the Lolo Trail. Consider a side trip east on UT 43 to the Big Hole Battlefield, along the Nez Perce Trail.

Salmon River Scenic Byway

The US 93 route to Stanley is Idaho's Salmon River Scenic Byway. You are never far from this mighty river, which Lewis and Clark dubbed "The River of No Return," as you roll along past gold-mining sites, wildlife, sunflowers on the rolling hills, rich bottomland, ranches, and even a smattering of red rock formations. The town of Salmon, once the winter campsite of Jim Bridger and Kit Carson, is at the fork of the Salmon and Lemhi rivers. It is also a favorite take-off point for float trips on the untamed Salmon river and for backpacking into the wilderness. Permits are required for summer float trips.

Special Events:
Salmon hosts Salmon River Days in early July—arts and crafts, a rodeo, a parade, raft and kayak races, and a staged bank robbery. In the second week of August is the Salmon River Balloon Fest.

Yankee Fork Historic Area

Follow the Salmon river along the climb to mile-high Challis. The attraction here is Land of the Yankee Fork Historic Area, which commemorates Idaho's first 100 years. The interpretive center at the intersection of US 93 and ID 75 features frontier mining history; ask for the brochures on the Custer Motorway Adventure Road and the Custer Walking Guide. Although most of this motorway is not for trailers, motorhomes, or low-clearance vehicles, it's not difficult if you enter the motorway via Forest Road 013 at Sunbeam and travel just 11 miles (18 kilometers) to Custer City. Continue from Challis on ID 75, past Bayhorse Campground, the East Fork of the Salmon River, and Clayton (which has 26 residents and one bar). Launch sites along the river and rafts floating through blue and white riffles can be seen as the river flows through a narrow chasm near Torrey.

Turn north for the side trip at Sunbeam and follow Yankee Fork Creek on a paved road past several campgrounds for about 5 miles (8 kilometers), where a good gravel road will take you to the 988-ton Yankee Fork Gold Dredge, a monster piece of mining equipment that you can tour. The road narrows somewhat for the next 2 miles (3 kilometers) to Custer, but smaller motorhomes seem to do fine for this short distance. The walking tour of Custer in this picturesque mountain valley is rewarding—you'll see a street of late-1800 buildings, including a schoolhouse that now houses a museum with displays of horsehide and buffalo-hide long coats, a papoose carrier, Chinese artifacts, and many more historic items.

Stanley: Gateway to Sawtooth National Recreation Area

The drive into Stanley is impressive. As if summoned by the wave of a wand, the Sawtooth Mountains rise majestically above the curving wide river in a scene reminiscent of the Tetons and the Snake River—a gorgeous setting. Although Stanley's population is 100 residents, it won't seem that small if you visit in midsummer. For miles along the highways entering Stanley from three directions, there is campground after campground. Even so, my arrival during the most popular summer weekend event, as well as during kayak/rafting activity on the Salmon River, forced me to settle for a forest service campground for boondockers, with no water, although it was a nice location by the river with room for horses. Don't be surprised to find two Stanleys—an Upper Stanley and a Lower Stanley—both lined with elegant-looking log homes, motels, and restaurants. Between are meadows with cows and a landscape where, in 1824, Hudson's Bay Company trappers found four acres of mostly plowed field with no fewer than nine grizzlies busily rooting away eating camas, onions, and wild celery.

For an excellent excursion into the Sawtooth National Recreation Area, take a 5-mile side trip south of Stanley to the heart of this mountain paradise at Redfish Lake. The visitor center has maps of both the Redfish Lake area and day-hike trails, plus scheduled talks. If nothing else, walk the Fishhook Creek Nature Trail to sample the sounds of this wilderness stream and see wildflower meadows and mountain vistas. Along the waterfront, Redfish Lake Lodge has a marina (canoes, kayaks, and paddleboats available), a beach for swimming, horses, a store, and public showers. The marina staff will also smoke your fish. Redfish Lake recreation complex has nine campgrounds; reservations are possible at three of them.

Ponderosa Pine Scenic Byway

The Sawtooths continue to enhance the tour as it leaves Stanley on the Ponderosa Pine Scenic Byway (ID 21). Subalpine meadows and forest are in the foreground as the highway climbs to an easy and quick 7,056-foot (2,151-m) summit, followed by some downhills with grades of five and six percent. The highway to the second summit, 6,118-foot (1,865-m) Mores Creek, is longer and more winding, but is not difficult and offers unfolding views. Campgrounds reappear at lower elevations, and you're soon in historic Idaho City, which was settled during the gold-mining excitement of the 1860s. A small, Sunday-tourist kind of city, Idaho City has a visitor center, old West exhibits, and history and map handouts for exploring the place.

It's all downhill now as you pass water recreation at Lucky Peak State Park on the dammed Boise River, with the byway ending at Interstate 84 in the Boise area. City lovers can make a detour into Boise if desired.

Snake River Birds of Prey Natural Conservation Area

For an appetizer before visiting the conservation area, take exit 50 south from Interstate 84 and follow the signs to the World Center for Birds of Prey, which is headquarters for the Peregrine Fund, a research and educational organization dedicated to raptor conservation that features live exhibits. With a map of the Snake River National Conservation Area, a driving tour will lead you through habitat for raptors near the Snake River. A guided boat trip on the Snake is an excellent way to view raptors.

For closure of this great loop tour, continue west on the freeway over the border into Oregon and visit Farewell Bend State Park, where Oregon Trail pioneers bid farewell to the Snake River, their visible route for over 300 miles. A fitting site for a modern campsite, it lures anglers with year-round catfish, bass, sturgeon, trout, and crappie fishing. New camping sleeping facilities include covered wagons and Tepees.

Perhaps it won't be easy to shake off images in your mind of travel on the Nez Perce, Lewis and Clark, or Oregon trails and those of glacial lakes and the Rocky Mountains, but then that's what good memories are made of, isn't it?

Special Event:
The Sawtooth Mountain Mamas Arts and Crafts Fair is scheduled in Stanley during the third week in July, with old-time fiddlers, a barbecue dinner, and a pancake breakfast.

CHAPTER 7

North Cascades International Loop:
Up Close with Mountains

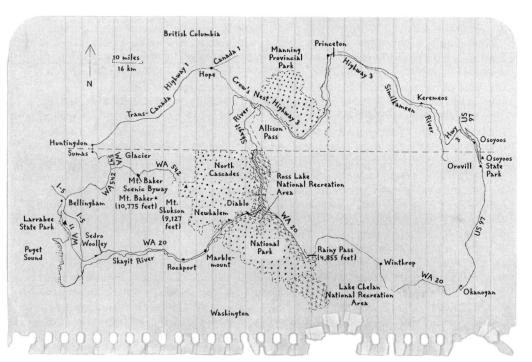

MILEAGE

Approximately 600 miles (965 km).

RESOURCES

- North Cascades National Park; Mount Baker Ranger District; Mt. Baker-Snoqualmie National Forest; Sedro Woolley: (360) 856-5700.
- Ministry of Parks, Zone Manager, Manning Provincial Park, Manning Park, B.C. V7G 1L3; (604) 840-8836.
- Mount Baker Scenic Byway: Contact Glacier Public Service Center, Glacier WA 98244; (360) 599-2714.

CAMPGROUNDS

ROCKPORT STATE PARK: Thirty-two miles (51 km) east of Sedro Woolley; campsites with hookups, restrooms with showers; reservations not accepted.

NORTH CASCADES NATIONAL PARK (RESERVATIONS NOT ACCEPTED): East of Sedro Woolley on WA 20; Newhalem Creek Campground (milepost 120 on WA 20) has tent and trailer sites, restrooms, dump station; Colonial Creek (milepost 130 on WA 20) has tent and trailer sites, restrooms, dump station.

OSOYOOS LAKE VETERANS' MEMORIAL STATE PARK: On the north edge of Oroville; campsites, restrooms with showers, dump station; reservations not accepted.

MANNING PROVINCIAL PARK: Campground reservations not accepted (east to west); Mule Deer has campsites and toilets, Hampton has campsites and toilets; Lightning Lake has tent and RV campsites, restrooms with showers; Coldspring has campsites and toilets; dump station at Visitor Center.

MOUNT BAKER SCENIC BYWAY: Douglas Fir (milepost 36 on WA 542) has tent and trailer sites, vault toilets; Silver Fir (milepost 47 on WA 542) has tent and trailer sites, vault toilets; reservations: (800) 280-CAMP.

LARRABEE STATE PARK: From exit 252, 7 miles (11 km) south on WA 11; RV and tent sites, restrooms with showers; (206) 676-2093.

Summertime in the northern Cascade Mountains is short but exhilarating. Snowmelt roars down waterfalls. Subalpine meadows burst into splashy wildflower colors. Wildlife experiences a time when survival is less harsh. Mountain lovers get the urge to travel and see what is happening at high elevations in the clear, invigorating air. It is a time to get close to the tallest mountains and experience the awesome emotion that only these geologic snow-capped peaks can inspire when you are within climbing and hiking distance of them. Camping in these lofty surroundings lures many back again and again to watch the burst of life in the warm weather and to tackle the wilderness of trees and rock. Experiencing wildness firsthand is even better than viewing a *National Geographic* special.

At this latitude, the best time for this tour is from mid-July to late August, when flowers edge many trails, although some of the higher elevations still have snow in July. Days are pleasant for such wanderings and nights are cool for sleeping. The western flank of the Cascades is the wetter side, with more sunshine on the eastern side. Interspersed between the high peaks along the tour are varied landscapes of warm valleys lush with fruit orchards and the delightful waters along Puget Sound.

Since the tour loops from northern Washington into southern British Columbia, proof of citizenship—birth certificate, voter registration, or passport—is required when crossing the border. Consider changing money soon after crossing into Canada to get more value for your dollars. Your pets need a recent veterinarian's certificate of health.

A fine starting point is the North Cascades Headquarters in Sedro Woolley, just east of Interstate 5 in northern Washington.

Rockport and the Skagit River

The North Cascades Highway, WA 20, runs east toward the mountains as it follows the Skagit River, which is winter habitat for bald eagles. For some forest wandering in a great grove spared from logging, stop at Rockport State Park and enjoy several trails. Named for Scotsman David Douglas, towering Douglas firs shade the campsites. Look for the bell-like flowers on waxy white stems of the saprophyte Indian pipe that sprouts in the rich humus. Listen for the distinctive sound of a pileated woodpecker among the trees.

At Marblemount, the 25-mile (40-km) dirt and gravel Cascade River Road branches off. This is the route to one of the best hiking trails for spectacular mountain hiking: the Cascade Pass Trail. This 4-mile (6.4-km) path was first used by Native Americans and is famous for dramatic, up-close alpine scenery—it's a designated Washington Centennial Trail.

North Cascades National Park

Often called "the most scenic mountain drive in Washington," the highway soon enters the North Cascades National Park Service Complex. This 684,000 acres of superlative beauty and recreation highs is a mostly undiscovered park with plenty of breathing space, which is a refreshing change from the overcrowding that plagues so many parks. An excellent road traverses Ross Lake National Recreation Area (open from April to mid-November), a developed corridor that divides the two vast designated wilderness

Ross Lake Overlook in North Cascades National Park.

units of North Cascades National Park.

The varied landscape of the park includes rich lowland valleys, dense forest, sheer-walled cliffs, cascading creeks, colorful wildflowers, tall mountains, permanent snowfields, and upwards of 318 glaciers—more than half of those present in the contiguous United States. It is a rugged place scarcely touched by human history—even explorers—although 1,500 species of plants and hundreds of birds, reptiles, and mammals find habitat in the park. Such endangered species as gray wolf, wolverine, grizzly bear, and peregrine falcon find space and the essentials for survival. The 386 miles (621 km) of maintained trails include some easy hikes in Ross Lake National Recreation Area, while longer trails often begin in this corridor and head into the backcountry, where some places have never felt the impact of hiking boots. Some trails are open to horseback travel.

NEWHALEM AREA

The North Cascades Visitor Center at Newhalem is strategically located to supply information, maps of the park trails, and a feel for the features of this park. Walk the boardwalk trail outside for excellent views of the Picket Range, or stroll the River Loop Trail to a peaceful river bar. The "To Know a Tree" Nature Trail helps you do just that. River runners can put in near the mouth of nearby Goodell Creek. The short Trail of the Cedars is across the river from the Newhalem Store. In upper Newhalem, cross the suspension bridge to the Gorge Powerhouse and hike the short Ladder Creek Falls Trail to view colored lights, beautiful pools, falls, and flower gardens. All of these trails can be enjoyed during a stay at the Newhalem Creek Campground. Rangers lead walks and evening programs both here at Newhalem and at Colonial.

Three miles (4.8 km) east, a viewpoint highlights the plunge of 242-foot (74-m) Gorge Creek Falls near Gorge Creek Dam, the first of three dams in this corridor built by Seattle City Light that capture some of electricity generating potential of the Skagit River.

Pasqueflower of subalpine meadows of North Cascade Mountains.

DIABLO LAKE AND COLONIAL CREEK

The second dam impounds Diablo Lake, which has a boat launch and offers boat trips and dam tours near camping at Colonial Creek. From this campground—where some sites are along the creek—hikers can sample the rambling 19.5-mile (31-km) Thunder Creek Trail. Starting at 1,200 feet (366 m), a 1.6-mile (2.6-km) round-trip hike to a suspension bridge is a fine family activity. This trail also accesses the popular 3,500-foot (1.067-m) Fourth of July Pass Trail, which is usually snow-free by June, for a 10-mile (16-km) day hike there and back. The pass features two pothole lakes and views of the Eldorado massif and glacier-draped Colonial and Snowfield peaks.

Northeast of Colonial is the spectacular Diablo Lake Overlook, a feast for the eyes, with views of Davis Peak and Sourdough Mountain to the north, along with Colonial Peak, Pyramid Peak, and the Skagit River drainage, all edging the milky, jade-green, glacier-fed water of Diablo Lake.

ROSS LAKE

As you approach Ross Lake, look for the 0.3-mile (0.5-km) Happy Creek Forest Walk, a barrier-free boardwalk through old-growth forest with interpretive plaques, although many visitors might enjoy stretching their legs while they listen for the sounds of water cascading and forest birds such as the varied thrush. Ross Dam and Ross Lake Resort, where you can rent fishing boats, is across the highway. The lake waters are too cold for swimming or waterskiing, but boating and fishing are popular (Washington state licenses and regulations apply).

The Ross Lake Overlook is nicely located where Ruby Creek enters the lake as a curving arm; the lake then begins an enticing S-shaped course shouldered by forested mountains as it heads north to the Canadian border. One way to travel to some of the park's wilderness areas is by launching a boat at Hozomeen—on the border—and boating to trailheads.

Rainy Pass, Rainy Lake, and the Pacific Crest Trail

The North Cascades Highway exits North Cascades National Park and turns south as it follows Granite Creek and climbs to Rainy Pass at 4,840 feet (1,475 m). This is a special stopping place in the Okanogan National Forest. In addition to being a delightful picnic area, three hiking trails invite exploring.

The 1-mile (1.6-km) Rainy Lake Trail to fishing and picnicking is one of an outstanding number of recently constructed trails for physically impaired travelers; it is also one of Washington's 25 Centennial Trails. A paved, level trail suitable for wheelchair travel, this trail's destination is a turquoise mountain tarn backed by the sheer walls of snow-capped cliffs, with rivulets of snowmelt forming several waterfalls that plunge into the lake. The walk itself is a delight as it borders a creek where deer are often spotted, and passes an array of wildflowers that include Lewis monkeyflower, rein orchid, lupine, and wild strawberry. The trail may be short and easy, but it compares to what backpackers see on

Destination of Rainy Lake barrier-free trail, North Cascades National Park.

long excursions into the wilderness.

A spur from this trail heads off to Lake Ann, where the cutthroat fishing is rumored to be good. Another mile on the trail leads to Heather Pass, and yet another mile brings you to Maple Pass and into the national park.

The Pacific Crest National Scenic Trail (PCNST), which begins at the Mexican border and goes into Canada, crosses the highway at Rainy Pass. If any backpackers are traveling this loop with RVers, they might consider being dropped off here. They can hike the last 69 miles (111 km) of the trail through flower-spangled high meadows and the Pasayten Wilderness before rejoining their group at the trail's terminus in Manning Park, which is along the route of this tour. Hikers also can sample the trail by heading 5 miles (8 km) north to excellent views at Cutthroat Pass.

The Methow Valley

It is not far from Rainy Pass to the Washington Pass Viewpoint (5,477 feet or 1,669 m), which is dominated by the granite pillar of Liberty Bell Mountain. Several trails are found in this vicinity. The highway heads east to Winthrop, a town in the Methow Valley near the North Cascades Smokejumper Base and Perrygin Lake State Park.

When an enormous glacier flowed south out of Canada some 15,000 years ago, it gouged out the Methow Valley, a place where residents enjoy a lifestyle that often revolves around the outdoors. Several rivers—the Twisp, the Methow, and the

Chewuch—come together in this valley, and the rafting is some of the best in the state after the winter runoff. These rivers, along with the many creeks and lakes, offer good fishing. Check with the locals on where to find whitefish, steelhead, small-mouth bass, and rainbow, brown, brook, cutthroat trout. Other wildlife abounds, so be alert.

Osoyoos Lake

The tour loop now swings north on US 97 from Okanogan through national forest and ranchland to Osoyoos Lake Veterans' Memorial State Park. Camping is a feature along this waterway, where the Osoyoos River widens into a 14-mile-long (22.5-km) narrow lake that straddles the border. The last town before the border, Oroville, has a good market and gas stations, so you can fill up with less expensive American gasoline before passing through customs and entering Canada. (Gasoline is sold in liters in Canada; 3.8 liters equal 1 gallon.) At the

Early morning paddlers on Lightning Lake, Manning Park, BC.

Canadian town of Osoyoos—the gateway to the Okanagan Valley (the name is spelled differently in Canada)—head west on Crowsnest Highway 3.

Okanagan Valley and Orchards

Visitors are in for a treat in this warmer, drier side of the Cascade Mountains in the Okanagan Valley, a landscape of lakes surrounded by high mountains, cliffs, and granite domes. Called Canada's fruit basket, orchards proliferate in this great mix of weather and soil. Be prepared when you drive through Keremeos for the multitude of fruit stands, with bins of ripe fruit that make delicious travel food; orchard tours are another attraction. This area is also one of North America's acclaimed wine producing regions. For an interesting look at the area's agricultural history, visit the restored Grist Mill, with its heritage gardens, historic wheat field, and heirloom apple orchard.

Manning Provincial Park

Crowsnest Highway 3 dips south at Princeton and follows the Similkameen River into the rugged Canadian Cascade Mountains in Manning Provincial Park, the equal of many a national park. The highway bisects this vast park of 66,500 hectares (164,255 acres) into two backcountry expanses that include historical trails—the Dewdney, Whatcom, and Hope Pass—that were explorer routes of the 1800s and connecting links between the coast and the interior until the early 1900s. History buffs can trek on these trails. In addition to the many trails that head off from the highway, two roads lead to recreation choices in the heart of this scenic park. Check the park map for trails permitting horse or mountain bike travel.

As the highway climbs into the park interior, the first self-guiding nature trail is Beaver Pond, an appealing short wetland walk. Although abandoned by the namesake beavers when their food source of willow and alder was used up, it is now habitat for muskrat, western spotted frog, dragonfly, belted kingfisher, mallard duck, and swallows. It's especially inviting in early morning as the sun warms up the place and mists and slanting sunbeams skim across the water. Also located here is the trailhead and terminus for the six-month trek along the Pacific Crest Trail to Mexico, a pickup point for long-distance backpackers, or a place to try out a section of the trail on a day hike.

LIGHTNING LAKE AREA

The visitor center for Manning Provincial Park is the most developed area at the core of the park. The Gibson Pass Road heads west to Lightning Lake and the most popular campground, where waiting lines form in early mornings on summer weekends. Try for a midweek morning for this excellent camping location. By overnighting here, you can enjoy that special early morning stillness that I found so refreshing when I walked quietly to the lake. The meadow seemed akin to a minefield because of the many holes made by ground squirrels that popped out to see what was happening. A doe and her fawn calmly continued browsing the vegetation. No one else was about except a family who had just tossed fishing lines into the lake and another young family who glided by in a canoe. The low morning sun cast reflections of tall forest and a Cascade Mountain peak on the water as it began to warm up. If you don't have your own canoe, rentals are available. A 9-km (5.4-mile) trail circles the lake, with longer trails continuing into the backcountry. Fly-fishing for rainbow trout is reported good in Lightning Lake; no power boats are allowed.

Farther west off the Gibson Pass Road is the Strawberry Flats Trail, which is a delightful walk among summer wildflowers that continues to three successive waterfalls. First, stroll past columbines and lilies edging a path backed by forests; the trees then recede and the strawberry flats area (aptly named) opens up replete with lupine, yarrow, cow parsnip, and a good representation of the park's many flower species.

On the drive back to the highway, consider walking the short Rein Orchid Trail. Smells are of the forest, and many

---

Campground Critters

Many of the basic needs of wildlife are found in campground areas, so overnighting provides an excellent opportunity for checking out some of the less shy animals. Being motionless and quiet helps. Black-tailed deer browse at dusk. Chickadees call from overhead tree branches. Hairy woodpeckers drum on trees. Chipmunks feed on seeds and fruit. Squirrels are active and noisy. Coyotes yap in the night. Paw prints that look like tiny human hands reveal the presence of raccoons. The snowshoe hare hops about on large furry feet. The Steller's jay mimics the calls of other birds, while the sapsucker laps up the sugary liquid on tree bark. Listing the many creatures you discover can be a good family game.

---

blossoming rein orchids are seen here from June through July, along with horsetail, bunchberry, fireweed, and other wildflowers. An added surprise attraction is a pond and wetland area. Notice the huge bear claw marks on a tree. The Canyon Trail at Coldspring Campground follows the Similkameen River past interesting plant life and geologic formations.

Insider's Tip:

It is illegal to pick berries in the park; leave them for the birds and wildlife. However, the park does provide an excellent booklet for identifying all types of berries and their edible characteristics, information that's helpful outside the park, too, if you choose to eat some berries while hiking. Anglers need a British Columbia license, obtainable at Park Headquarters.

SUBALPINE WILDFLOWER MEADOWS

For panoramic views and wildflower displays, take the paved but winding, steep-edged Blackwall Road just west of the Visitor Center and head 15-kilometers (9 miles) north to a parking lot to see the surrounding mountains at Cascade Lookout, with exhibit information on identification of the peaks. Golden-mantled squirrels and marmots are easy to spot here. I wouldn't advise taking trailers or large motorhomes on this road. A gravel road continues another 6 kilometers (4 miles) to spectacular subalpine wildflower meadows and trails. Blackwall Road is usually open July through September.

The self-guided Paintbrush Interpretive Loop begins at the Naturalist Hut at Blackwall Peak, where brochures are available, although you can also reach the trail from the lower parking lot. Common red paintbrush provides plenty of nutritious nectar for the energetic rufous hummingbird; try to see how many other species of birds you can identify. Peak wildflower blooms occur from mid-July to August, although the western anemones bloom as soon as the snow melts and by late July their picturesque seed heads dot the meadows before their feathery parachutes are dispersed into the wind. Snow-peaked mountains in the distance add to the charm of the trail, which begins on the Hozameen Range, where the peaks were shaped by the last Ice Age and this ridge was under several hundred meters of ice. Nearby summits more than 2,100 meters (7,000 feet) high poked their tops above the ice sheet and managed to retain their jagged appearance.

This multihued carpet of flowers stretches 24 kilometers (14 miles) from Blackwall Peak to Three Brothers Mountain. At the lower parking area by Blackwall Peak you can sample some or all of this terrain on the Heather Trail; it traverses a vast subalpine meadow to Buckhorn Camp and continues for a total of 21 kilo-

meters (12 miles) to Nicomen Ridge and Nicomen Lake. Register for an overnight tent site in the backcountry or turn around whenever you wish on a day hike. As always in fragile subalpine meadows, please stay on the trail.

While on your walks, keep in mind that subalpine plants and animals arrived after the last glaciers retreated. Sitka valerian, lupine, hellebore, lance-leaved stonecrop, woolly pussytoes, spreading phlox, fan-leaf cinquefoil, and red heather are some of the subalpine flowers. A rare find at these high meadows is the alpine larch, a deciduous conifer, but whitebark pine and subalpine fir are common. Often overlooked, tiny Piper's woodrush, green-leaf fescue, and showy sedge have reddish leaves from the presence of the pigment anthocyanin, which serves as a sunscreen to protect the plants against the strong ultraviolet rays at this elevation.

MANNING'S NORTHWEST CORRIDOR

As the highway veers northwest from the Visitor Center area, it ascends to 1,341-m (4,400-foot) Allison Pass near where the Similkameen River heads downhill from its headwaters. Within a couple of kilometers of losing the Similkameen, the Skagit River emerges from its high-country beginnings and borders the highway route through an enormous wilderness area.

Eleven kilometers (7 miles) from Manning's West Gate, the Rhododendron Flats Nature Trail, a 20-minute forest walk, features rhododendrons, rain-dependent shrubs typically found in temperate rainforest areas of the northwest. Although these rose-colored, flowering plants are especially beautiful in late spring, this trail is still interesting at other times and is an exemplary rain forest tract along the Skagit River. I found rein orchids blooming in late July. Some 1,000 rhododendron species are found worldwide.

Another 1.6 kilometers (1 mile) west, the self-guiding Sumallo Grove Trail through old-growth forest offers insights into the components of this temperate rain forest on the wet side of the Cascade Mountains. This is a wheelchair-accessible loop

Pasqueflower seed heads off the Paintbrush Trail in Manning Provincial Park, BC.

of 700 m (0.5 mile). The short drive from the highway weaves through large trees on a road reminiscent of those among the redwoods in California. Magnificent stands of western red cedar are found, along with western hemlock, Sitka spruce, cottonwood, alder, vine maple, sword fern, spring wood fern, mosses, foamflowers, sugar stick, mushrooms, devil's club, rotting trees, and ginger, with its distinctive smell. A picnic area is situated along the Skagit River.

Mount Baker Scenic Byway

It is not far via Trans-Canada Highway 1 to the border crossing at Huntingdon, where you can pick up Washington 547 at Sumas and then head east on Washington 542 at Kendall. This highway becomes the 24-mile (39-km) Mount Baker Scenic Byway at the Glacier Public Service Center (milepost 34), in the Mount Baker-Snoqualmie National Forest. This native stone-and-timber building constructed by the Civilian Conservation Corps (CCC) in the late 1930s, and now listed on the National Register of Historic Places, serves as an information center operated in the summer by the Forest Service and National Park Service. A good camping base is just 2 miles (3.2 km) east at Douglas Fir Campground, or at Silver Fir (milepost 47). You can relax at these forest camps along the North Fork Nooksack River and then choose one or more of the many forest hikes, climb one of several mountains, visit energetic Nooksack Falls (milepost 41), do some birding, scout for berries or mushrooms, participate in a wild,

Mount Baker Scenic Byway, WA.

white-water trip on the river with one the available concessionaires, and enjoy the byway attractions to its terminus at Artist Point.

This is the third major encounter with the North Cascades along this tour, and it is the one that serves well as the climactic experience. I promised an "up-close-with-the-mountains" experience, and here it is: you can drive almost right up to these peaks, an extravaganza of alpine splendor that is so close you should have no difficulty feeling the sensual excitement of this rare and wonderful place.

HEATHER MEADOWS RECREATION AREA
Although RVers can get to the two campgrounds without difficulty, trailers and large motorhomes simply cannot manage the remainder of the byway—and this is where mountains are so close. The last 10 miles (16 km) of the highway, although in excellent condition, have sheer drop-offs and hairpin turns with no barriers. I drove this in a pickup camper with a pop-up top, but anything larger should not be taken to road's end. Leave your trailer in the campground and use your tow vehicle if you have one.

The first special stop in the recreation area is at Picture Lake, where craggy Mount Shuksan is often reflected on the water surface. This beautiful scene is one you've probably seen in photographs, but it's better to be there in person. Take a leisurely walk around the tiny tarn on the wheelchair-accessible 0.5-mile (0.8-km) trail, stopping to notice the profusion of flowers and plants in the lakeside wetland.

The Wild Goose Trail offers connections to other trails and area facilities; it starts at the ski area parking lot and ends at Artist Point. Several trails—some self-guiding and wheelchair accessible, some longer hikes into the surrounding Mount Baker Wilderness—begin along the remaining section of the byway.

The stone Heather Meadows Visitor Center is a good place to stop, ask questions, and learn about the cultural heritage of Heather Meadows. In the 1920s, a grand lodge accommodated guests from around the globe. Tragically, it burned. After the Great Depression, the Civilian Conservation Corps constructed trails and the picnic grounds that form the core of facilities at Heather Meadows. Bring a picnic lunch to Austin Pass Picnic Area and feast on food and views of Terminal Lake and the rugged expanse of mountains.

The eastern end of Mount Baker Scenic Byway has miles of rolling meadows with heather, huckleberry, and other subalpine vegetation. Lakes sparkle in the sunlight. Nine-hundred-year-old mountain hemlock perch on mountain ridges, and all around are eye-catching rock formations with their lava origins and glacial carvings.

 Insider's Tip:
Do not take the mountain experience lightly if you enter the backcountry. Be well informed, carry good maps, and the essentials necessary for a safe wilderness experience. And please always protect the delicate natural resources.

The road ends dramatically at 5,140-foot (1,567-m) Artist Point. Snow is sometimes present in mid-July, so August would be a better time to sample the Artist Ridge Trail, with its excellent views east that include nearby Mount Baker and Mount Shuksan, which is actually in North Cascades National Park. Sometimes, mists and clouds swirl about and seductively reveal only hints of these glacier-carved peaks, but these days have their own charm. Hikers and mountain climbers will love the area, but so will anyone who drives to the end of the byway.

Larrabee State Park

For a mind-expanding finish to the tour at sea level with a sunset lighting the water, travel Washington 542 to Puget Sound and then head south from Bellingham on WA 11 to Larrabee State Park. Located right on the water on the seaward side of Chuckanut Mountain, a self-guiding walk lets you explore the ecosystem along the shore of

Nooksack Falls along the Mount Baker Scenic Byway, WA.

the sound where low tide exposes the inhabitants of this rocky shore. Longer trails begin across the highway to both Fragrance Lake and Lost Lake within the park. I strongly recommend doing at least the first part of this longer hike, 0.9 mile (1.4 km) of switchbacks to a cliff-edge viewpoint. This vista offers a dazzling sight across Puget Sound that includes nearby Samish and Chuckanut Bays and the rugged offshore islands—Lummi, Orcas, and others. If you're lucky, a bald eagle may fly out from a nearby tree.

Your thoughts will no doubt focus on the spectacular and varied scenery of the Cascade Mountains as you drive home. I hope that you, too, find that up-close-to-the-mountains experience that sent me out on this discovery trip. The northern Cascade Mountains offer such experiences and you can drive to them if you know where to go. As a transported Midwesterner who first saw real mountains when I was over 30 years old, snow-capped mountains and summer go together like ice cream and hot-fudge sauce. The alpine environment still works its magic on me.

CHAPTER 8

Southwestern Oregon: Two Extraordinary Rivers and Crater Lake

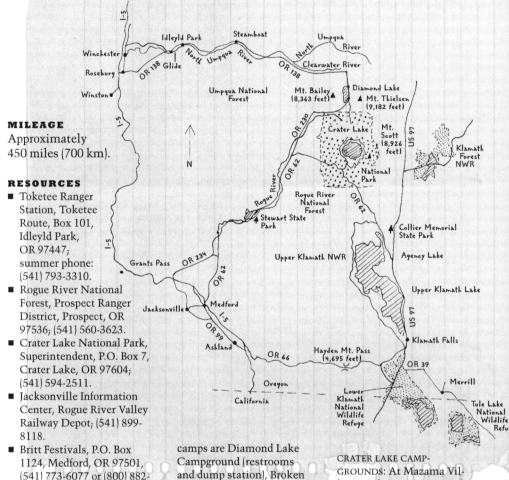

MILEAGE

Approximately 450 miles (700 km).

RESOURCES

- Toketee Ranger Station, Toketee Route, Box 101, Idleyld Park, OR 97447; summer phone: (541) 793-3310.
- Rogue River National Forest, Prospect Ranger District, Prospect, OR 97536; (541) 560-3623.
- Crater Lake National Park, Superintendent, P.O. Box 7, Crater Lake, OR 97604; (541) 594-2511.
- Jacksonville Information Center, Rogue River Valley Railway Depot; (541) 899-8118.
- Britt Festivals, P.O. Box 1124, Medford, OR 97501; (541) 773-6077 or (800) 882-7488.
- Oregon Shakespeare Festival: Tickets at (541) 482-4331.

CAMPGROUNDS

SUSAN CREEK CAMPGROUND: 12.5 miles (20 km) east of Glide; restrooms with showers; reservations not accepted.

DIAMOND LAKE CAMP-GROUNDS: On Diamond Lake off OR 138; Forest camps are Diamond Lake Campground (restrooms and dump station), Broken Arrow (restrooms), and Thielsen View (vault toilets): reservations at (800) 280-CAMP; hookups and showers are available at Diamond Lake RV Park: reservations at (541) 793-3318.

ROGUE RIVER CAMP-GROUNDS: From Prospect, south to north along the river, forest camps are River Bridge (no fee), Natural Bridge (no fee), Union Creek, Farewell Bend (flush toilets), and Hamaker.

CRATER LAKE CAMP-GROUNDS: At Mazama Village is a huge campground with restrooms, public showers available; tents only at Lost Creek Campground (on Pinnacles Road), with restrooms.

FAREWELL BEND CAMP-GROUND: 12 miles (19 km) north of Prospect; campsites with restrooms and playground; reservations not accepted.

JOSEPH P. STEWART STATE PARK: 35 miles (56 km) northeast of Medford; campground with restrooms, showers, and electrical hookups; reservations not accepted.

COLLIER MEMORIAL STATE PARK: 30 miles (48 km) north of Klamath Falls off US 97; tent and full hookup sites, restrooms with showers, dump station; reservations not accepted.

The bounteous rainfall in western Oregon has spawned a wealth of streams that flow to the ocean from the Cascade Mountains. The North Umpqua and Rogue rivers of southern Oregon are two of the most well known among outdoor enthusiasts, whether for rafting, fishing, or hiking the trails that skirt them. Summer is a great time to visit the upper portions of these rivers, with their close proximity to the high mountain peaks of southern Oregon. Waterfalls, wildlife, green forests, and wildflowers abound.

Near the headwaters of both rivers, Crater Lake National Park is Oregon's crown jewel of parks, a one-of-a-kind deep blue lake rimmed by a glorious looping drive full of surprises. With so much winter snowfall at this elevation, it's best to visit the park in mid-August when the wildflowers are at their peak.

The tour finishes with great music at the Britt Festival in the historic town of Jacksonville and Shakespeare performances in Ashland. Klamath Basin national wildlife refuges are nearby. The tour starts at Roseburg on Interstate 5 and follows a designated scenic byway most of the route.

Wildlife Safari

Begin the tour a few miles west of Roseburg, via exit 119 on Interstate 5, with extraordinary wildlife viewing at Wildlife Safari, a 600-acre drive-through zoological park where hundreds of animals from around the world roam freely in natural surroundings and offer some unusual sightings. Live animal programs along with African elephant (weather permitting) and train rides are features. Children will like the petting zoo. Wildlife devotees and photographers will want to allow plenty of time.

Rental cars and kennels are available; no convertibles are allowed in the lion or bear drive-throughs. The adjacent village includes the White Rhino Restaurant and the Casbah gift shop. Summer is often hot, so it's best to come early or late in the day.

North Umpqua Highway

The North Umpqua Highway, a designated scenic byway, begins at Roseburg and heads east via OR 138. If you first head north from Roseburg to Winchester—perhaps stopping at the Winchester Dam to look through the underwater viewing windows—you can soon turn east and follow the North Umpqua River immediately along a pretty stretch. You'll intersect with the byway at Glide, a scenic stopping place to witness the confluence of the North Umpqua and Little rivers.

A few miles past Glide, the 79-mile (127-km) North Umpqua Trail follows the North Umpqua River—named for the Umpqua Indians who once fished the river for salmon—to its headwaters at Maidu Lake, where it meets the long-distance Pacific Crest Trail. Many trailheads, with parking, restrooms, and sometimes campgrounds, divide the North Umpqua Trail into eleven segments that are easily walked as day hikes. Several short trails lead from the main trail to waterfalls and geologic at-

Rock formations along the North Umpqua River.

tractions. These hikes pass fishing holes, sections of old-growth forest, and calypso orchids and maidenhair fern, with frequent sightings of osprey, water ouzel, and common merganser. You might even hear a northern spotted owl. Horses and mountain bikes are allowed on some segments of the trail.

Insider's Tip:

A detailed brochure on the North Umpqua Trail that includes highlights, difficulty factors, and fishing, historical, and facilities information is available from the Umpqua National Forest. The North Umpqua River from 700 feet (213 m) above Rock Creek is open only to fly-fishing. Check for current regulations before fishing.

The Deadline Falls Watchable Wildlife Site is only 0.25 mile (0.4 km) from the start of the trail at Swiftwater Park. From June through October you may see salmon and steelhead jumping the falls along this easy, barrier-free section of trail. A little farther along are two special stops at Fern Falls and Allilo Creek Canyon.

The first campground along the byway is Susan Creek Campground, with excellent sites in mature forest along the river, where rafters have fun weaving around rocks and through riffles in the river. Once a state park, the Bureau of Land Management has recently upgraded the campground; barrier-free trails provide views of forest and river, while longer trails head for Susan Creek Indian Mounds and Susan Creek Falls.

Steelhead fishing on the North Umpqua River was so exciting that Zane Grey gave up on the Rogue River after it received too much publicity, "to camp and fish and dream and rest beside the green-rushing, singing Umpqua." Anglers still hang out at Steamboat Inn.

After you pass several forest camps and other trails, you'll arrive at another watchable wildlife site at Weeping Rocks, with excellent views of Chinook salmon spawning. Look for gravel depressions (redds) on

Eagle Rock in the mist along the North Umpqua River.

the river bottom where eggs are deposited. The main trail crosses the river near here to continue along the north bank of the North Umpqua. The geology gets more interesting a few miles past Weeping Rocks; notice Eagle Rock and columnar basalt and perhaps some canoes or kayaks on the river. Between these two rock formations the Boulder Creek Wilderness borders the north bank, with a trail taking off north along the creek.

Near the forest service road turnoff to Toketee Lake, the byway loses the North Umpqua River and now follows the Clearwater River upstream past a series of spectacular waterfalls that are easily accessible from the highway. (The North Umpqua Trail continues to follow the North Umpqua River.) The first waterfall is 272-foot (83-m) Watson Falls—the highest in southern Oregon—followed by Whitehorse Falls tumbling through a forest camp into a shady pool, and then Clearwater Falls (another forest camp) near the headwaters of the Clearwater River.

Diamond Lake

The byway soon turns south and heads for Diamond Lake. If parking your rig on the shore of a mountain lake is on your wish list, try Diamond Lake, 4 miles (6.4 km) north of Crater Lake National Park. You have the option of viewing either Mount Bailey or Mount Thielsen—and sunsets or sunrises—across the lake from your campsite, as three forest camps are located on a road that circles the lake. The rufous hummingbirds gathering nectar from the wildflowers are great entertainment.

At an elevation of 5,182 feet (1,579 m), the lake covers nearly 3,000 acres, so there is plenty of room for waterskiing and boating. Stocked with rainbow trout, anglers have success here and swimmers find the surface water warm enough for swimming in the afternoon.

Hiking trails are many and go in all directions into the mountains—up Mount Bailey, Howlock Mountain, or Mount Thielsen, with a connection to the Pacific Crest Trail. Short easy walks past streams, ponds, and meadows are near the lake, and there are bicycling and horse trails.

The Upper Rogue River— First Segment

Although the north entrance to Crater Lake National Park is not far, entering via the south entrance lets you make a complete loop around the lake and ensures your seeing some special attractions in the park and along the Upper Rogue River. So choose OR 230 and head south.

Diamond Lake and Mount Thielsen viewed from the Mount Bailey Trail.

When the present Cascade Mountains were being uplifted by fluid basalt lava, the ancestral Rogue River was forced to cut a channel through basalt rocks. From north to south along the trail, watch for these spectacular geologic features.

In contrast to the well-known "Wild and Scenic" portion of the lower Rogue River, few people are aware that the Upper Rogue River Trail borders a wild and unfloatable section of the river at the beginning of its 210-mile (338-km) downstream journey. Several easily reached stops along this route let you day hike segments of the trail, which covers easy to moderate terrain. Situated near special aspects along the trail, many of these stops have picnic areas and campgrounds, with parking for picking up hikers doing one-way hikes.

Crater Rim Viewpoint is the northern trailhead for the 45.5-mile (73-km) Upper Rogue River Trail (No. 1034) that follows the river. If you wish to see the headwaters of the river in Crater Lake National Park, take the left spur 0.5 mile (800 m) from the trailhead to Boundary Springs. Here the Rogue has mossy beginnings, where torrents of snowmelt from the Cascades collide with logjams of downed trees, as it joins the water from the fragile environment of the springs.

Heading south on the highway—or on the trail—a pumice chasm, Ruth Falls, Rough Rider Falls, and another unnamed falls are along the river north of Hamaker Campground and Hamaker Meadows. The next waterfall south, appropriately named Highway Falls, is easily viewed from the road. Just north of the Foster Creek Trailhead, the river crosses the highway where the creek enters the Rogue.

South of Foster Creek, the river has cut through once molten pumice from the Mount Mazama explosion, leaving 250-foot (76-m) cliffs of compacted pumice called "Winding River Canyon." The trail is not through stark landscape, however, but traverses a richness of tiny plants and mature forest much of the way along the river. Anglers enjoy the quiet solitude while fishing for rainbow and cutthroat trout.

Below Big Bend Trailhead, OR 62 heads

off east to Crater Lake, and this is a good time to head for the national park.

Crater Lake National Park

About 7,700 years ago, the Modoc Indians witnessed a catastrophic event. Legend says that mountains shook and crumbled. Red-hot rocks as large as hills were hurled through the skies. An ocean of fire spewed out, devouring the forests, with the flames sweeping on until they reached the homes of the Modoc near the mountain called Mazama, which was once 12,000 feet (3,658 m) high. The Modocs believed that this violence resulted from a battle between two gods, Llao and Skell. After a living sacrifice was made by the Modoc, the high mountain collapsed and the tears of the Modoc filled the dark abyss, which became a sacred lake to the Indians.

Causal forces were mysterious then, but in fact Mount Mazama collapsed because of the incredible amounts of magma released from beneath its summit. Even those who witnessed the May 1980 eruption of Mount St. Helens cannot imagine these explosions, which were forty-two times more powerful. The huge caldera was too hot and full of cracks to hold water for a time, but eventually rain, snow, and springs began to fill this 4,000-feet (1,219-m) deep hole that is up to 6 miles (9.6 km) wide—and beautiful Crater Lake resulted.

Today the lake, at 1,932 feet (589 m), is the country's deepest. Surrounding it is a circle of cliffs on the crest of the Cascade Mountains that include Watchman, Hillman Peak, Llao Rock, Pumice Point, Cleetwood Cove, Skell Head, Mount Scott, Kerr Notch, Sun Notch, and Garfield Peak. To the north are the Pumice Desert, Mount Bailey, and Mount Thielsen.

The lake's intense blue color is breathtaking, a result of sunlight and the lake's purity and depth. All other colors of the spectrum except the short blue wavelengths are absorbed by water molecules; and the color blue is scattered from great depths and radiated anew in all directions. The low concentration of dissolved minerals and organic matter reinforces this vision of blue, which delights spectators. A research vessel monitors the clarity of the water.

A newspaper editor from Jacksonville, James Sutton, gave the lake its permanent name, and photographer Peter Britt loaded his cumbersome gear into a wagon and was off to take the first photo of the lake, a picture that appeared widely and helped make Crater Lake a national entity.

It was a 16-year-old schoolboy, William Gladstone Steel, who became the father of this national park. He first became captivated by Crater Lake when he read a short piece about it in a newspaper—in which his luncheon sandwich was wrapped! After seventeen years of lobbying by Steel, Crater Lake became the country's fifth national park in 1902. Steel even carried the first 600 fingerling trout to seed the lake. Today, introduced rainbow and kokanee trout are still part of the lake's ecosystem.

ANNIE SPRING ENTRANCE

The south entry to the lake is open all year to Rim Village for cross-country skiing and snow play. The northern entrance and the Rim Drive are usually closed from mid-October to late June during an average snowfall year, which can vary from 252 inches to 614 inches (640 cm to 1,560 cm). In summer, Mazama Village is open near the Annie Spring Entrance Station where there is a large campground, a store, gas, and a laundry.

The Annie Creek Loop trail heads down into a canyon from Mazama Campground,

Crater Lake rim reflections and Sinnott Memorial structure.

a hike past wildflowers along the creek where dipper or ouzel birds are often seen, as well as pinnacles that are remnants of ash flows. Hot gases from the climactic eruptions emerged through fumaroles in this area. Eventually, water washed away loose pumice and left more resistant, cemented rock as spires.

The Steel Information Center near Park Headquarters shows a film called the *"Crater Lake Story."* Across the road is Castle Crest Wildflower Trail, a park highlight. Summer comes late at the 6,176-foot (1,882-m) elevation of Crater Lake and snow rules much of the year, but an exuberance of color blazes in special locations, and this is one of them. I highly recommend walking this short trail. The melted snow of picturesque Castle Creek meanders through a meadow and nourishes a quilt of color. Pink Lewis monkeyflowers, shooting stars, yellow buttercups, bleeding hearts, and blue stickweed are a few of the flowers that contrast with the lush green along this 0.5-mile (800 m) walk over stepping-stones.

RIM VILLAGE

Arriving via the south entrance, the first lake views are near Rim Village. You'll want to linger and gaze at the incredible scene; its serenity belies its violent beginnings. Always stunning, the lake landscape changes with the light and weather, and at sunrise and sunset. Sun is the norm in summer, and the white clouds that gather in the afternoon enhance the impact of the brilliant blue of the lake. You'll be entertained by the friendly antics of Clark's nutcrackers, chipmunks, and golden-mantled squirrels.

Stroll down to Sinnott Memorial Overlook and then on to the fully restored Crater Lake Lodge that reopened in 1995 after years of withstanding heavy snowfalls. Near the lodge is the strenuous trail up Garfield Peak, which is a fine day hike with panoramic views. For a slower, more intense viewing of the lake, try some or all of the section of the Pacific Crest Trail from Rim Village to North Junction on the Rim Drive.

Today the lake environs are full of wild

beauty that has recovered quite a bit from the geologic upheaval of the past. New life emerged after the plants and animals were obliterated. One of the first was probably the whitebark pine, since it seeds are scattered by Clark's nutcrackers. Other birds and animals, along with the wind, spread other seeds—Shasta red fir, old growth mountain hemlock, and lodgepole pine. Several pairs of northern spotted owls inhabit the park, some nesting and producing young. The rare Mount Mazama collomia flower is also being monitored in the park.

THE RIM DRIVE

Magical vistas and more than thirty overlooks—several with trails—are along the 33-mile (53-km) Rim Drive. Names such as Wineglass, Skell Head, Cloudcap, Castle Rock, and Devil's Backbone hint of the scenery. This is not a place to rush, and the many picnic areas provide great spots for lunch. Head clockwise, where the first excursion is a short trail that climbs to a lookout on Watchman Peak, the best viewpoint for Wizard Island. Past North Junction, Cleetwood Cove offers the only safe and legal access to the water via a steep trail that drops 700 feet (213 m) in 1.1 miles (1.8 km); the trek back out of the crater is definitely aerobic. If you'd like to take the ranger-narrated boat tour on the lake you must hike the trail. Ask about a stopover at Wizard Island, where a trail leads to the crater on the summit of the island. Tickets are sold at the parking lot near Cleetwood Cove Trailhead.

The east side of the Rim Drive accesses the drive's quintessential hike to the historic fire tower on the summit of the tallest mountain edging the lake, 8,926-foot (2,721-m) Mount Scott, a 5-mile (8-km) round-trip with a 1,500-foot (457-m) gain in elevation. Out in the open, with the lake far below and vistas that include the Williamson River Valley to the southeast, the hike is one of my all-time favorites. Watch for glacier lilies and pasqueflowers along the trail.

An easy walk through lovely meadows at Sun Notch provides close views of the

Phantom Ship, whose "sails" are upright dikes of hardened lava that radiated out from fissures. Phantom Ship is part of the original cone of Mount Mazama. As the drive meanders away from the lake near the Vidae Ridge, Vidae Falls plunges over a series of rock ledges through vivid green vegetation.

To continue the tour, head back to the Upper Rogue River along OR 62 and proceed south.

Upper Rogue River—Second Segment

Almost immediately after reaching the Rogue River, the popular Farewell Bend Campground fronts the lovely colors and sounds of the river. Quiet sections of water mix with wilder areas. I once camped here at the edge of a miniature gorge, a special site. It's always fun to pick a site with the most ambiance, if available, but doing so often means parking and walking the complete campground because such sites are not always obvious.

You can walk south along the river at Farewell Bend and see where daisies and wild strawberries have inched their way up through openings in swirls of lava. Orbiting rocks in the violent surge of water have carved potholes in the lava riverbed. The noisy tumble of miniature waterfalls demonstrates how the Rogue is still working away at the ancient basalt rock. This walk leads to another spectacular place on the river—the Rogue River Gorge. A wild, raging passage through a channel of basalt—a collapsed lava tube—the Rogue roars like a caged lion. Yellow and black swallowtails sometimes hover above the turbulence. A walk back through the conifer forest may reward you with sightings of Columbia windflowers, a delicate, solitary white flower above a whorl of three leaves. The main access to the Rogue River Gorge, however, is past the campground via a parking lot off the highway. A paved trail skirts the gorge, which is probably the most visited spot on the upper river; exercise extreme caution.

The larger Union Creek Campground and Union Creek Resort are just south of the gorge. The Civilian Conservation Corps built many rustic structures near the resort in the 1930s that are now on the National Register of Historic Places. Two trails begin in the campground. One continues south from the gorge between the campground and the river to Natural Bridge. The second begins where Union Creek joins the Rogue, crosses the highway, and continues following the creek for several miles through majestic examples of old-growth Douglas fir through a forest called a "five star" ancient grove.

The section of the Upper Rogue River Trail in this area begins at Big Bend Trailhead and moves to the west riverbank, where it passes rapids that alternate with a placid river. The trail crosses the river on a bridge just north of Natural Bridge Campground.

Natural Bridge is another must-see geologic attraction and is easily reached by road, where an interpretive wheelchair-accessible trail is found. When the Rogue River was re-establishing a channel over basalt lava, it was diverted into partially collapsed and intact lava tubes. At Natural Bridge, much of the river's flow disappears into a maze of these tubes and then bursts out into a surface channel where the tubes collapsed with incredible pent-up gravitational force. It's an awesome sight, and a place to exercise caution. A man once slipped here and was never found. Late summer is the best time to see this because the winter and spring runoff often overflows the basalt bridge.

A short section of Trail No. 1034 continues to Woodruff Bridge, where you'll find a picnic area. Along the first part of the next section of trail south to River Bridge Campground, foot-long, sugar pine cones are scattered on the forest floor, which would have pleased David Douglas. The attraction at 1.5 miles (2.4 km) is the unique Takelma Gorge, a narrow, deep channel in basalt that follows a series of rapids and a sharp turning arm of hardened lava for a little over a mile; this is a good destination for a day hike. Yellow Pacific sedum and purple asters bloom on the brink of the gorge.

Bunchberry flowers at Union Creek Campground, Upper Rogue River.

The Upper Rogue Trail ends at Prospect, at the boundary of the Rogue River National Forest, but both OR 62 and another 30 miles (48 km) of the Rogue River National Recreation Trail continue to follow the river as it flows southwest.

Joseph P. Stewart State Park

The Rogue has been dammed several miles downstream from Prospect, creating Lost Creek Lake in a mountainous and timbered canyon. Joseph P. Stewart State Park is pleasantly situated along the southeastern shores of the lake, where some sites have lake views. The Park was once the location of a pear orchard established by A. J. Weeks, the son-in-law of Joseph P. Stewart, one of the country's foremost horticulturists.

Whether your sport is boating, waterskiing, bicycling, hiking, or fishing, you'll find good opportunities here. A marina, ramp, fish-cleaning stations, store, cafe, and swimming area are located at the day-use area not far from the campground. Both the bicycle and walking paths will lead you there, or consider a longer ride or hike to Peyton Bridge at the lake's eastern end. The bike trail is nearer the highway, while the Rogue River National Recreation Trail is nearer the lake.

The hiking trail is high above the lake and soon merges with meadows; it then crosses bridges and continues on the high

bank of the river. Wildflowers are varied and numerous in summer and include California poppies, vetch, wild rose, Oregon grape, mock orange, ocean spray, striped coral root, self heal, fireweed, and chicory. The dried flower head of a salsify is a wonder of golden spokes that swirl out like a comet spewing a multitude of tails that are all silver fluff. Other wild things are about: monarch and swallowtail butterflies dart among madrone, pine, fir, oak, red cedar, and red huckleberry trees. The river has mothered a land awash in color and life.

The North Shore Trail makes it possible to circle the lake and, although that's a distance of approximately 18 miles (29 km), campgrounds and toilets are located in several places in this roadless area. Boaters have easier access to sections of this trail. Another hiking choice is the state park's 10-km Volkswalk.

Casey State Park

The highway and recreation trail continue to Casey State Park (day use only) just west of the McLeod Bridge. This picnic area is the beginning of good salmon fishing downstream along the Rogue.

The park also easily accesses Lost Creek Dam, the Cole M. Rivers Fish hatchery, the last part of the North Shore Trail, and a visitor center at McGregor Park. Designed specifically for handicapped visitors, McGregor Park has drinking fountains, restrooms, fishing pads, picnic areas, and barrier-free, hard-top trails. It's a lovely spot just downstream of the dam, a great place for a rest stop and lunch in this wetland habitat. Oregon grape, blackberry, ferns, mock orange, and ocean spray grow beneath cottonwood, California laurel, alder, dogwood, and bigleaf maple trees. Horsetail grows to three feet tall, and beaver, muskrats, western gray squirrels, porcupines, and chipmunks are at home in this ecosystem. Small rocks in the river attract resting merganser ducks.

Painted paw prints on the pavement guide you past the fish diversion dam and the hatchery, and the trail begins again in an open field, where you may spot great fishing birds—bald eagle, osprey, great blue heron, and kingfisher. More birds are attracted by the millet planted as a nutritious seed. Human anglers practice catch-and-release in this area of the river. Continue on the trail to see the powerhouse, where released water is temperature controlled for the fish downstream. Stop and watch the salmon struggle to ascend the fish ladder, where they leap and leap until they are successful.

Weekenders love the river downstream from Casey State Park as it rocks and sings with a wild voice. They launch rafts and dories and get thrown around in the boisterous river as they move quickly downstream. Meanwhile, the salmon fight to go upriver during their swim from the Pacific Ocean at Gold Beach. Anglers on the river bank can be seen pulling in salmon. A little farther downstream, the Rogue Elk County Campground is nicely situated along the Rogue.

As the Rogue flows into the Rogue River Valley, it becomes a sedate affair for a time in this place of vineyards and country living. Just north of Medford, Tou Velle State Park provides good access for flyfishing on the Rogue—prime salmon and steelhead fishing—with trails weaving through the wildlife refuge that adjoins the day-use area of the park. Bring binoculars to see the wildlife.

The Historic Town of Jacksonville

Five miles (8 km) west of Medford, the town of Jacksonville, which was founded in 1851 with the discovery of gold in Rich Gulch, is a National Historic Landmark. The pioneer spirit prevailed here after the gold ran out, even though epidemics, floods, and fires threatened to destroy the town. Today it is a quaint and beautiful community replete with more than 80 well-maintained Victorian homes and pioneer businesses. A stroll along the self-guiding walking tour (brochures available at the information center) reveals beautiful lawns, flowering shrubs, and shade trees.

The Jacksonville Museum of Southern Oregon History has an exhibit that tells the story of photographer Peter Britt, who set out on foot on the Oregon Trail with a cart containing several hundred pounds of photographic gear and arrived in Jacksonville in late 1852. In addition to his many photographic achievements, Britt had an interest in horticulture and planted a subtropical garden, fruit trees, and Oregon's first commercial vineyards. His Valley View wines were once common in southern Oregon homes. Today he is remembered by the music festivals that bear his name and that are held on the hillside estate he bequeathed to Southern Oregon College. Since 1963, the Britt Festivals have gained a reputation as premier outdoor music and performing arts festivals. Held from June through August, events include classical, country, jazz, pop, folk, and dance performances. Spectators enjoy everything from champagne breakfasts to Sunday Mornings (classical music) to evening picnic concerts under the stars (bring your own blanket, food, and drink)—a wonderful experience in this small-town ambiance.

Shakespeare at Ashland

From Jacksonville it's a quick jaunt south to Ashland, a town that attracts visitors from great distances to its Tony Award–winning Oregon Shakespeare Festival, which is presented on three unique stages: the outdoor Elizabethan Theater, the Angus Bowmer Theater, and the Black Swan. The season is from February through October. Performances are outstanding, even if you've never been a big fan of the Bard.

Although Shakespeare memorabilia is the rage throughout Ashland's downtown, Lithia Park is a natural town jewel. Designed by John McLaren, who also designed San Francisco's Golden Gate park, visitors can watch ducks and swans, enjoy an array of outdoor sports, and listen to summer concerts at the bandshell. An outdoor market is held on weekends from May through October on Water Street behind the plaza.

A recent addition to the Ashland scene is the Pacific Northwest Museum of Natural History, which is a great place to learn more about the diverse ecosystems of the

Pacific Northwest. Interactive displays using videos, microscopes, and computers engage the five senses to inform you about the ocean, the rain forest, the high desert, and the wetlands. See a lava tube, discover what species are threatened or endangered, and uncover facts on wildlife crime detection. The U.S. Fish and Wildlife Service's National Forensics Laboratory is located in Ashland.

Explore the surrounding countryside where fruit orchards are a specialty and several commercial operators feature raft trips on the nearby Rogue River.

Klamath Basin National Wildlife Refuges

A trip east on OR 66 across a lower elevation of the Cascades unfolds a region rich in wildlife, especially birds. The Klamath Basin contains five national wildlife refuges that stretch from the upper end of Klamath Lake to south of the Oregon-California border: Lower Klamath, Tule Lake, Clear Lake, Klamath Forest, and Upper Klamath. Although numbers of birds are highest during the fall and spring migrations, Lower Klamath and Tule Lake are two of the most exciting refuges in the country to visit at most any time, especially in early morning and evening.

The visitor center is at Tule Lake. Lower Klamath (the country's first waterfowl refuge), and Tule Lake has rewarding auto tours. In addition to the profusion of bird species, sightings of otters, deer, coyotes, and muskrats are also frequent. Both Tule Lake and Upper Klamath have canoe trails, which is a quiet way to observe birdlife without disturbing them. The Klamath Basin has the largest population of wintering bald eagles in the lower 48 states.

Collier Memorial State Park

Just east of the northern reaches of Klamath Lake, along US 97, is a unique state park—Collier Memorial State Park. One of the country's finest collections of logging equipment is featured in an open-air museum. Walk past huge sections of Douglas fir and sugar pine trees, skidding equipment, steam tractors, loggers' "cats," road graders, mighty circular saws, steam-powered Dolbeer donkey engines used to skid logs to landings, and the last boat to haul log rafts across Klamath Lake. Exhibited on a railroad track are a narrow-gauge locomotive, a one-person handcart, a stiff-boom loader, a log buncher, a swing-boom loader, and a track-laying car. A steam-generating plant once powered a sawmill.

Continue past the logging exhibits to the pioneer village on Spring Creek, complete with authentic log cabins that include a doctor's office, a store, a sheepherder's wagon, and an explorer's cabin. A glimpse of the interior furnishings provides hints of pioneer life in the area. Signs identify native plants along the paths.

Some visitors come to the park specifically for the excellent trout-fishing in the Williamson River and Spring Creek, where great blue herons and ducks also hang out. Hiking trails connect areas of the park on both sides of the highway. A road north on the highway leads to the campground that is located on the opposite shore near the confluence of the creek and the river.

Begin or end your stop at the authentic logger's homestead, which is now an information center and gift shop. You'll see a huge, stuffed Alaskan timber wolf mounted on the wall along with historical artifacts of the area.

Now you can head for home with memories of a unique blue lake, wildlife, and two extraordinary rivers.

Elizabethan Shakespeare Theater at Ashland, OR.

Autumn Trips

The best weather on the Pacific Northwest coast is in September. The summer winds and many of the tourists are gone, yet the storm season has not arrived. On the Olympic peninsula, fall is an excellent time to walk the wild beaches and rainforest trails. The riches promised by summer are fulfilled in autumn. Flowers are resplendent at Butchart Gardens near Victoria, British Columbia, which is an easy RV trip by ferry. Throughout the country, residents and travelers partake of the edible feast of the harvest season. On the Colorado Plateau, RVers can camp near orchards planted by Mormon pioneers in Capitol Reef, perhaps enjoying an apple while they view spectacular red rock surroundings at sunset.

Along the rivers of many of southern Utah parks, autumn foliage reflects fluttering abstract designs across the waters. In the Colorado mountains, the foliage colors climb the mountain sides

Sand milkweed
(Asclepias arenaria)

.and are mirrored by lakes in a spectacle proclaiming nature's climax to the growing season.

The wildlife plays an even more dramatic role in this golden-bronze season, when the harvest moon seems more luminous than ever. Rocky mountain elk bugle for mates and all the animals prepare for the harshness of winter. For many birds this means migrating to warmer climes. Wildlife refuges across the western landscapes are stopping places, with one being Dungeness in Washington. In New Mexico, Bosque Del Apache attracts great numbers of wintering birds; there is even a festival in November to celebrate their arrival.

CHAPTER 9

Olympic Peninsula Loop:
Wilderness Beaches, Rain Forests, and Mountains

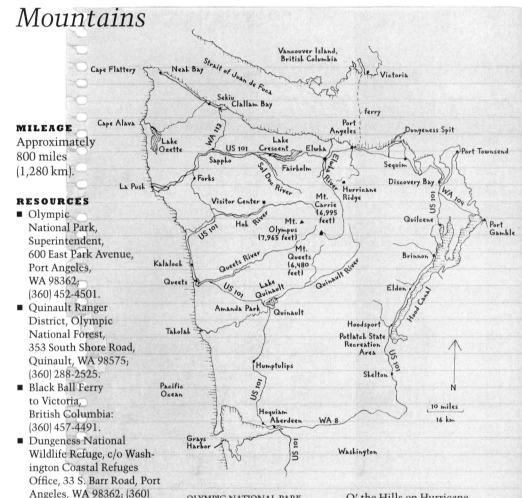

MILEAGE

Approximately 800 miles (1,280 km).

RESOURCES

- Olympic National Park, Superintendent, 600 East Park Avenue, Port Angeles, WA 98362; (360) 452-4501.
- Quinault Ranger District, Olympic National Forest, 353 South Shore Road, Quinault, WA 98575; (360) 288-2525.
- Black Ball Ferry to Victoria, British Columbia: (360) 457-4491.
- Dungeness National Wildlife Refuge, c/o Washington Coastal Refuges Office, 33 S. Barr Road, Port Angeles, WA 98362; (360) 457-8541.

CAMPGROUNDS

QUINAULT VALLEY CAMPING: 42 miles (68 km) north of Hoquiam; national forest camps along Quinault Lake at Willaby and Falls Creek with restrooms; longer hookup sites at Rain Forest Resort on lake; forest camp upstream at Graves Creek with restrooms.

OLYMPIC NATIONAL PARK COASTAL STRIP: Kalaloch area north; free primitive oceanfront camping with restrooms at South Beach; fee campgrounds at Kalaloch and Mora have restrooms and dump stations.

INLAND AT OLYMPIC NATIONAL PARK: Heading clockwise, campgrounds at Hoh, Sol Duc, Fairholm on Lake Crescent, Elwha and Altaire in Elwha Valley, and Heart

O' the Hills on Hurricane Ridge road have campsites, restrooms, and dump stations (except for Elwha and Heart O' the Hills); reservations not accepted.

DUNGENESS RECREATION AREA: Three miles north of US 101 off Kitchen Road between Sequim and Port Angeles; campsites, restrooms with showers, dump station.

A glance at a map of the northwest corner of Washington shows no roads crossing the interior of the Olympic Peninsula. Bordered on three sides by the waters of the Pacific Ocean, the Strait of Juan de Fuca, and the Hood Canal, a highway circles the mystical core that is the glacier-cloaked Olympic Mountains. What is hidden beyond the eclipsing forest in this mountain wilderness? It sounds like a place for adventure, for exploration, and for solitude away from madding crowds. Yet, an incredible assortment of enlightening experiences—for other than those who seek a release of adrenaline—exists in every mile of this outermost tip of the northwest.

This peninsula is an obvious place for a tour loop, with side trips on roads that edge rain forests and penetrate a short distance into the vital center of Olympic National Park—where you can take off on foot if desired. Roads in the opposite direction lead to waterfront recreation, whether it's a trek on a wild ocean beach or gathering clams and oysters along the Hood Canal. Only one paved road reveals panoramic views of the many mountain ridges, valleys, and innermost peaks that are so often hidden.

Weather is a dramatic affair on the peninsula. As the southwest winds of wild winter storms move inland from the Pacific, rain is dumped on the coast and on the windward side of the mountains, creating a rain shadow on the lee side. Thus, although

Black-tailed deer at Hurricane Ridge in Olympic National Park.

the crown of the park, 7,965-foot (2,428-m) Mount Olympus, attracts some 200 inches of precipitation annually—mostly as snow—Port Townsend averages only some 15 inches.

The good news is that a high pressure area hovers near the Gulf of Alaska and sends northwest winds and rather dry, temperate summers to the peninsula. Late summer or early fall are optimal times to visit, before the winds shift and the rains arrive. Weather can be spectacular for outdoor activities at this time, although there is never any guarantee against rain anywhere and any time. And remember, without this rain these cathedral-like rain forests would not be here. One of the ten most visited national parks, Olympic National Park is definitely a favored travel destination.

Entry into this tour loop is via ferries at Port Angeles and Port Townsend; across the Hood Canal Floating Bridge that connects the Kitsap Peninsula; by road at Aberdeen or west from Interstate 5 at Olympia; or at many points on the peninsula.

Gateway North at Aberdeen

At the head of the deep ocean bay called Grays Harbor—where roads head west to developed beaches along Washington's south coast—US 101 crosses the inlet waters of the Chehalis and Wishkah rivers. Sprawled along the bay is the city of Aberdeen, a gateway north into the Olympic Peninsula. A replica of Captain Robert Gray's ship, the *Lady Washington*, is exhibited at Grays Harbor Historical Seaport. Gray sailed this ship along the northwest coast in 1792 and established the claim of the United States to Oregon country.

Lake Quinault and the Quinault River Valley

The lowland rising gently from the sea along Washington's northwest coast is dominated by dense, lush, and unspoiled rain-forest valleys along three rivers generated by glaciers and by raindrops, sleet, and snow. Nourished by twelve feet of precipitation each year and a warm, humid climate that includes summer fogs, this landscape exists in a natural greenhouse. The Quinault Valley is the first of these river corridors along the tour, entered via the South Shore Road along Lake Quinault. Stop at the ranger station by the lake for hiking maps. The rustic Lake Quinault Lodge is impressive and worth a look-see, and perhaps even a stay for a dinner of fresh grilled salmon or trout. Colorful canoes beached along the glacier-carved lake are inviting. Fishing is good for trout and dolly varden.

Insider Tips:

Lake Quinault is part of the Quinault Indian Nation and a special permit is required from them for lake fishing. A Washington State Personal Use Food Fish License is required in national forest areas (not in Olympic National Park except when fishing from the ocean shore). A special state catch record card is required for steelhead and salmon caught in state waters.

In 1890, the Seattle Press Expedition was the first to cross the interior over the mountains. They arrived in Quinault Valley after an impractical beginning up the Elwha River in January. Led by James Christie, their north-south journey took five-and-a-half months, a trip backpackers can do now in five days.

National forest campgrounds among towering trees are strung out along the lake and make fine base camps for exploring the area. Two excellent trails for viewing the magnificent rain forest are within walking distance. The Rain Forest Nature Trail is a short distance southeast of the entry road to Willaby Campground. A longer excursion is via the Quinault Loop Trail, which can be hiked in several ways for a 4- to 8-mile (6.5- to 13-km) hike that includes views of the lake and a boardwalk through a cedar swamp.

South Shore Road continues 19 miles (30.4 km) east of the lake—with good views of the forest for vehicle-bound travelers—as it climbs along the Quinault River into the rugged wilderness of the national park and

to Graves Creek. Most of this road is gravel. The Graves Creek Nature Trail, a campground, and the trailhead to the 13-mile (21-km) Enchanted Valley Trail are at the end of the road. This backpacking trail heads upstream to a log chalet (a sometime-ranger station) set in a spectacular gorge rimmed with waterfalls. Hikers can continue past this to the world's largest western hemlock and on to Anderson Pass. South Shore Road branches off along the North Fork of the Quinault River to trailheads that lead to the world's largest yellow cedar and to the Low Divide, the pass between the Quinault and the Elwha rivers, one of the main "through the park" trails.

Insider's Tips:

A use permit is free and required for all overnight stays in the backcountry. Know wilderness regulations. Plan carefully for long hikes into the inner Olympics, boil your drinking water or carry potable water, consider the possibility of a good rain, and leave only footprints. Stop, stay calm, and do not run if you sight a cougar. Sites with water for interior backcountry overnight stays are numbered. If your destination is one of the largest trees, make sure to ask a ranger whether it is still standing; after all, nature changes.

As US 101 heads west to the coast through the Quinault Indian Reservation, it passes the second impressive river corridor that flows downhill from glaciers to surf, the Queets, where a trail from the road's terminus leads to the Park's largest Douglas fir.

Olympic National Park Coastal Strip

The highway crosses the boundary into the coastal section of the Olympic National Park just before a sign for South Beach, a no-fee campground (no potable water) on the oceanfront. This is the beginning of 57 miles (92 km) of wild natural coastline dominated by dramatic surf, cliffs, log-

Ruby Beach at low tide, Olympic National Park.

strewn beaches, sea stacks, and wildlife. Except for beach hiking, access is via a few paved roads that take visitors within sight of the Pacific. A few miles north is the Kalaloch Information Station, Kalaloch Lodge, and the more developed Kalaloch Campground, with lots of beach for walking and beachcombing.

Along this south stretch of the coastal strip are short, sometimes steep trails to six numbered beaches and to Ruby Beach. The best time to explore any of these coastline jewels is at low tide, so carry tide tables. The warm Japanese ocean current is responsible for a water temperature of 45° to 55° all year and over 330 frost-free days. These conditions—and the quite strong surf and currents—don't bode well for swimmers, but the coastal marine life is bountiful. The plentiful nutrients from near-shore upwelling attract more then 75 species of coastal birds. Schools of cod, halibut, and salmon swim offshore.

Most intriguing, with a Brigadoon-like accessibility during low tides, is the intertidal area of these rocky shores—an arena of dramatic and constant daily changes in this merging of air, land, and sea. You might think that life would be difficult in the midst of booming surf, shifting sand, changing tides, and drastic variations in temperature and salinity. Yet this unique blend of habitats is a fascinating place in which to see a rich assortment of plants and animals and you can begin to understand how complexities often spur biological organisms to adapt. As you explore the tide pools from the beach toward the sea, the inhabitants change, reflecting different zones as you move seaward that vary with

the amount of air time creatures must endure. It's a fun experience to see how many different creatures you can find. If you turn over rocks to look for these curiosities, please leave them as you found them.

Walk out onto Beach No. 4 to view uplifted rock strata that hints at its origin, although it is now being slowly ground down by the ceaseless action of the waves. At low tide, you can view the great diversity of species in the tide pools. Look for sand dollars, fittings from shipwrecks, green anemones, sea stars, mussels, barnacles, limpets, hermit crabs, scampering small crabs, and more creatures than you can name. Popular activities are beachcombing, birding, digging for razor clams (license required; check with a ranger station), catching smelt with dip nets, and surf fishing.

A few miles north on the east side of the highway, a short road leads to 130-foot-high (40 m) Big Cedar Tree. Ruby Beach, the most northerly of this stretch of beaches, is named for the pinkish sand that contains tiny garnet crystals. It is a picturesque location with large tree-crowned sea stacks just offshore and a vast expanse of rocky shelves where intertidal life is exposed at low tide.

Hoh River Valley

The third, and most visited, of the coastal river corridors is along the Hoh River, inland on US 101 and then 19 miles (30.4 km) east on a park road to the Hoh Rain Forest Visitor Center. Humans build cathedrals; nature assembles temperate old-growth rain forests—outdoor green temples where we can visit and find peace. These natural constructs allow our "biophilia" to have expression. If a poem cannot match the magnificence of a tree, how can we ever describe the power and majesty of an old-growth rain forest?

For a sensual connection, try one of the nature trails. The Hall of Mosses Trail, with mosses and ferns hanging from giant trees, will impart that "jungly" atmosphere associated with lush vegetation, as will the longer Spruce Nature Trail and a shorter, wheelchair-accessible minitrail. For a more peaceful connection with the ecology of this forest—and a chance to see some of the more secretive wildlife—try a few (or all!) of the miles that make up the 17-mile (27-km) Hoh River Trail that climbs—easily at first—to summer wildflowers at Glacier Meadows and to Blue Glacier. This trail is the shortest route to Mount Olympus. Don't go onto the glacier nor climb to the summit without proper training and equipment.

An overnight at the Hoh Campground offers further opportunities to catch the changing show of hues in the forest, to view the moving shafts of light that penetrate it, and to check out the flora and fauna. Chances are good for sighting some Roosevelt elk. The predominant giant trees are Douglas fir, western hemlock, and western red cedar, with bigleaf maple and alder along the wet edges of streams. Young trees sprout in a row on old fallen logs called "nurse logs." Sword ferns and other varieties of ferns are thick on the forest floor; mushrooms pop up as fall approaches. One acre of this forest can grow some 6,000 pounds of mosses, lichens, and epiphytes. Vanilla leaf, western trillium, salal, Oregon grape, and Pacific bleeding heart all provide flowers. Huckleberries, salmonberries, thimbleberries, and blackberries are tasty edibles that grow wherever they can get some sun and are good eating on hikes.

You probably won't see the northern spotted owl or the marbled murrelet that are around, but wrens scurry about on the forest floor and kinglets, varied thrushes, chickadees, finches, vireos, and other small birds are around—even though they are heard more often than seen. Watch for a green flash—it might be a tree frog.

Second and Third Beach at La Push

After crossing the Bogachiel River and passing through the logging town of Forks, a spur road heads west again to some spectacular ocean beaches. To reach La Push, travel left at the main fork in the road. La Push, located in the Quileute Indian Reservation at the mouth of the Quillayute River, is a fishing port where brave fishermen still climb aboard their boats to tackle

what nature throws them as they harvest the natural riches of the sea.

National park beaches begin at the south boundary of Indian land, and there are two outstanding day-hike offerings near La Push. A 0.6-mile (1-km) trail leads to a wonderful walk along Second Beach, where I spotted a pair of bald eagles in a snag. The 1.6-mile (2.6-km) trail to Third Beach leads to another dreamscape of mesmerizing waves and giant sea stacks, tide pools at the north end, a stream halfway along the beach, a waterfall on a high bluff at the south end, and illuminating sunsets. The view south is called "Graveyard of the Giants." Third Beach is also the beginning of the 15.8-mile (26-km) South Wilderness Coast Hike to Oil City (no oil and no city), a demanding piece of backpacking where dangerous overland trails must be climbed over headlands. Those tackling these adventure trips must be strong hikers who value rewarding experiences.

 Insider's Tips:
Although Second Beach and Third Beach are adjacent, they are connected by Teahwhit Head, a point that can be neither rounded nor climbed. A tide table, park hints and regulations, and a trail map, with danger and caution markings along the trail, are a necessity for the long wilderness beach trails. Camp safely above the high tides.

Rialto Beach

The influence of natural elements on the park is obvious along the surf-swept wilderness beach so easily viewed at popular Rialto Beach north of La Push. Huge wave-tossed trees are scattered high on the berm of the beach by the booming surf, a feat demanding considerable force. Picturesque James Island lies just offshore, although it is sometimes connected to the mainland at low tide; it's part of Indian land. The beach is a mix of sand and round, polished stones; rock formations to the north beckon beachwalkers. Be on the lookout for scavenging bald eagles and wave-riding cormorants tossing glittering fish down their gullets. Black-tailed deer sometimes come to the beach to eat the iodine-rich seaweed.

You can walk south along the sandspit to the Quillayute River or north a little over a mile to tide pools on a rock reef at Hole-in-the-Wall (a sea tunnel), wading Ellen Creek along the route if it's not high tide. If you wish to learn intriguing details about the tide pool creatures, join a ranger-led walk. You might learn that kelp can be pickled and seaweed can become candy. A 21.8-mile (35-km) wilderness hike heads north, via Cape Alava, to Ozette. Or you could enjoy an overnight on the beach anywhere north of Ellen Creek.

Although excitingly beautiful, this wild coast was—and still is—very dangerous for sailing ships. Two memorials, one Chilean and one Norwegian, are along the wilderness trail to Ozette at sites where ships and most of their crews were lost in the early 1900s.

Lake Ozette and Cape Alava

To approach the northern section of the park's coastal strip, continue north on US 101 to WA 113 and then west along the Strait of Juan de Fuca to the turnoff to Lake Ozette, just past the town of Sekiu. This lake—the largest natural one in the state—is off the beaten path and offers solitude and rich outdoor experiences that include wildlife sightings. It also offers a ramp, potable water, and campsites.

Two trails lead to the ocean, and a longer loop trail combines them. The level 9.3-mile (15-km) Alava-Sand Point-Ozette triangle heads west from the lake past salal, evergreen huckleberry, cedar, Sitka spruce, and meadows on a wooden puncheon walkway for 3.3 miles (5.3 km) to Cape Alava, the most westerly point in the contiguous states.

An Ozette Indian village was located just north of the cape, situated near the sea for netting smelt and salmon and for excursions out through crevasses between beach rocks to harpoon whales from dugout canoes. The village was buried by a mud slide

Petroglyphs along the Cape Alava-Sand Point-Ozette trail, Olympic National Park.

300 to 500 years ago and is now closed and sealed, but some of the artifacts from this site can be seen at the Makah Cultural and Research Center at Neah Bay. Hike 3 miles (4.8 km) south along the beach past petroglyphs at Wedding Rocks for views of Ozette Island and tide pools among the rocks at low tide, which is the best time to walk the beach section.

I was caught in some rain on the beach, but snacked on my lunch of nuts and ripe cherries under a spruce tree. A raccoon came looking for a handout, although it didn't get one. A doe and her fawn lay quietly in the grass undisturbed by the few people hiking in the area. A pair of blue herons were not very skittish as they intently searched for food in the sea and then flew to a nearby rock. At Sand Point, another mostly planked 3-mile (4.8 km) trail heads back to the starting point through forest dotted with photogenic bright-red bunchberries.

Consider a side trip to Neah Bay to see the Makah Cultural Center and more wild coast at the confluence of the ocean and the Strait of Juan de Fuca. The strait was named for a Greek who sailed under the Spanish flag and who claimed—although this is somewhat disputed—that he found this waterway in 1592; he did give the correct latitude. On returning to US 101, you might want to stop for some fishing at Callam Bay.

Up the Sol Duc River

Back in the national park, the Sol Duc River has its share of enchanting lowland forest and recreational activities. Follow the river south for 14 miles (22.4 km) past a stopping point at Salmon Cascades and a park campground to road's end. The trailhead to Sol Duc Falls is located here, an easy 1-mile (1.6-km) walk through a forest of old-growth trees of western hemlock and Douglas fir to a waterfall viewed from a bridge overlooking this powerful plunge. The Lovers Lane Trail is a loop trail that can be hiked from site 62 in Loop B of the park campground to the Sol Duc Falls trailhead; it then continues just past the bridge as it loops back on the opposite side of the river to the Sol Duc Hot Springs Resort, where you can pick up a trail to the park campground—a distance of 6 miles (9.6 km).

Several other hiking options extend from the Sol Duc area into the interior of the park. One trail climbs from the resort to Mink Lake and connects to other trails. Or you can continue into the inner Olympics from the waterfall to the Seven Lakes Basin—and even farther.

Many travelers can't wait to immerse themselves in the soothing waters at the hot springs resort. Named Sol Duc after the Quileute Indian words for "sparkling water," the resort was built in 1912 and includes mineral pools ranging in temperature from approximately 98° to 106°F. Camping is available both at the resort and at the national park campground.

Lake Crescent

A lovely section of US 101 hugs the south shore of Lake Crescent, with many places to pull over along the winding route. On sunny days the lake's clear waters resemble a vivid blue sapphire. Carved some 600 feet (183 m) deep by an ancient glacier, the lake's fishing (the unique Beardslee trout is here), boating, and hiking possibilities have long attracted vacationers. Years ago, they flocked to spend the summer in this cool spot, taking a train to Port Angeles and then a jitney through the mountain scenery to the lake, where they boarded a ferry to reach resorts on the west end. Today, Fairholm Campground is in that area.

Lake Crescent Lodge and the Storm King Visitor Center are midway along

Marymere Falls, near Lake Crescent, Olympic National Park.

South Shore Road. The Barnes Point Parking Area at this location is the trailhead for a 1-mile (1.6-km) hike through a forest of large cedar and fir trees—and perhaps a sighting of tiny Indian pipes—to 90-foot (27-m) Marymere Falls, a pretty fern-framed waterfall. Along this trail, the more demanding Mount Storm King Trail branches off to the east and climbs this mountain in 1.7 (2.7 km) more miles—a difficult 1,700-foot (518-m) climb that seems like it's straight up. Notice the beautiful bark of the madrone trees along the trail, a peeling, deep red underlaid with pea green. The view of the lake and nearby mountains is fabulous, even before you've quite reached trail's end, and the motorhomes parked below along the lake seem like toy rigs on a child's playground.

From this high elevation, ponder the similarity between Indian legend and geologic theory concerning the lake's formation. Legend says that Mount Storm King once grew so tired of watching Clallams and Quileutes fighting that he broke a rock off his head and rolled it down on them. The rock was so big that it dammed a river and the lake formed. Geologists think an ancient landslide of different material than the glacier-deposited rock in the area did dam the Lyre River and create the lake.

One trail open to bicycles—the Spruce Railroad Trail—begins at Crescent Parking Area on the North Shore Drive of Lake Crescent. At one point during World War I, the old Sitka spruce trees were considered prime raw material for airplane components, but fortunately manufacturers were able to find other sources.

Elwha River Valley

The Elwha River Valley offers nice varied terrain with campgrounds along the river and a fine network of trails, some from the campgrounds, others along Lake Mills and near Boulder Creek. If you can manage the narrow dirt Whiskey Bend Road, the Elwha River and Krause Bottom trails loop around easily to spots for trout fishing on the river and continue past an old cougar-hunter's cabin and the Humes Ranch homestead site.

Hurricane Ridge

From sea level at Port Angeles, the park road to Hurricane Ridge climbs past curves that overlook valleys edged by mountains. Fog rides sidesaddle on the ridges, and sweeping views include Port Angeles, Mount Baker, and Vancouver Island. The destination is a 5,200-foot (1,585-m) overlook of the glacier-covered inner Olympic Mountains. Forced upward by the collision of two giant coastal plates, ocean-floor sediments were the building ingredients of these awesome peaks. Still crowned by many glaciers, notice the horn peaks, knife ridges, craggy landscape, and U-shaped valleys that were sculpted by moving ice masses.

The combination of the actual landscape and the three-dimensional park model at the Hurricane Ridge Lodge afford a better understanding of how the geologic landforms nurture the temperate rain forests. Using the model, you can trace the flow of melted snow and rain from the tip of the Olympic Mountains down the rivers and creeks to the sea. You can also follow some of 600 miles of trails in the park to visualize the terrain. No wonder that this 922,626-acre park is an International Biosphere Reserve and World Heritage Park, with some 1,200 plant, 200 bird, and 70 mammal species found in its many habitats. The geographic isolation of the Olympics led to such endemic species as the Flett's violet, Piper's bellflower, Olympic Mountain daisy, and Olympic chipmunk.

Looping paths invite you to wander among the flower-salted subalpine meadows edging the road while looking for a black-tailed deer—perhaps with a fawn. One path continues along Klahhane Ridge for views across the Strait of Juan de Fuca and into Canada, a trail where you'll no doubt discover the piercing whistle and antics of whistling marmots, a social species unique to the Olympics. Or hike up Hurricane Hill for international views and perhaps sight some grouse and chipmunks. A longer trail continues to the Elwha River Valley.

Insider's Tip:

The black-tailed deer seem so tame at Big Meadow that visitors feed them the strangest things, even potato salad, which is definitely not good for their health. Signs remind people not to feed the animals; please care for the wildlife by simply observing them.

Ferry Trip to Victoria, British Columbia

A lovely side trip from Port Angeles is a short ferry ride to Victoria, British Columbia. Touring this provincial capital in Canada is easily managed by strolling its streets and using public transportation, so you can park your RV and go for the day. Or drive your rig onto the ferry and camp along the picturesque waterfront in Victoria. Called one of the top ten cities in the world by Condé Nast *Traveler*, Victoria is awash in old-world charm and exciting ambiance.

Consider hiring one of the horse-drawn carriages—plush affairs with color-coordinated debonair drivers—for a quick look at the city. Then walk across the street to inspect the spacious grounds and interior of the stately Victorian-style Parliament Building, seat of the provincial legislative assembly. Sparkling fountains, a statue of Queen Victoria, and an Indian totem pole are backed by a golden statue of Captain George Vancouver atop a green copper dome.

Next door is the Royal British Columbia Museum, easily western Canada's finest museum. Its award-winning exhibits reflect the human and natural history of British Columbia, including the Haida Indians of the North Coast. Allow plenty of time for this attraction.

Cougar Hunter Cabin in Elwha River Valley of Olympic National Park.

Flanking the harbor to the east is the brick facade of the famed Empress Hotel, where bright-red, London-style double-decker buses drop off passengers for English afternoon tea. Four extraordinary establishments are Rogers' Chocolates, the Quest Gallery, the Gallery of the Arctic, and Munro's Books, a Victorian building that writer Allan Fotheringham regards as "Canada's most magnificent bookstore." Enter Chinatown through the red, gold, and black Gate of Harmonious Interests. A day excursion will allow time for the short bus trip to the world-class Butchart Gardens, where paths border the rose,

sunken, Japanese, and Italian gardens and the dancing water designs of choreographed Ross Fountain.

Dungeness National Wildlife Refuge

For a change of pace west of Sequim—back in Washington—take Kitchen Road north and follow signs to the Dungeness National Wildlife Refuge. In this rain shadow area, you'll pass farmland with picturesque old barns alternating with new homes, a golf course, and then flowering fields with horse trails, cattail marshes, upland forest, and ponds near the county's Dungeness Recreation Area. You'll find picnicking and camping here, and a path connects to the Dungeness National Wildlife Refuge along the coastal bluff that is scented with the rich aroma of honeysuckle and wild roses.

The highlight of this side trip is a walk on the Dungeness Spit, a narrow sandy finger of land generated by the combined forces of wind and ocean currents. If you're up to it, you can spend a day doing the 11-mile (18-km) round-trip walk to the New Dungeness Lighthouse, but any distance short of that is yours to choose. If it's a good low tide, vast areas of the protected inland harbor will be exposed as mudflats, with clamming a possibility—the only allowed collecting activity in the refuge.

Wildlife rights have priority at the refuge and, although people are allowed, their noisy jet-skis are not. Kite flying and windsurfing are also banned in the refuge so the peace is not broken. Visitors to the spit can, however, ride on a separate horse trail, explore the quiet harbor on an inflatable raft, or paddle a kayak offshore. Bring binoculars, spotting scopes, or telephoto lenses for excellent wildlife viewing—as many as 30,000 waterfowl inhabit this area during the spring and fall migrations. Look for harlequin ducks, widgeon, scoters, bald eagles, and harbor seals in this protected habitat with its rich feeding grounds.

If you're hungry for oysters, visit the oyster farm just east of adjacent Cline Spit and buy some for a feast back at the campground. When returning to the US 101 loop, head east and then south and check out the street names. See if you can find the one that leads to the chicken farm that inspired the movie *The Egg and I*.

Port Townsend

Past Sequim Bay, consider heading north off US 101 for a look at Port Townsend at the tip of a finger of land jutting out into the entrance to Puget Sound. One of the oldest cities in the state, Port Townsend boasts elegant Victorian architecture: highlights such as the Jefferson County Courthouse, Rothschild House, and St. Paul's Church can be enjoyed on a stroll. Much of the waterfront near Point Wilson is occupied by Fort Worden State Park, an historic coastal fortress complete with parade ground, the 248th Coast Artillery Museum, Victorian houses along Officers' Row, the Marine Science Center, the Point Wilson Discovery Walk along Admiralty Bay, and picnicking and camping facilities.

The Hood Canal

Shaped by glaciers (as was Puget Sound), the Hood Canal, which is along the third side of the peninsula, is a totally different waterfront area. The canal is first visible as its waters lap close to Quilcene. Maps of trails and campgrounds are available at the ranger station.

Although the weather didn't cooperate during my visit, a good sunrise or sunset should bring spectacular views of Puget Sound, Quilcene Bay, and an array of mountain peaks from the two viewpoints on the summit of 2,804-foot (855-m) Mount Walker. A narrow, steep gravel road 5 miles (8 km) south of Quilcene will take you there (the road is not recommended for trailers or motorhomes), or, if you'd rather hike, a 2-mile (3.2-km) trail that switchbacks up the mountain through forest and rhododendrons begins 0.25-mile (400 m) up the road.

One of the public harvesting places for oysters (in season; check with a ranger station) is the Seal Rock Forest Campground, north of Brinnon. The Hood Canal is an amazing sight at low tide. Great blue herons and astounding numbers of human figures are scattered about the mud flats clamming, crabbing, shrimping, or enjoying the water in canoes and kayaks or small boats. Returning clammers are often muddy but happy. An Interpretive Trail along the waterfront includes exhibit information on Japanese and Olympia oysters.

Several rivers—the Dosewallops, the Duckabush, the Hamma Hamma, and the North Fork of the Skokomish—flow down from the steep east side of the Olympic Mountains into the Hood Canal. Roads follow these waterways for some distance, accessing some campgrounds and rugged trails in the national forest, two wilderness areas, and the national park. Hamma Hamma oysters, which have a salty-sweet taste and cucumber-like finish, grow where this river meets Hood Canal. The Skokomish has been dammed and the result, Lake Cushman, has the usual dead shoreline of such reservoirs. Continue farther on this road, however, to enter the national park and the feeding stream where Staircase has a pleasant campground and short trails with connections to the backcountry.

The last place to stop along the canal is at Potlatch State Park, a pleasant overnight with water access and mudflats dotted with oyster shells at low tide. The site of the park was once used for potlatch ceremonies, special events of the Northwest Indians where the host divested possessions and gave extravagant gifts to those present. Beyond Potlatch State Park, you can connect to major routes home or continue west on WA 8 back to the Aberdeen area.

There is little doubt that Olympic National Park is the highlight of this RV trip. Myth suggests that Jupiter chose Mount Olympus as his second home when he became disenchanted with Greece. It's a peak that does overlook an extraordinary landscape, from a heartland of trails between the craggy peaks to the incredible dynamics of the wilderness beaches. Perhaps it is while facing the vast Pacific Ocean that we mortals can best ponder the power of the raindrops so important in shaping this landscape.

CHAPTER 10

Colorado Foliage Color:
High Country Magic

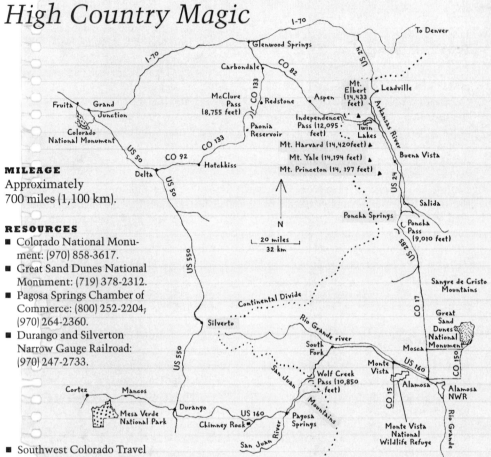

MILEAGE
Approximately
700 miles (1,100 km).

RESOURCES
- Colorado National Monument: (970) 858-3617.
- Great Sand Dunes National Monument: (719) 378-2312.
- Pagosa Springs Chamber of Commerce: (800) 252-2204; (970) 264-2360.
- Durango and Silverton Narrow Gauge Railroad: (970) 247-2733.
- Southwest Colorado Travel Region in Durango: (970) 382-8767; (800) 933-4340.
- Mesa Verde National Park: (970) 529-4465.

CAMPGROUNDS

COLORADO NATIONAL MONUMENT: Four miles (6.4 km) from West Park (Fruita) Entrance; Saddlehorn campground has restrooms, but no hookups; reservations not accepted.

GREAT SAND DUNES NATIONAL MONUMENT: 38 miles (61 km) northeast of Alamosa; Pinyon Flats Campground has two loops of campsites, wheelchair-accessible sites, restrooms; reservations not accepted.

MESA VERDE NATIONAL PARK: Morefield Campground is 4 miles (6.4 km) from US 160 (midway between Mancos and Cortez); several loops are available, some for tents, others for RVs, some for the physically impaired, with some hookups available; restrooms, showers and laundry near the store; reservations not accepted.

One state in the lower forty-eight has more high-country magic than any other: Colorado. In autumn, the slopes of its many mountain ranges are the stage for a stunning panoramic color show. With 56 peaks over 14,000 feet (4,267 m), that's quite a performance. Leaves of white-barked aspen trees burst into blazing golds and rich oranges that contrast with the deep green of the coni-fers. The scene is like a plush tapestry hung on rock walls. It's a great time to visit, to stand still, and say, "Wow! This is incredibly beautiful."

Sometimes an over-night dusting of fresh snow on the granite peaks produces a second feature in the warm light of sunrise. Alpine lakes capture images and flip them upside down on the smooth water. Leaves fall on soft paths through gold tunnels where the walking is good.

This autumn scene is a fleeting one. Timing your visit is the trick. The colors pop out early in September and peak in the high mountain passes midmonth in the north before gradually moving south and to lower elevations. It's not too difficult to partake of the color feast as it moves around.

Cool nights are followed by warm afternoons for exploring. Although this tour is satisfying even if you just drive the scenic byways and relax at a campground with a view, Colorado invites you to try some special outdoor activities. Choose from mountain biking, river running, fly-fishing, horseback riding, hiking, a llama trip, soaking in hot springs, a chuckwagon dinner, skiing down a sand dune, or a narrow-gauge railroad excursion. Woven throughout the countryside are hints of cowboys, mining, and ghost towns. If you're lucky, as I was once in these mountains, Rocky Mountain elk might serenade you near your campground as they bugle for a mate in this season of rutting.

Colorado National Monument

It may seem strange, based on the route I've chosen—with lots of considerations for RVers—that the trip's first destination is a red rock landscape, but it's right there where I want to begin, just after Colorado's Welcome Center at Fruita, via CO 340. And the canyon country of Colorado National Monument is special.

From the Fruita, or west, entrance of the park, it's 4 miles (6.4 km) of steep, winding uphill—with sheer drop-offs—and through a couple of short tunnels to the Saddlehorn Campground and nearby visitor center. It's amazing how quickly the valley below becomes a distant sprawl of lines and fields. When I camped there, I found several fairly long RVs already set up in the campground, so the road is do-able, although slow.

Colorado National Monument from Window Rock Trail.

Both the Window Rock and Canyon Rim trails (they connect) wander easily through the terrain between the campground and visitor center. Such walks offer an excellent way to begin exploring the monument. Picturesque juniper trees perch at the edge of slickrock drop-offs and small plants poke out golden flowers from among the rocks. Beyond the path, below in the canyon areas, rise weathered and eroded monoliths and spires with names such as Pipe Organ, Sentinel Spire, and Balanced Rock, all consisting of the rusty-hued sandstone that dominates the park. The terrain easily hides some of the large mammals that live here: cougar, mule deer, elk, and even bison. Rim Rock Drive continues another 23 miles (37 km) to the east entrance near Grand Junction and connects with the longer Monument Canyon and Liberty Cap trails, or you can return to the west entrance.

West Elk Loop Scenic Byway

From Grand Junction, a stretch of the famed cross-country highway, US 50, heads for Delta via a very pleasant valley bordered by varied foothills and pretty canyons, with a few picnic tables along the way. This landscape has yielded some important dinosaur fossils and the quarries where paleontologists still dig for bones may be visited. Switch to CO 92 at Delta and head for Hotchkiss; the timing is perfect for partaking of the harvest of area orchards at fruit stands.

Taking CO 133 out of Hotchkiss puts the tour on the Scenic West Elk Byway and it soon passes rippling giant footlike appendages of badlands. To the north is the Redlands Mesa, with the Rocky Mountains to the east as the byway closely follows the North Fork of the Gunnison River. Sometimes you'll glimpse a house on the side of a mountain that seems impossible to get to, let alone build on. Just off the highway is the town of Paonia—more orchards and more mountains—and then the historic coal-mining town of Somerset. The road is now in a canyon with great mountain views as a gravel road heads east to Crested Butte—sometimes called the mountain bike capital of the world. As the byway turns more sharply north, West Muddy Creek joins the Gunnison River, an area now dammed and the site of Paonia State Park, with streamside camping and fishing and views of the Ragged Mountains. The elevation has climbed enough for some autumn color to appear in the aspens. Going over 8,755-foot (2,669-m) McClure Pass should satisfy expectations of mountain scenery and autumn foliage color. In addition, you'll get a surprise backside view of the famed Maroon Bells that are so often seen from the opposite side near Aspen. The good news is that RV rigs shouldn't have any trouble with this pass.

On the downhill side of the pass, it's surprising to immediately enter a different kind of scenery, also stunningly beautiful. Walls of the canyon are now purplish sandstone rock formations with hues ranging from mauve to red as you wind past a singing mountain stream, the Crystal River. This is the Crystal River Valley Historic Area, and it's easy to see why some people have chosen to make their homes here. The Ute Indians once chose this area. Later, the coal baron John Cleveland Osgood (cousin to President Grover Cleveland) built a village called Redstone for coal

miners (the coke ovens are still here). Now a National Historic District, Redstone's Victorian-era character is retained in the resort amenities of Osgood's Redstone Castle, Inn, and Museum.

Carbondale is a place for route decisions. Choose either to travel CO 82 over 12,095-foot (3,687-m) Independence Pass, or take CO 82 just to Aspen and the famed Maroon Bells and then turn around and travel Interstate 70 east to Glenwood Springs. There, you can soak in the famed hot springs or paddle a kayak on the Colorado River before rejoining the tour via US 24 to the Twin Lakes area. Vehicle length on Independence Pass is restricted to a maximum of 35-feet (11-m), but I wouldn't want to travel this route in anything wider than a pickup truck or car and nothing longer than a small van. I saw no one driving anything larger. There are many small pullovers along the route.

Aspen and Independence Pass

First, let's consider what Aspen has to offer. It's definitely very busy and touristy, but it also provides the only access for trails to the exquisite, much-photographed blocks of mountain peaks called the Maroon Bells. Tune your radio to AM 1610 for weather conditions and information on the frequent mandatory shuttles (Rubey Park Transit Center) to these trailheads at the terminus of Maroon Creek Road. A 1.25-mile (2-km) trail circles Maroon Lake, a popular 1.75-mile (2.8-km) trail heads for Crater Lake, and other long distance hikes lead farther into the Maroon Bells-Snowmass Wilderness Area. The views of lakes and mountains are spectacular; autumn colors add to the allure.

Those who can manage the long, slow drive over Independence Pass—and the Continental Divide—will find breathtaking foliage colors, some lingering wildflower blooms, and rocky mountain highs. On the way, look for ruins of mining structures. Approximately 10 miles (16 km) southeast of Aspen, the mining town of Independence once had some 1,000 residents and was a main stop for three stagecoach lines. A short trail leads to The Grottos along the Roaring Fork River at 10.2 miles (16 km), and at 13 miles (21 km), a green sign alerts drivers to the Braille Trail, a short path where a guide wire connects 22 interpretive stations. The longer Lost Man Trail heads into the Hunter–Frying Pan Wilderness Area at 14 miles (23 km) at a Forest Service campground. The summit pass has an overlook with great views of the downhill route as it travels more easily than the squiggly, looping river through a slot between Mount Elbert and La Plata Peak, both over 14,000 feet (4,267 m). High meadows, creeks, and a quilt of gold and orange aspens checkered against the deep green conifers roll by. This portion is easier, with more open views, and very pretty as the road descends to Twin Lakes, where a campground is perched at water's edge for viewing the autumn scene up in the mountains.

Route choices converge near Twin Lakes—an area not to be missed. US 24 and US 285 (the "Pan American Highway") follow one of the ten most popular recreational rivers in the country, the Arkansas, through a lovely mountain-lined valley. The names of the peaks in the Sawatch Mountains to the west honor universities—Harvard, Princeton, Yale, Columbia, Oxford, and so forth—with fifteen peaks over 14,000 feet. For 148 miles (238 km), the Arkansas Headwaters Recreation Area provides access and some primitive camping along the river, whether you choose to raft, kayak, or enjoy the gold-medal trout fishing, as it is officially designated by the Colorado Division of Wildlife. Commercial companies in both Buena Vista and Nathrop offer scenic rafting day trips and more challenging white-water excursions on the Arkansas.

High Country Cautions

- Since warm midafternoons are followed by quite cool evenings and nights, bring layers of clothing and appropriate bedding to be comfortable.
- The sun is more intense at higher elevations, with ultraviolet radiation increasing approximately four percent for every 1,000 feet; that's almost a 50 percent increase at Independence Pass. Protect your health with a hat, sunscreen, and sunglasses if outside in the sun.
- The human body often sends signals above 5,000 feet (1,524 m). Your heart may beat faster and the lower oxygen levels may cause your rate of breathing to increase. Although individuals respond differently, some may experience dizziness, headaches, nasal congestion, fatigue, nausea, and sleeping difficulties. Some helpful suggestions: stay at 5,000 feet and go easy on physical activities for a couple of days; eat high-carbohydrate foods; minimize intake of alcohol, caffeine, and salty foods; and drink lots of water. Most people experience little difficulty.
- Even in the summer, snow can fall at high elevations, although it's certainly not common. Be prepared, however, if hiking long trails into the wilderness.
- Autumn brings the opening of hunting season, so be cautious if you're hiking in areas where there are hunters. Wear international (hunter) orange.

Great Sand Dunes National Monument

The river veers east as this tour continues south on US 285 over the Poncha Pass, which is an easy, fairly short affair. It is now a fast, straight drive to Six Mile Lane, just north of Mosca, which shoots east past San Luis Lakes State Park to the entrance to Great Sand Dunes National Monument and an inviting change of scenery in the San Luis Valley.

You wouldn't expect to find North America's tallest sand dunes at 8,000-foot elevation and nestled against the snow-dusted peaks of the Sangre de Cristo Mountains. Yet, that is the wonder of these nearly 750-foot-high curving hills of golden sand that spread over 39 square miles. Windswept sand has met the mountains and fallen into an artistry of light, texture, and contour. Much of the year, shallow Medano Creek weaves along the foot of the dunes and adds water play to the fun of climbing the dunes. Autumn splashes foliage color against the granite rock while the dunes capture the colors of the sunset.

Author's tent site in Great Sand Dunes National Monument, CO.

September temperatures are just right for exploring these sinuous dune mountains where intriguing tracks tell of the passing of a Great Sand Dunes tiger beetle and a giant sand treader camel cricket, a couple of endemic creatures that roam the sand. Do pace yourself, however, because this is energetic exploring. Several trails offer hiking in varied terrain. Little Medano Trail traverses pine forests and grasslands along foothills skirting the dunes; another trail heads into the Sangre de Cristo Wilderness and follows the route of pioneers traveling over the Mosca Pass. Imagine the surprised looks when they came over this pass the first time and discovered the dunes.

Some campsites with spectacular views are in the Pinyon Flats Campground, which is adjacent to grasslands where bright yellow prairie sunflowers are still blooming in September, the grasses are heavy with sprays of seeds, and mule deer are not intimidated by campers. Other animals are more secretive in the surrounding forest. Check out the wondrous dune photos and books in the visitor center.

Insider's Tip:
Black bear sometimes wander into the campground in the middle of the night, so keep coolers in your vehicles. Don't tempt a bear to be a "problem." Although a "problem" bear is relocated the first time, it is destroyed after the second offense.

Alamosa and Monte Vista National Wildlife Refuges

You have already traveled the first segment of the Los Caminos Antiguos Scenic Byway on Six Mile Lane, and continuing out of the park along CO 150 affords excellent close views of the west face of the Sangre de Cristo Mountains on the drive to US 160—the "Navajo Trail." A west turn on this highway will take you across southern Colorado and through the vast natureland of the San Juan Mountains. Before you climb into this high country, you may want to stop at a couple of wildlife refuges along the way in the San Luis Valley. Alamosa National Wildlife Refuge is 4 miles (6.4 km) east of the town of Alamosa and 2 miles (3.2 km) south on El Rancho Lane, with a visitor center, bluff overlook, and a hiking trail along the Rio Grande River. Monte Vista National Wildlife Refuge is 6 miles (9.6 km) south of the town of the same name via CO 15. Although the nondescript drive doesn't seem to promise much in the way of scenery, birds moving on the ponds and among cattails and other wetland vegetation against a mountain backdrop turn out to be a scenic destination. September is a month before peak migration, but even so, I found enough birds to keep me entertained at midday. I didn't find the sandhill cranes or any rare whooping cranes, but I roused a Harris hawk into flight, and sighted coots, grebes, avocets, killdeer, an ibis, and several species of ducks. A self-guiding auto tour winds through this wildlife sanctuary for quiet observations.

Wolf Creek Pass

Anglers might wish to stop along the Rio Grande River between the towns of Del Norte and South Fork, another "Gold Medal" trout water area. The headwaters of this mighty river are not far upstream, near Creede, but we will continue west and head for 10,850-foot (3,307-m) Wolf Creek Pass in the Rio Grande National Forest.

The San Juan Mountains of southwest Colorado are young mountains, jagged and precipitous terrain where the Continental Divide weaves around before heading northeast. These rocky reaches provide some of the best rock climbing in Colorado. Explorer John C. Fremont lost a third of his men in 1848 in a winter expedition here. Vast areas of rugged wilderness still occupy much of this corner of the state, but enough roads have followed the intense silver and gold mining activities that resulted in many of the settlements.

Wolf Creek Pass over the Continental Divide gets high enough for patches of tree color and it is not a particularly difficult pass for RVers to negotiate. It's obviously a favorite recreational area—a large number of campgrounds are on both sides of the pass, as are a wide range of amenities, from miniature golf to trail rides. A summit pullover has trails leading into the forest.

The Town of Pagosa Springs

Gliding downhill from the pass, the San Juan River edges the road from its headwaters just east of the pass. It flows right through the middle of Pagosa Springs, located in a valley that the Utes called "Pagosah" or "healing water." Fall is lovely here at 7,000 feet (2,134 m) in this southern reach of Colorado, and the small population—just over a thousand residents—and wonderful amenities provide a relaxing base for exploring the San Juan Mountains and nearby waterways, which are replete with trails, horseback riding, kayaking, fishing, bird watching, and waterfalls.

Pagosa Springs is laid out astutely along the river. At a "Y" heading off the main street, a tall sign alerts visitors to "The

Sand dune formations backed by Sangre de Cristo Mountains in Great Sand Dunes National Monument, CO.

Springs" in the center of town. There, a river walk, a visitor center with picnic facilities by the river, a post office, a campground, and parking are all easily accessible. A restaurant in this area has an interesting menu, patio dining, and overlooks the water. Stroll along the waterfront and try the mineral hot baths.

Chimney Rock Archeological Area

As you travel to Durango, Chimney Rock is quite a sight as it rises high above the lowland along the highway. It is a landmark that guided prospectors, missionaries, and conquistadors who settled this country. Shaped like a tall pyramid with a chimney atop it, the rock is four-sided with sharp stone edges at its corners. A drive to the site on CO 151 reveals a row of high rock structures that were home and sacred shrine to the Anasazi Indians, an outlier of the Chacoan culture, with the same core-and-veneer masonry found at Chaco Culture National Historical Park in northwest New Mexico.

Managed by the Forest Service, Chimney Rock Archeological Area is accessible via a guided walking tour through September. Lasting approximately two hours—weather permitting—the tour visits a ravine that is wheelchair-accessible and another trail that climbs approximately 200 feet (61 m) to one of these structures in a quarter of a mile. The High Mesa community contains 16 excavated sites of Chacoan

Special Event:

Pagosa Springs celebrates its Colorfest the third weekend in September, with hot air balloons, a community barbecue, and a bike race. Some twenty-one communities in southwest Colorado have their own Colorfest celebration, with more than seventy special events.

Chimney Rock Archaeological Area in southern Colorado.

structures, among them the Great House, a Guardhouse, and a Great Kiva. Some 200 other structures that reflect the native architecture rather than the imported Chacoan influence are found across the 6 square miles of the archaeological area. Recent studies suggest that Chimney Rock Pueblo was built solely for reasons of religion and astronomy; research continues today.

Durango and Mancos

Not only is Durango a crossroads for local industry, ranching, commerce, and culture, it is a gateway to the north. To see this area, consider taking a relaxing trip—rather than the winding drive—on the Durango and Silverton Narrow Gauge Railroad, which offers 90-mile (145-km), 9-hour trips via a coal-and-steam engine that traverse the San Juan National Forest and Animas River Valley to the old mining town of Silverton in the high country. Upon arrival obtain a map for the self-guiding walking tour of this National Historic Landmark. You'll have time for a stroll, and perhaps lunch before returning to Durango. The train departs Durango from 479 Main Street; return from Silverton is also available by bus.

Mancos is very small, with just a few amenities, including a couple of eating places. I always get a kick out of seeing the old Mesa Verde Stage Coach parked along the street curb. And the mural of old-time fire-fighting equipment next to the post office is worth a look.

Mesa Verde National Park

Mesa Verde National Park is a special place: an outdoor museum of Anasazi cliff dwellings atop a green mesa above the Montezuma and Mancos valleys. These Indians chose this site some 1,400 years ago. For 700 years, their culture flourished here before they walked away from their homes, leaving a city of incredible sandstone structures tucked under sheltering cliffs.

To absorb a smattering of this culture, pick a campsite in Morefield Campground, 4 miles (6.4 km) into the park, and stay a while. The Morefield store has essential supplies, and you can even mosey to the patio there for a pancake breakfast or a traditional western barbecue dinner. Three hiking trails—Knife's Edge, Prater's Ridge, and Point Lookout—begin in the campground, each different and scenic. Check the campground map for access points.

It's another 11 miles (17.6 km) of sharp curves and steep grades along the park road to the Far View Visitor Center, with its display of contemporary Indian arts and crafts, and the beginning of the Ruins Road on Chapin Mesa. Trailers and towed vehicles are prohibited beyond Morefield campground. One way to visit the ruins is via a bicycle; there are also bus tours from Morefield Campground.

Although you can see most of the major cliff dwellings from overlooks, it's not the same as wandering through these dwellings. Some of the ruins are a bit more strenuous than others to visit because you have to climb steps and ladders. Also, don't forget that the altitude of the park varies from 6,000 to 8,000 feet.

The first major ruin, Spruce Tree House, is easy to visit and large enough, at

Special Event:
Durango holds its annual Cowboy Gathering the first weekend in October.

approximately 216 feet (66 m) by 89 feet (27 m), to have provided a home for about 100 people. As you wander through the 114 rooms and eight kivas, try to imagine the lives of the Anasazi. They were fortunate to have shade and a spring near this ruin, which can be viewed along the 2.1-mile (3.4-km) Spruce Canyon Trail.

The 2.8-mile (4.5-km) Petroglyph Point Trail also begins in this area. It weaves around and under sandstone formations, past caves, and offers excellent views of Spruce Canyon and Navajo Canyon plus a good example of Anasazi rock art at 6,800-foot Petroglyph Point. Many plants used by the Anasazi are along this trail. I found this walk to be a wonderful way to try to understand the Anasazi way of life; it's a quiet place to make personal connections to the past. I envisioned agile people at home among the cliffs, enjoying feasts of roast turkey—a fowl kept for their decorative feathers—and gathering for their ceremonial dances in sacred paraphernalia. Register for hikes on either of these trails at the ranger's office.

The largest cliff dwelling in America is Cliff Palace, with 217 rooms and 23 kivas, a wondrous architectural construction in an alcove that was obviously selected with considerable thought for the possibilities. The short trail to this dwelling is narrow, winding, and strenuous but definitely worthwhile.

The third major dwelling on Chapin Mesa is Balcony House, a 45-room affair that is difficult to visit. Access is via a 32-foot (10-m) ladder, a 100-foot (30-m) climb up a cliff face; the exit is via a 12-foot (3.7-m) tunnel. It does make you marvel at the dexterity and agility of the Anasazi who used so many hand and toe trails—often requiring a specific foot to start—to negotiate these living areas.

The Mesa Top Ruins tour provides a chronological sequence of Anasazi architecture and culture before the cliff dwellings were constructed. Along this loop is the Square Tower House, a cliff dwelling that was built later and that is photogenic from the overlook.

Excellent brochures are published for each of the major ruins, and you can learn much about the intriguing Anasazi Indians from these, particularly if you take the time to slowly tour the ruins with one in hand, questioning and pondering the fit of the information to the site. Mesa Verde illustrates how this ancient culture advanced from Basketmakers to the Classical period. It was a vigorous civilization that accumulated many skills, arts, traditions, and accomplishments in community living.

Autumn in southwestern Colorado is a collage of mesas, canyons, Anasazi history, whitewater rivers, sand dunes, and especially the high-country magic of autumn colors. In your mind—and your photographs—the most pervasive images of these landscapes may remind you of the song "America the Beautiful." Katherine Lee Bates wrote some of the words to that standard while gazing at these "purple mountain majesties." It is inspiring territory.

Cliff House in Mesa Verde National Park, CO.

CHAPTER 11

Southern Utah: *River Canyons and Red Rock Magic*

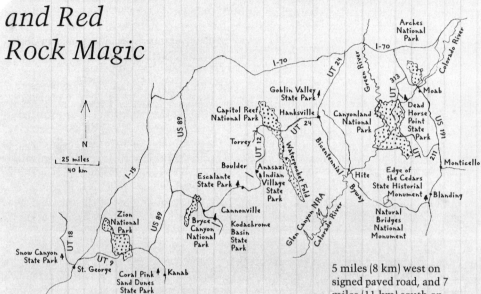

MILEAGE

Approximately 1,000 miles (1,600 km).

RESOURCES

- Utah Travel Council, Council Hall/Capitol Hill, Salt Lake City, UT 84114; (800) 200-1160.
- Utah State Park information: phone (801) 538-7220.
- Arches National Park, P.O. Box 907, Moab, UT 84532; (435) 259-8161.
- Canyonlands National Park, Moab, UT 84532; (435) 259-7164.
- Capitol Reef National Park, Torrey, UT 84775; (435) 425-3791.
- Trail Head Station at Kodachrome Basin State Park: (435) 679-8536.
- Bryce Canyon National Park, UT 84717: (435) 834-5322.
- Zion National Park, Springdale, UT 84767-1099; (435) 772-3256.

CAMPGROUNDS

ARCHES NATIONAL PARK: The park is 5 miles (8 km) north of Moab; campsites and restrooms (through October); reservations not accepted.

DEAD HORSE POINT STATE PARK: 11 miles (18 km) northwest of Moab on US 191 and 23 miles (37 km) southwest on UT 313; Kayenta Campground has sites with electric hookups, restrooms, dump station, through October; because of water shortage, arrive at the park with full water tanks; reservations at (800) 322-3770.

CANYONLANDS NEEDLES DISTRICT: Squaw Flat has campsites and vault toilets; reservations not accepted; Needles Outpost, just outside the park, has a campground (no hookups) with restrooms and showers.

GOBLIN VALLEY STATE PARK: 20 miles (32 km) north of Hanksville, off UT 24, then 5 miles (8 km) west on signed paved road, and 7 miles (11 km) south on gravel road to park; campsites and restrooms with showers; reservations at (800) 322-3770.

CAPITOL REEF NATIONAL PARK: Just east of Torrey; Fruita Campground has campsites and restrooms; reservations not accepted.

ESCALANTE STATE PARK: One mile west of the town of Escalante off UT 12; campsites and restrooms with showers, dump station; reservations at (800) 322-3770.

KODACHROME BASIN STATE PARK: 7 miles (11 km) south of Cannonvile off Cottonwood Canyon Road; campsites and restrooms with showers, dump station; reservations at (800) 322-3770.

BRYCE CANYON NATIONAL PARK: South of Visitor Center; North and Sunset campgrounds have tent and RV sites, restrooms; reservations not accepted.

CORAL PINK SAND DUNES STATE PARK: 5 miles (8 km) north of Kanab off US 89 via either Hancock Road or Sand Dunes Road; tent and RV sites with restrooms with showers (to late October), dump station; reservations at (800) 322-3770.

ZION NATIONAL PARK: South of Visitor Center; South and Watchman campgrounds have tent and RV sites, restrooms; reservations not accepted.

SNOW CANYON STATE PARK: 11 miles (18 km) north of St. George off Utah 18; tent and RV sites with hookups, restrooms with showers, dump station; reservations at (800) 322-3770.

Part of the famed scenery of the Colorado Plateau, the canyon country of southern Utah is so magnificent and convoluted that the many geologic formations have thwarted much development. As a consequence, the natural beauty has been preserved in a stunning array of parks. A few good roads—many of them designated scenic byways—let you visit these landscapes and pursue whatever level of intimacy with nature you desire. Superlatives abound. You could spend a lifetime exploring these natural wonders, so you may want to pick and choose. Or you may want to do the whole tour and select favorite spots for return trips.

From September to early November, autumn foliage and green conifer trees add startling color contrasts to the existing richness of the multihued rock hoodoos, arches, and natural bridges that stand out against the clear blue skies of the high desert. And although this is a popular destination, the crowds of visitors are diminished in the fall and temperatures are not so high. Arrival at the Mormon-planted orchards of Capitol Reef in September or October offers the treat of picking fruit off trees next to the campground.

Insider's Tip:

If you have bicycles hitched onto your rigs, know that the Utah Travel Council has a Bicycle Utah Vacation Guide that contains information on exciting rides—from easy to demanding—at locations throughout the state.

Keep in mind that this is the Colorado Plateau, where high elevations are the norm, so consider sunglasses and a hat as protection from the intense sun in the clear air. From Interstate 70 in southeast Utah, begin your tour by heading south on US 191 to Arches National Park.

Arches National Park

Arches National Park has the greatest density of natural rock arches in the world; more than 200 have been catalogued. About a quarter of the park is stone, mostly pale orange Navajo Sandstone and salmon-colored Entrada Sandstone (most of the arches are in this layer). Upwarping and 100 million years of erosion of sandstone overlying a salt bed have produced these arches. And they continue to form and erode in this park immortalized by Edward Abbey in his book *Desert Solitaire*.

From the visitor center just off the highway, a 20-mile (32-km) road first climbs a bit and then squiggles through the park past natural creations. The first stopping place is the South Park Avenue Trailhead, where you can take a delightful mile-long walk on the rocky marvel of Park Avenue and intersect with the road farther on, where the Organ, Three Gossips, and the Tower of Babel formations are attractions. Balanced Rock—a bit of nature wizardry—stands out just before the turnoff to the Windows section.

The "windows" are various and remarkable; you'll want to get out and walk among most of them; you'll also want to note the Parade of Elephants. Double Arch is probably the most unusual and intriguing. Back on the main road, you'll pass Fiery Furnace, a dense array of red rock fins that glow at sunset. Rangers lead visitors on a guided tour along the tricky route among the fins.

At the end of the road is Devils Garden, where an exciting trail passes a number of outstanding arches, including 291-foot (89-m) Landscape Arch, the longest known natural stone span in the world. The walk up to this arch is easy; from there, the trail gets more primitive but continues past several more arches en route to Double O Arch and finally, Dark Angel. The campground is adjacent to Devils Garden, with beautiful sites among the rock formations; it's very popular, so arrive early.

The well-known landmark of the park, which appears on Utah license plates and on postage stamps, is Delicate Arch, which can be seen via either a 3-mile (4.8-km) round-trip hike over slickrock or from Delicate Arch Viewpoint. I can assure you that it is an emotional experience to stand beneath this span.

Insider's Tip:
Although scampering up and around red rock formations is okay in the campground, climbing any feature named on US Geological Service maps is prohibited.

Dead Horse Point State Park

For an impressive look at the powerful carving of sandstone layers by the Colorado River, head a short distance north on US 191 and take UT 313 to Dead Horse Point State Park. From an overlook 2,000 feet (610 m) above the river, view the maze of twists and turns as the Colorado heads toward its merging with the Green River in Canyonlands National Park. The views here are so spectacular that the park was one of three Utah state parks featured on the CBS Morning News on location.

The road through the park to the point is on a natural rocky promontory, and the point is almost cut off from the rest of the park. Cowboys used the point as a natural corral for wild mustangs by fencing the narrow neck, which provided the only escape. After the mustangs were roped and broken, the unwanted culls, or "broomtails," were left there. On one occasion, all the broomtails died of thirst, although the gate was supposedly left open—hence the name.

Trails loop around the edge of the promontory, providing access to great viewpoints, slickrock passages, and desert terrain with microbiotic crusts and a few flowering plants. You can park your rig at the campground—where there is access to

all the trails—and enjoy the outdoor exercise. Consider making this your base for exploring Island in the Sky.

Island in the Sky

The turnoff to the Island in the Sky section of Canyonlands National Park is also along UT 313. Island in the Sky is the high mesa left by the cutting power of the Colorado and Green rivers. Rafters slice through the park on these whitewater waterways; hikers penetrate the park's secrets with a different perspective.

A good paved road leads past the visitor center and the entry to the Shafer Trail, a dirt road that is sometimes passable to small two-wheel-drive vehicles, but is more easily traveled by mountain bikes and four-wheel-drive vehicles; it descends into the backcountry and leads past dinosaur tracks and Indian rock art to Moab in 38 miles (61 km). This road also connects to the 110-mile White Rim Road (four-wheel-drives only) that was made by uranium

Archaeological and Historic Sites

Even if the impact is unintentional, the increasing numbers of travelers threaten the preservation of many informative and interesting treasures from the past, so consider this before you visit.

Look at and photograph rock art, but do not chalk or chisel it, repaint it, wet it, make molds of it, trace it, shoot bullet holes in it (yes, people have), or even touch it, as the oil on hands attracts dirt and hastens the destruction.

At the sites of ruins, do not walk through middens—old trash piles. Stay on trails and do not climb on roofs or walls. Camp and cook away from these areas. Learn from these ancient cultures and visit ruins with respect. The Archaeological Resources Act of 1979 imposes stiff penalties for desecrating these treasures, as well as a reward for information leading to a conviction. Contact a ranger, federal land management authorities, or the local sheriff if you discover any illegal activity.

Balanced Rock in Arches National Park, UT.

miners. The Shafer Trail Overlook offers a good view of the White Rim Road, which was first an Indian path and later a cattle trail down to the White Rim, the unique rim that wriggles around Island in the Sky and is easily viewed from above.

Atop the mesa, the 0.5-mile (0.8-km) Mesa Arch Trail loops through pinyon-juniper woodland to a sandstone arch and panoramic views into Buck Canyon, the La Sal Mountains, and the Washerwoman Arch. Past this trail, the paved road forks. The logical choice is to continue south to Grand View Point for a better overview of the park, its convoluted rock formations, and glimpses of its rivers. A picnic area is near the point, with an easy 1-mile (1.6-km) trail that offers spectacular vistas of the White Rim. Another short trail heads off from Grand View Point.

The other fork in the road provides access to the Willow Flat Campground (no water) and the Green River Overlook; a view into the Maze, which is the most isolated and wild district of Canyonlands; and Stillwater Canyon on the Green River, a tranquil stretch named by John Wesley Powell. Upheaval Dome and its picnic area are a few miles farther, near the end of the road. Take the short Crater View Trail to the rim of this unusual geologic feature and try to theorize what caused this deeply eroded mile-wide crater. Another view of this feature is seen along the nearby Whale Rock Trail.

Moab

Just before you cross the river heading southeast into Moab, consider following the river in either direction to enjoy the scenery. Heading northeast on UT 128—the Colorado River Scenic Byway—provides access to the popular Negro Bill Canyon Trail to Morning Glory Bridge. The southwest route is via the Potash Road Scenic Byway (UT 279), which connects to the Shafer Trail. The first interesting stop is the slickrock trail (watch for cairns) that switchbacks up to the Portal Overlook, with its grand vista of the Moab area. Ten miles (16 km) west is the Corona Arch Trail, which is marked by cairns and has safety cables and a ladder at certain points. A brochure available in Moab is helpful in following these trails. Steep drop-offs call for close supervision of children.

Moab has changed. Once a cozy little desert town, it now lures upscale tourists with its shops, lodging, and restaurants. It is also the center of an extremely popular mountain biking area, with two famed trails beginning in Moab. The strenuous and difficult Moab Slickrock Bike Trail is marked by white blazes on rock and heads for overlooks of Negro Bill Canyon. The 128-mile (348-km) Kokopelli's Trail is a series of easy to strenuous sections of canyon back roads to Loma, Colorado, a much-used trail managed by the Bureau of Land Management that connects to other bike routes.

Moab is also a center for river rafting, with several commercial operators offering various river runs that range from fairly easy to wild. Cataract Canyon in Canyonlands National Park offers some of the largest rapids in North America. You can also do you own river floating, even canoeing, on the water near Moab. It's a curious fact that some of the West's best river runs are in Utah's desert country.

The Needles Section: Canyonlands National Park

Squaw Flats Scenic Byway (UT 211) heads west from US 191 to the Needles District of Canyonlands National Park. Along the way, a large number of ancient Indian petroglyphs from several distinct periods can be seen on Newspaper Rock, a 50-foot-high (15-m) rock face. Once a state park, this area is now managed by the Bureau of Land Management.

A few miles of paved road and many more roads passable only to four-wheel-drive vehicles penetrate some areas of Canyonlands National Park, but the park offers more territory to those who trek into this rewarding chunk of wild America. But what you can see and do from the those few miles of paved road is tantalizing. This landscape was more familiar to the Anasazi Indians, and traces of their lives can be found in almost every canyon in the Needles District. Pictographs made by the Fremont Indians are also found.

The entry road leads to Squaw Flat, a grassy park surrounding Squaw Butte, where there is a modestly developed campground (water available through September). The massive rock formations that resemble needles blaze with fiery color at sunset. Roads branch off from this central point to several areas. A paved one heads for the Big Spring Canyon Overlook, where an all-day hike leads to the Confluence Overlook of the Green and Colorado rivers. A jeep road gets you much closer.

A paved road takes you to the 0.6-mile (1-km) Cave Spring Loop Trail, a path that climbs onto slickrock and descends via two ladders to Cave Spring and an old cowboy line camp located in a vast cave opening. Head left at the trailhead just to visit the cowboy camp. The spring here was vital for both the Anasazi and the Fremonts, who left soot-blackened ceilings under the cliff overhangs as well as panels of handprints on the rock. Cowboys also valued the year-round source of water. Pioneering cattleman John Albert Scorup managed to establish a large, successful cattle operation in this harsh land that evolved into the largest ranch in Utah. Such large operations required cowboys to stay out with the herds for weeks at a time at line camps. You'll see many of the items they used in this cave from the late 1800s up until 1964, when the park was established.

An interesting day hike begins at Squaw Flat: the Squaw and Big Spring Canyons Trail. I enjoyed this trek but could never have made it up over the strenuous rock pass without a helping hand; it's always a good idea to check with a ranger on what you might encounter. I would encourage you to head out on this trail for some distance and enjoy the surroundings and plant life.

The Needles District has its share of awesome arches. Particularly noteworthy is Angel Arch, the creation of weathering by wind and water that is reached by a short hike from the end of a long, wiggling jeep road. Energetic hikers will find many rewards along the long day-hike and backpacking trails. From Elephant Hill—via a dirt road accessible to two-wheel-drive vehicles—long trails lead to the Colorado River, to the Needles of Chesler Park, and to Druid Arch.

The nearest services for gas, food, and a campground (among red rock formations) is just outside the park entrance at Needles Outpost. Continue the tour south on US 191 to the state park near Blanding.

Edge of the Cedars State Park

When Mormons chose to settle on the fertile White Mesa, they thought the Utah juniper trees were cedars and the name has stuck. Edge of the Cedars State Park is noted for its Anasazi ruins, home of several families from about A.D. 700 to 1220. On this ridge above Westwater Canyon, archaeologists have identified six living quarters and ceremonial complexes made of stone and adobe. A planked-walkway and interpretive brochure help you explore this site. Among the curiosities are the remains of a Great Kiva in Complex 4, the northernmost one of its kind in Utah. Atypically, this one was probably roofed and used for intercommunity ceremonies and perhaps as a playground for children while their mothers ground corn, prepared meals, and made baskets and pottery. Nearby, the men crafted tools or added on to a pueblo. Some rooms were entered through the roof. One kiva in complex 6 can be entered from above.

The museum built here in 1978 was closed in 1993 while an antiquities workshop was held. Artifacts were sorted and catalogued according to individual sites to aid in tracing the settlement and in the dating of each site. Now reopened, the focus of the museum is the Native American cultures of San Juan county. Featured is one of the best exhibits of Anasazi pottery in the Four Corners area. Other exhibits are related to the contemporary Navajo and Ute Indian cultures, with some exhibits of nineteenth-century white culture to complete the historic picture of the various peoples who have inhabited the Four Corners region.

Corn grows behind the museum and intriguing outdoor sculptures complement its exterior. The park includes an authentic Navajo hogan, Navajo sunshades at picnic areas, and an observation tower.

Natural Bridges National Monument

South of Blanding, head west on the 122-mile (196-km) Bicentennial Highway (UT 95), which was completed in 1976 and traverses a beautiful and undeveloped landscape to Hanksville.

Turn north onto UT 275 to enter Natural Bridges National Monument, the world's largest display of natural bridges. Confusion sometimes arises over the difference between an arch and a natural bridge, but the distinction is easy if you know that natural bridges are formed in deep canyons in the path of streams that wear away and penetrate the rock. Natural arches are not dependent on stream erosion and are found on skylines.

Stop at the solar-powered visitor center before beginning the 9-mile (14.5-km), one-way, paved loop through the park. Water is only available at the visitor center. Please leave all towed units in the visitor center parking lot, since limited parking is provided along the drive. The primitive campground is accessible before you enter the drive.

Bridge View Drive—at an elevation of over 6,000 feet (1,829 m)—is atop a mesa dominated by pinyon-juniper forest of the high desert, with the bridges in canyons below where streams once flowed. The three natural bridges were discovered by prospector Cass Hite while he was exploring White Canyon in 1883. Although they were originally named after explorers or their relatives, President Howard Taft affixed Hopi Indian names to the bridges since the Hopi are descendants of the Anasazi Indians—about 200 of their dwelling sites have been found here. Horse Collar Ruin is accessible from the trail between Sipapu and Kachina bridges.

Several overlooks provide stopping places, some with bridge views and/or trails leading into the canyon, past hanging gardens on the stairstep walls created by erosion of different rocks. All three bridges are connected to the drive via trails, so you can walk to them. Various loop trails may be hiked for a more intimate acquaintance with the canyon. Always carry water. Climbing on the bridges is prohibited.

Sipapu, the first bridge, has the longest span (268 feet or 82 m) and greatest height (220 feet or 67 m). These fragile rock structures are transient creations of water and erosion that reflect three general states: youth, maturity, and old age. Now far from the streambed that created it, Sipapu is considered a mature bridge.

Kachina Bridge is a youthful structure and, as such, is huge and bulky, with a greater width and thickness than any of the three. Rock art on this bridge resembles the symbols found on kachina dolls, thus the name Kachina or "ghost dancer."

The third natural bridge, Owachomo, is in its late phase, with a thin rock span that could crack at any time (or remain standing for centuries in this dry country). A wetter climate between 4,000 and 900 years ago probably began the erosion of most spans, so only this bridge is believed to be over 5,000 years old. The shortest and easiest trail leads to Owachomo.

Insider's Tip:
Please don't take UT 261 from Goosenecks to the Bicentennial Scenic Byway; the southern part of this highway is extremely dangerous even for passenger cars. It's the scariest highway I've encountered in the West.

Glen Canyon National Recreation Area

The byway continues northwest along White Canyon to Hite Crossing at Glen Canyon National Recreation Area, the only highway water crossing in the recreation area in Utah. A marina, boat rentals, fuel, and a campground are here, and you'll probably see some RVs parked along the water. If you are carrying a boat, you can explore some hidden areas on this lake, which is rimmed with red rock walls. Autumn is an excellent time for some quiet fishing. You might even want to pack a tent and camp overnight on a secluded beach. Do get maps and information before doing that. The Colorado has been dammed below Glen Canyon and has changed considerably since one-armed Major John Wesley Powell explored the river.

Soon after the Hite Crossing you'll cross the Dirty Devil tributary, named when Powell and his men remarked that the stream "stinks like a dirty devil." Before long, the Henry Mountains to the west should grab your attention. In this vast roadless area, bison that were introduced in 1941 have become one of the few, wild, free-roaming herds in the country. Other wildlife abounds. This landscape has lured gold prospectors and cattle rustlers hiding their bounty, and it is also the site of Robbers' Roost, an important stop along the "Outlaw Trail."

Hanksville is one of the few towns in this isolated area where you can stock up on supplies. Then consider a side trip north to Goblin Valley in the southeastern corner of the San Rafael Reef.

Goblin Valley

Geologic events produce many strange and unusual creations that intrigue human wanderers; they happen frequently in the West. Turn west off UT 24 at Temple Mountain junction, almost 20 miles (32 km) north of Hanksville, to Goblin Valley where you'll pass Wild Horse Butte and find a valley of eroded sandstone of intricate shapes resembling strange life forms. It's a place for the imagination. These shapes evoke thoughts of giant mushrooms, comic-strip shmoos, a band of dwarfs huddled against the wind, or the head of a steer complete with horns and eye sockets. Some even look like hamburgers on pedestals. Children will love wandering among these natural sculptures. When it rains, chocolate-colored streams flow between the figures and, like magic, the shapes don different disguises.

The smells, however, are of the desert, not a fast-food restaurant. Above the valley the greenish-white Curtis Formation looms in sharp contrast to the red siltstone of the cliffs and goblins. A couple of short trails meander through canyons and badlands, offering views of an impressive butte called Molly's Castle and of the Henry Mountains. A campground is near the park entrance that is backed by sandstone walls, but there aren't any trees for shade; it's a fine camp if the weather's not too hot.

Return south and head west on the Hanksville Scenic Byway (US 24) that slices through Capitol Reef National Park.

Capitol Reef

Several stops along the highway near the Fremont River hint at the wonders of Capitol Reef National Park. The Hickman Bridge Trail leads through desert curiosities to a spectacular 133-foot (40.5-m) natural bridge accompanied by good views of Capitol Dome. Short paths by the river get you close to enigmatic rock art left by the Fremont Indians, and you'll also see the historic Fruita schoolhouse. Turn south at the visitor center and you're at the site of the Mormon set-

Egyptian Temple along Scenic Drive in Capitol Reef National Park.

tlement of Fruita, a site selected because of its proximity to the river. Fruit orchards planted by the Mormons are still vital and producing apples, cherries, pears, and other fruits from June to October. It's only a few steps from the adjacent campground to a stroll among the fruit trees. Horses and a barn are a pastoral scene against a backdrop of stunning red rock formations, with the Castle a fiery red high rock structure at sundown. Across the road is the Cohab Canyon Trail (it's only strenuous the first short climb into the canyon); inquire about the origin of its name. What a place to live!

A scenic drive heads south a few miles past views of the Egyptian Temple and Golden Throne and provides access to trails. Easy walks are through either Grand Wash or Capitol Gorge (with petroglyphs and waterpockets or "tanks"), which connect to the strenuous Golden Throne Trail. Another strenuous trail heads for Cassidy Arch, with a connection to the Frying Pan Trail that continues to Cohab Canyon.

As you continue out of the park, interesting stops are at Goosenecks, Chimney Rock (a nice trail loops around here), and Twin Rocks. Several unpaved roads that are usually passable to passenger vehicles lead to other spectacular park areas: Cathedral Valley, Strike Valley, Circle Cliffs, and Boulder Mountain. Inquire about road conditions relevant to your vehicle. Geology is fantastic here. It's noted for the Waterpocket Fold, but you'll get a better view of this soon.

Outside the park, at Torrey, the tour heads south on Highway 12 Scenic Byway for some of the most varied scenery in the state. You might want to stop at Capitol Reef Cafe, a combination gift and restaurant affair with a nice selection of books and surprisingly delicious food in this isolated region. Everything is fresh and freshly baked.

Highway 12 Scenic Byway

Also called the Clem Church Memorial Highway, the 122-mile (195-km) byway begins a slow but not difficult climb to the 9,200-foot (2,804-m) summit of Boulder Mountain, with viewpoints and campgrounds in Dixie National Forest. This is

Farm among the red rocks of Capitol Reef.

the place to stop for an illuminating perspective on unique Waterpocket Fold of Capitol Reef National Park. A major geologic feature, the fold is a giant wrinkle in the Earth's crust that was uplifted by the same forces that built the Colorado Plateau 65 million years ago; its ridgeline stretches some 100 miles (161 km).

The byway now winds downhill through forest to Boulder and Anasazi Indian Village State Park. On a mesa at 6,700 feet (2,042 m), this site is believe to represent one of the largest Anasazi communities west of the Colorado River. Excavations by the University of Utah uncovered 87 rooms, but the village is largely unexcavated. Informative artifacts, maps, exhibits, and a diorama of village life are at the visitor center. Pottery and tree-ring studies (dendrochronology) have established occupation dates between A.D. 1050 and 1200. A selfguiding trail leads through the site past a sixroom replica of an Anasazi dwelling of Jacal and Kayenta masonry, which is a different technique than that used at Mesa Verde and Chaco. You'll also see an authentic pithouse. Picnicking facilities are available.

Boulder is said to be the last town in the United States to have had mule-train mail delivery; the paved byway is not very old. The Burr Trail Road, which is used by rugged vehicles and mountain bikes to more intimately view the Waterpocket Fold and backcountry of Capitol Reef, terminates here. The byway now continues through excellent views of red rock country on the shoulder of the Aquarius Plateau. An early explorer-geologist, Clarence Dutton, wrote that this plateau "should be described in blank verse and illustrated upon canvas."

South and east of this byway is Grand Staircase–Escalante National Monument, a beautiful chunk of wild country designated in 1996 and administered by the Bureau of Land Management. It encompasses a geologic sampler of formations and features—and world-class paleontologic sites—the last place in the continental United States to be mapped, and a landscape that is still a frontier for explorers. No services are in this new park, although hikers and photographers know some of its special places. Gateway cities are Escalante, Boulder, and Kanab as well as Kodachrome Basin State Park.

Serious and experienced explorers will find that Utah has places in the backcountry where the truly wild and solitary hike has many forms and destinations. In fact, you could get lost in the rugged terrain of the Colorado Plateau in the southeast corner of Utah. One young man named Everett Ruess, a savvy traveler and writer, did that deliberately and was never found again—although he enjoyed a considerable period of time there—so go forewarned into unknown territory.

CALF CREEK RECREATION AREA

The Bureau of Land Management manages the beautiful Calf Creek Recreation Area at the edge of the Grand Staircase–Escalante National Monument. It is a very special place. The day-use area, where you can picnic or dangle your feet in the creek, can be reached from the byway a few miles south of Boulder. The adjacent campground borders this year-round waterway, which slides over red slickrock amid soft green surroundings.

The popular attraction here is the 5.5-mile (8.8-km) round-trip Calf Creek Falls Trail. Pick up an interpretive brochure at the trailhead and begin to absorb this smashing walk past unexpected wetlands and wildlife between cliffs of Navajo sandstone. Except for loose sand—or summer hot weather—this is easy hiking that follows the creek to a magnificent waterfall. The 126-foot (38-m) falls are enhanced by the wet brown, gold, and mossy green colors of the sandstone, a colorful vision in good light. The sand-edged pool is enchant-

ing and inviting on a hot day. Both the Fremont and Anasazi Indians visited this area; some settled this canyon as evidenced by the rock art and granaries. Both cultures were knowledgeable about using available plants and animals for survival, and planted squash, corn, and beans in the canyon bottoms. Trout swim in the creek.

ESCALANTE STATE PARK

With so many fantastic national parks in Utah, a lot of visitors miss the enchantment of a quiet hike through a petrified-wood strewn landscape at Escalante State Park. In addition to offering a lovely campground that edges Wide Hollow Reservoir—which has great fishing for rainbow trout and bluegills—the park is listed in the *Utah Wildlife Viewing Guide* as one of the few wetland bird-viewing sites in southern Utah. Start your visit with a trip to the visitor center.

The Petrified Forest Nature Trail (pick up a brochure) climbs initially but then levels out for most of the hike through a pygmy forest. Deposits of petrified wood soon become frequent, particularly in washes. The loop ends near a 5-foot (1.5-m) section of a fossilized log and expansive vistas of the surrounding geology, the lake, and the town of Escalante.

The Sleeping Rainbows Trail branches off the Petrified Forest Trail and goes past large deposits of petrified wood, but it is a strenuous, scrambling affair over rocks as the path descends sharply and then climbs again to return to the nature trail.

 Insider's Tip:
It is very tempting to pick up an exquisite piece of petrified wood for a souvenir when walking along the petrified wood trails. It is strictly forbidden!

You may be surprised at the richness of the colors of petrified wood. The colors of the wood no longer predominate; rather, any spaces that could collect minerals are filled with a variety of colored crystals: rosy red, amethyst, gold, purple, amber, silver, and orange. Adding to the intrigue is the weaving of these colors, the patterns of the cracks, the variations of the veins, and the overlays of contrasting lichens. The nearby Morrison Badlands, long called the "Painted Desert," are rich in the minerals that infuse petrified wood with crystalline colors. Erosion loosened these jeweled rocks from their previously buried positions and washed them down to this location.

KODACHROME BASIN STATE PARK

As indicated by its name, Kodachrome Basin is another of Utah's special state parks. Campers might see a full moon rising above the kaleidoscope of rocks that range from gray and white to several shades of red and orange. Swirling layers of slickrock invite scrambling explorations near the campground. A geologic fascination is the park's unique sand pipes—monolithic spires often called chimneys—are the remains of filled-in underground springs.

The wealth of trails here suggest setting up a base camp in this quiet place—although it is not so quiet on weekends and holidays. Cottontail rabbits and various birds, particularly chukars, might entertain you at your site. Accessible from the campground, a nature trail is informative about the plants, geology, and ecological interconnections. The 3-mile (4.8-km) Panorama Trail (the only trail that allows mountain bikes, except on the steep spur to Panorama Point) includes short side paths to rock formations such as the Ballerina Spire and the Secret Pass. The optional 2-mile (3.2-km) Big Bear Geyser Trail veers off the main trail.

Two 1-mile-long (1.6 km) trails—Angels Palace Loop Trail and the Grand Parade Trail—reveal more rocky curiosities. Another trail—Eagle View Trail—involves a strenuous and treacherous hike to the top of a white sandstone cliff. You need to be surefooted and energetic to reach the Eagle View Overlook on the top.

The park also claims an arch that was discovered recently by the park manager while looking for a coyote den, and it is appropriately named the Shakespeare Arch after its discoverer. A nature trail now loops by the arch, although you may want to check the conditions of the rutted dirt road that takes you to the trail.

Trail Head Station offers Scenic Safaris for viewing the park via a variety of guided horseback tours. Physically impaired or senior travelers might prefer the horse-drawn stagecoach.

BRYCE CANYON NATIONAL PARK

Back on the byway, our tour takes us through the north end of Bryce Canyon National Park. UT 63 then turns south and provides a road tour through this long, narrow park as it climbs to an elevation of 9,015 feet (2,748 m) at road's end. Much is learned from the 18-mile (29-km) park road, with its multitude of stopping points, but the 50 miles (80 km) of trails are like no other. Offering a different perspective than Zion and other parks, where the views are seen by looking upward, you enter the magical intimacy of Bryce Canyon's surroundings by descending on foot. Keep in mind, however, that the climb out is the strenuous part.

Picked by many foreign travel writers as their favorite place in this country, it is an enchanting salmon and pink-hued fairyland of rock pagodas, windows, and spires called hoodoos. Bryce is an amphitheater, rather than a canyon, of alternate layers of hard and soft rock eroded by time, raindrops, snow, and ice. Sunsets and sunrises are spectacular. Two campgrounds are available: North Campground is along the edge of the canyon, with easy access to Rim Trail, which wanders up high all the way to Bryce Point before it descends into the canyon and continues as the Under the Rim Trail to Rainbow Point. Sunset Campground is across the park road from Sunset Point. (No trailers are allowed on the road beyond this campground.)

Along the drive, the sunken aspect of the canyon allows incredible views. Many visitors miss the side trip to the Fairyland Canyon northern trailhead, with its viewpoint of colors and bizarre shapes. You can take a day hike from the southern trailhead near North Campground, looping past the Chinese Wall and Tower Bridge, into Fairyland Canyon and return via the Rim Trail.

This is a strenuous 8-mile (12.8-km) loop.

Stops along the drive include Sunrise Point, Sunset Point, Inspiration Point, a side trip to Bryce Point and Paria View, Swamp Canyon, Fairview Point, Natural Bridge overlook, Agua Canyon, Ponderosa Canyon, and finally Rainbow Point and Yovimpa Point, where a trail leads to ancient bristlecone pine trees on the rim edge.

The most popular trails are near the campgrounds. The Queen Garden Trail and the Navajo Loop Trail can be done individually or combined for a 3-mile (4.8-km) round-trip loop by beginning most wisely at Sunset Point and returning via the less strenuous ascent to Sunrise Point. Twenty-nine switchbacks down from Sunset Point, hikers enter Wall Street, a narrow "street" where tall conifers stretch upward in slots between eroded rose-orange pinnacles. Thor's Hammer and a spire christened Queen Victoria are along the trail. Complete the loop by walking the Rim Trail back to Sunset Point. Elevations are approximately 8,000 feet (2,438 m), so hiking is not easy. In winter and spring this is snow country.

The UT 12 Scenic Byway ends after a flourish of more color as you pass through Red Canyon, where you'll find forest camps along the road.

US 89 Scenic Byway

No sooner does one byway end than another fine one begins; this time it's US 89 heading south to Kanab. This route traverses Long Valley along the Sevier and Virgin rivers before reaching Kanab, a place called Utah's "Little Hollywood" because more than 70 movies have been filmed in this vicinity.

CORAL PINK SAND DUNES STATE PARK

The appeal of this jaunt off the tour's main route is Coral Pink Sand Dunes State Park, which is reached by two roads that branch off US 89 before Kanab. You can hike or ride off-highway vehicles (OHVs) on 2,000 acres of rose-colored hills surrounded by mountains and the Vermillion Cliffs. At night there is clear stargazing in this wild back-

Mesa Arch, Canyonlands National Park.

country park, which is developed enough to include a campground with some amenities.

The nature trail offers an introduction to the dunes and their vegetation. The fun, although strenuous, involves climbing one or both of the two enormous dune formations—a barchan and a star dune. A longer trail loops around the southern edge of the dunes.

Intrepid sand explorers will find many other areas full of delightful discoveries, such as mule ears, sunflowers, yucca, cactus, and a threatened species of milkweed that sprouts on sandy hills. Ponderosa pines grow at the higher elevations, where small pools of water attract animals. Bird tracks are visible on the sand, along with the uniform footprints of the camel cricket and scurrying beetles. Harder to discover are the spadefoot toads and tiger salamanders.

Off-highway vehicles are allowed in certain areas, but this park is noted for enforcing Utah's OHV regulations, so please be familiar with them.

Zion National Park

Return to US 89 and head west again. Zion Park Scenic Byway (UT 9) heads west at Mount Carmel Junction. The road passes through Zion National Park, a roller coaster of a ride that zigs and zags via an engineering marvel of a highway that begins mildly as it skirts the White Cliffs and Checkerboard Mesa. Watch for the self-guiding Canyon Overlook Trail between the two tunnels, with its views of lower Zion and Pine Creek Canyon. You emerge from the second and longer tunnel to fantastic views of Zion Canyon and the Great Arch of Zion as you descend to Zion Canyon Scenic Drive, where you turn north.

Insider's Tip:

Many recreational vehicles are too large to pass safely through the long tunnel in two-way traffic; therefore, an escort is required for large vehicles and a fee is charged. During the busier seasons, large vehicles are restricted in where they may park in Zion Canyon. Plans are underway to prohibit vehicular traffic in Zion Canyon, with transport to be by shuttle, except for bicycles and hikers.

Zion Canyon Scenic Drive is a 6-mile (10-km) route that follows the North Fork of the Virgin River, which almost single-handedly carved Zion Canyon. Since so much is packed into this short drive, and the park is so popular, arrive early to find parking by trailheads and try to avoid weekends and holidays. Two campgrounds near the visitor center and nature center allow camping in lovely surroundings and early starts in the morning. The Watchman Trail begins near South Campground.

Zion is resplendent with massive peaks rising elegantly into the sky, marvels of burnt-orange, whites, and every shade in between among their fractures and layers, as if shoved upward from a fiery furnace as a monument to be praised as fine art on a giant scale. A Mormon homesteader was so impressed with the magnificence of this area that he persuaded friends to visit and they agreed with him and called it Zion. Brigham Young, however, said it was not Zion, and for years it was called Not Zion. Names on the map hint at the beauty.

In sequence heading north along the scenic drive are stops at Court of the Patri-

archs and the Sand Beach Trail. Next is the trailhead to Emerald Pools, a highly recommended trail that climbs to three magnificent waterfalls and views. Guided horseback rides are available at Zion Lodge. Past the Lodge is a picnic area at the Grotto with access to the long West Rim Trail, which wanders into the backcountry and also intersects with the trail to Angels Landing. This trail will take you to great views fairly quickly, but it's not a good one if you have vertigo.

Past the Great White Throne is Weeping Rock Trail, a short trek to a rock alcove with dripping springs and hanging gardens. The drive ends at the famous Temple of Sinawava, the Gateway to the Narrows Trail. The first mile is wheelchair accessible with assistance. This is also where hardy backpackers risk weather changes on the demanding 12.5 miles (20 km) along the Virgin River, often wading through narrow canyons (permit required).

Groves of box elder, willow, cottonwood, and ash flourish along the canyon floor and excellent autumn foliage often turns the green waters of the Virgin River into a flaming fluid reflection.

Snow Canyon State Park

At an elevation of only 2,600 feet (792 m) on the canyon floor, Snow Canyon's name is deceiving. A special park, it occupies a red rock landscape strewn with lava flows in the warm ambiance of year-round camping, hiking, and golf at nearby St. George. The camping area is scattered among slickrock formations that are great for exploring.

Trails include the Hidden Pinyon Trail, one to Johnson Arch, and another to lava caves that continues to West Canyon Overlook, where the rock textures urge close-up camera shots. A longer hike or a horseback ride leads into West Canyon. Or you can climb the short, steep trail up a cinder cone. The geology of the park is stunning in its variety and intrigue. There's even a patch of sand dunes for the children as well as a rock-climbing wall.

Southern Utah is an RVer's fantasy trip; it will dazzle you with its natural beauty.

Special Event:
Springdale, near Zion, is famous for its Southern Utah Folklife Festival in early September.

CHAPTER 12

New Mexico's Camino Real:
Pueblos, White Sand, and Migrating Birds

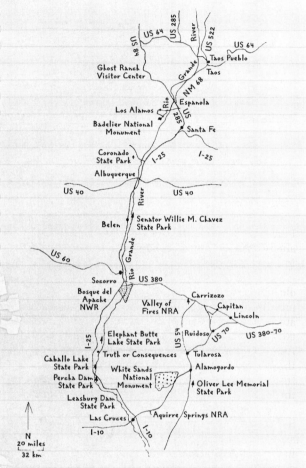

MILEAGE

Less than 1,000 miles (1,600 km).

RESOURCES

- Santa Fe Chamber of Commerce: (505) 984-6760 or (800) 777-2489.
- Bandelier National Monument: (505) 672-3861.
- Albuquerque Convention and Visitors Bureau: (505) 842-9918.
- White Sands National Monument: (505) 479-6124.
- Geronimo Springs Museum: (505) 894-6600.
- Bosque del Apache National Wildlife Refuge: (505) 835-1828.

CAMPGROUNDS

BANDELIER NATIONAL MON-UMENT: West of US 285 and Pojoaque on NM 502 and then south on NM 4; Juniper Campground has campsites, restrooms, and a dump station.

CORONADO STATE MONU-MENT: One mile (1.6 km) northwest of Bernalillo on NM 44 off Interstate 25; campsites with long pull-throughs, some with electric hookups, restrooms with showers, dump station; for information, phone (505) 867-5351.

VALLEY OF FIRES RECREATION AREA: Four miles (6.4 km) west of Carrizozo; campsites (some with electric hookups), restrooms and planned showers should be available; for information, phone (505) 648-2241.

OLIVER LEE MEMORIAL STATE PARK: Ten miles (16 km) south of Alamogordo; campsites (some with electric hookups), restrooms with showers, dump sta-

tion; for information, phone (505) 437-8284.

ELEPHANT BUTTE LAKE STATE PARK: Five miles (8 km) north of Truth or Consequences; varied campsites (some with electric hookup), restrooms with showers, picnic shelters; reservations at (505) 744-5421.

New Mexico is a provocative mixture of stimulating landscapes and cultural influences. Indian pueblos, white sand dunes, Spanish missions, high desert, Anasazi ruins, lava flows, high mountains, wild rivers, and colorful badlands are a few of its enticements for travelers. And road travel is not new here. One road—the Pueblo Indian Trail—sliced through this state long before Columbus discovered America. The route was used by Indian traders traveling from Taos to El Paso. Roughly following the flow of the Rio Grande River from north to south through the center of the state, the trail was used and extended to Mexico by Spanish explorers, the first being Francisco Vasquez de Coronado. Traders, settlers, sheep, cattle, horses, and carts were part of the highway traffic on the Camino Real de Tierra Adentro, or "Royal Highway of the Interior Land." Today a modern scenic byway parallels this old road, which can still be found in a few places.

Wild birds have chosen a similar route along the wetlands of the Rio Grande. This provides an excellent reason for traveling in autumn, when sweeping flocks of sandhill cranes and snow geese arrive at Bosque del Apache National Wildlife Refuge to spend the winter. Approximately 100,000 people from around the world visit yearly to see the migrating birds.

By beginning your tour at Taos and heading south in October, fine weather should accompany you, with daytime highs in the sixties and nights near freezing in the north. The lower elevations in southern New Mexico are warmer.

Outdoor oven at Taos Pueblo, NM.

Entering New Mexico on US 64, stop at the observation platforms and picnic area by the Rio Grande Gorge Bridge for a view of the river and the sculpturing it has created. It's impressive from 650 feet (198 m) above the water. One of the two "Wild and Scenic" rivers in northern New Mexico, it is popular with river rafters and, although the "white knuckle" seasons are spring and summer, some portions are negotiable year-round.

Taos Pueblo

When the Stone-Age Anasazi people searched for new homes in new landscapes, for whatever complex reasons, many settled in New Mexico's Rio Grande Valley, where they built multistoried earthen pueblo structures. About A.D. 1500, the Spaniards estimated that at least 30,000 people speaking several languages inhabited some 100 pueblos. Even today they comprise a mix of native people.

The wonder is that one of these pueblos, the Taos Pueblo, has been continuously inhabited for 700 years. Although its sunlit appearance mistakenly lured Coronado in his search for the fabled Seven Cities of Cibola, the earthen hues of these "apartment houses" of flat-roofed, stair-stepped cubes of adobe provide a magical setting of architecture that is open to the public.

Two miles (3.2 km) north of the newer town of Taos, North and South Taos Pueblos edge the waters of Rio Pueblo Taos in the foothills of the Sangre de Cristo Mountains at 7,000 feet (2,134 m). The Tiwi-speaking Indians who live here have opted for a simple life without electricity or indoor plumbing, with handmade ladders leaning against walls and outdoor ovens, or "hornos," in sheltered corners for baking bread (do try some; it's delicious). A few shops carrying jewelry, weavings, leather goods, and hand-stretched drums are open to the public daily, but please respect the privacy of those areas off-limits to the public. An entry fee and an additional camera-use fee are charged to wander about the grounds. During festivals and religious celebrations, visitors are requested to respect the sacred dances and not photograph them.

Near the entrance to the pueblo, notice the ruins of the Mission San Geronimo de Taos, a structure burned in the 1680 rebellion, restored twenty-five years later, and then damaged again by U.S. troops during the 1847 revolt. The massive walls and bell tower that remain are impressive. White geometric shapes topped with white crosses contrast with the beige adobe walls. An interior courtyard is laid with irregular slate slabs. I found this mission extremely attractive in its simple, effective design complete with ladders, wood beams, and decorative balcony.

The Artistic Community of Taos

Ever since wandering artists discovered the inspiring location of Taos and formed the Taos Society of Artists, this town, which was originally Spanish—legally, Don Fernando de Taos—has attracted writers, artists, musicians, and artisans who have consistently earned Taos fame as a center of creativity. Writer D. H. Lawrence lived here in a pretty adobe house furnished with handcrafted furniture, Mexican and Navajo rugs, and lovely pots. Surrounded by desert and the sacred mountain of the Indians, he remarked that the environment changed him forever.

Frontiersman Kit Carson had a home in Taos and is buried along with other notables in Kit Carson State Park. The Taos Historic Walks start from the Kit Carson Home and Museum; the guided tours last 1.5 hours and take place from June through October.

It's a little confusing at first to discover that there are three villages called Taos.

Old Mission San Geronimo de Taos at Taos Pueblo, NM.

The third one is the older farming community of Rancho de Taos (San Geronimo de Taos), New Mexico, 4 miles (6.4 km) south of the artistic and tourist Taos. It is well known for its picturesque Spanish church, San Francisco de Asis.

Abiquiu and Georgia O'Keeffe

Before continuing south on the Camino Real, a side trip to Abiquiu, northwest of Espanola, reveals some enchanting country. This landscape not only inspired the paintings of Georgia O'Keeffe, but inspired her to make this her home. Imagine her wandering the landscape: "I have wanted to paint the desert and I haven't known how. . . So I brought home the bleached bones as my symbols of the desert." I knew I had to see whether the landscape would speak to me as powerfully as it did to O'Keefe, and I was not disappointed.

The Ghost Ranch Living Museum is north of the town and the Abiquiu Reservoir, which is an Army Corps of Engineers recreation area that's popular with windsurfers. The Reservoir has picnic areas, campgrounds, a visitor center, and offers boat tours. The museum is a National Forest Service operation—with support from the Ghost Ranch Living Museum Foundation—and combines conservation and ecology education and cultural history. It was designed by educator William Carr of Arizona-Sonora Desert Museum fame. Wildlife that is representative of the Carson National Forest—beaver, bear, badger, mountain lion, bobcat, trout, and other species—can

Special Event:
The San Geronimo Vespers Sundown Dance and Feast Day are held at Taos Pueblo during the last week of September, with Comanche and Corn dances, foot races, a pole climb, and an arts-and-crafts sale part of Feast Day.

be viewed from a walkway. The "Gateway to the Past" exhibit was where I felt connected to O'Keeffe, with exhibits and actual furnishings decorating small rooms reminiscent of her life in the area. Outdoors are trails through the area vegetation.

The landscapes here are a dramatic and sudden change from that to the north and the south. Near the reservoir are vivid badlands of deep purplish red and rust that have hardened at the foot of colorful cliffs. Even more dramatic hoodoos and soaring rock formations are to the north; in one place they border a creek that is lush with green vegetation and trees. The scenic climax in the north is the Echo Amphitheater, which features an adjacent primitive campground-picnic area and short walkway through desert vegetation to view this natural "theater" that was hollowed out of sandstone by years of erosion. Incredible patterns of "desert varnish" from water runoff at the top edge of the cliffs and the blend of gold, gray, and light orange of the surrounding rock formations are all beautiful—an artist's paradise.

Bandelier National Monument

Some of the Anasazi who relocated settled on the Pajarito ("little bird") Plateau, in what is now Bandelier National Monument. They occupied pueblos there until about A.D. 1550, when they moved to present-day Rio Grande pueblos. This plateau consists largely of tuff (consolidated volcanic ash) and basaltic lava ejected thousands of years ago by a great volcano. The most accessible ruins are in Frijoles Canyon. This deep gorge carved by a mountain stream, Rito de los Frijoles ("Bean Creek"), provided an oasis in a dry land, and was an excellent location for these farmers who used cotton cloth and made decorated pottery.

The Frey Trail leads down from Juniper Campground to the Tyuonyi ruins (a shorter trail takes off from the visitor center), where you can climb short ladders and peek into cave dwellings created in the soft tuff that were gouged out with harder stone tools. Other trails lead to Ceremonial Cave,

pictographs, petroglyphs, and into the vast backcountry wilderness, which encompasses most of the park.

The Falls Trail is a particularly appealing day hike because it follows the creek through the deep gash of Frijoles Canyon down to a vista point of Upper Falls. The wood of the narrowleaf cottonwood trees along the stream was used by the Indians to make drums, and the roots became part of Kachina dolls. Hikers will pass good examples of tuff called "tent rock," ruins, ponderosa pines, and intriguing geological formations. You might also see some birds. The view of the falls is lovely in its surrounding mix of pinkish striated rock and resistant dark basalt. The 1.5-mile (2.4-km) trail to this point continues another 1 mile (1.6 km) down to the Rio Grande River in White Rock Canyon; it's a steep climb back out of the canyon. Fortunately, fall is a cooler time for the uphill trek. I was amused by the trail register. Someone commented that they felt like Dorothy in the Land of Oz: "This is not Kansas."

Travelers can loop west past Los Ala-

Upper Falls on Frijoles Creek in Bandelier National Monument, NM

mos before returning to the main highway north of Santa Fe and see the historic place where the Manhattan Project resulted in "Little Boy" and "Fat Man," the atomic bombs that ended World War II. It was here that scientist J. Robert Oppenheimer named the test of the weapon "Trinity" and helped guide that device to completion. The route passes the Los Alamos National Laboratory, a University of California research center.

Historic Santa Fe

A number of Indian pueblos are clustered near the freeway heading south to Santa Fe and Albuquerque. Several have gaming casinos. Tewa-speaking Tesuque Pueblo north of Santa Fe has a casino and a campground across the highway next to the unique natural rock sculpture called Camel Rock.

Charming Santa Fe has been named the "most livable small city" of communities under 100,000 population. Its unique ambiance is a blend of cultures—Indian, Spanish, and Anglo—that challenges foreign locales with its special flavor and look. The rough-hewn woodwork, adobe walls, and decorative door and window trim of its buildings reflect a city that fits beautifully into the sunlit environment as the warm tones and rounded corners lift upward.

The oldest capital city in the United States, Santa Fe was established by the Spaniards in 1610, ten years before the Pilgrims arrived in the East. The core of the city was the Plaza. Once the "end of the Santa Fe Trail," the Plaza was a scene of freight wagons, donkeys kicking up the dust, and horseback riders with sombreros and silver-studded trousers. The marketplace was found here, too, with hanging slabs of buffalo meat, bear, turkey, and goat, plus beans, chili peppers, and corn-husk cigarettes.

The Plaza remains essentially intact and is an exciting place to begin a stroll. (Parking lots for RVers fringe the historic area.) On the Plaza's north side, the porch of the Palace of the Governors is a gathering place where Native American artisans display their wares.

Galleries and shops exhibit Western art that is rich in history: paintings, serigraphs, and photographs of Tepees, cowboys, buttes, mountains, and pueblos alongside turquoise squash-blossom jewelry and exquisite black pottery. Hotel lobbies are splashed with the hues of bright tiles, Navajo rugs, and potted cactus. Restaurants feature Mexican food, with green and red chile sauces, although menus also reflect Native American and continental flavors.

The oldest house in Santa Fe is three blocks south of the Plaza on the Old Santa Fe Trail. Across the street is the Mission of San Miguel. Around the next corner is New Mexico's new capitol, a round building that represents the "circle of life" belief of the Native Americans.

Santa Fe embraces a richness of museums. The Museum of Fine Arts is impressive without even going inside, but you should check out the contemporary and historic art. Other museums feature Indian arts and culture, international folk art, and works of Georgia O'Keeffe, along with other subjects. Featuring well-known artists in an open-air theater, the Santa Fe Opera is another example of this city's sophistication.

The tour zooms south past small hills and juniper trees on Interstate 25, with mountains looming to the east. Follow signs on the north side of Bernalillo to Coronado State Monument, the site of the Tiwa-speaking village of Kuaua ("sacred evergreen"), which was established about A.D. 1300. When visited by the Spaniards in 1540 and 1542, several hundred Indians inhabited it. The explorers first came marching through with an expedition numbering 1,200 people, along with numerous pigs, chickens, and cattle. Troubles erupted as a result of attempts by the Spaniards to dom-

Special Event:

The Annual Feast Day of Tesuque Pueblo is held in mid-November. The public is welcome to attend.

Indian ruins and museum, Coronado State Monument, NM.

inate the area. By the early 1600s, the village was a ghost town.

Today, visitors can walk the interpretive trail through the partially reconstructed adobe village and view artifacts and exhibits in the museum that illuminate our understanding of the early settlement of the Rio Grande Valley. Bright-colored tropical bird feathers, shell necklaces, chunks of turquoise, corn, beans, sea shells, and tales of distant places were brought here from time to time by travelers. A visitor in 1610, Gasper Perez de Villagra, wrote that resident Indians had structures up to seven stories high, with paintings of gods on the walls. The women wore shawls of many colors. "A man sits at the door playing a fife while the women grind food, moving the stones to music and singing together."

A stay at the adjacent park campground provides an opportunity to inhabit this his-

toric landscape along the Rio Grande River, with a view of the Sandia Mountains across the water. Campground trails connect to the museum area. Adobe-sheltered picnic tables are decorated with striking Indian paintings.

The Vicinity of Albuquerque

The countryside south of Albuquerque is flat and boring until mountainous surroundings appear shortly before Socorro. Senator Willie M. Chavez State Park is just east of Belen, an older park along the Rio Grande, with camping, hiking, and good viewing of birds migrating along the river.

Valley of Fires National Recreation Area

Crossing a lonely terrain of flat desert, US 380 heads east as it gradually climbs into the mountains and reaches a final stretch of lava rocks peppered with tall cactus near Valley of Fires National Recreation Area, an inviting Bureau of Land Management facility complete with a visitor center. This area is called the Malpais (*mal-pie-ees*), Spanish for "bad country." The expansive Carrizozo Lava Flow poured out of vents in the valley floor 1,500 to 2,000 years ago, and is one of the younger and most pristine lava flows in the continental United States. Amongst this basalt landscape are plants of the Chihuahuan Desert and habitat for many animal and bird species. A covered wildlife viewing shelter is situated at the beginning of the 0.5-mile (0.8-km) Malpais Nature Trail. The first part of the trail is paved and wheelchair accessible with handrails; a more difficult dirt trail loops back to the trailhead.

On an island of older rock called a kipuka—higher ground not covered by the lava flow—an inviting campground offers great views of the surrounding Tularosa basin-and-range landscape, much of which is designated a Wilderness Study Area. Although the sites have no shade trees, the shelters and campsites are spread out and offer considerable privacy. A hilltop overlook trail is located in the campground area.

Special Events

In early October, more than 700 balloonists participate in the annual Kodak Albuquerque International Balloon Fiesta. In mid-October, Albuquerque also takes part in the Dia del Rio, events along the Rio Grande River from Colorado to Mexico that celebrate, preserve, and restore life along the river.

Historic Lincoln County

Continuing east on US 380 offers a tour of historic Lincoln County. The highway soon winds through blocks of Lincoln National Forest and passes the visitor center for Smokey the Bear State Park and a short trail to the original Smokey's burial site. The town of Lincoln, the main attraction, began as an Hispanic farming community along the Rio Bonito River in the late 1800s. It became famous in 1878 for the Lincoln County War, a bloody five-day series of ambushes and killings started by rival businessmen who brought in lawless elements—including Billy the Kid, who escaped before his scheduled hanging, but was later shot and killed by Sheriff Pat Garrett at Fort Sumner.

It takes some imagination to picture Lincoln as a place of violence. It is now a peaceful small town where old rocking chairs adorn porches. A few houses have seen a bit of restoration, but none are gussied up and painted. Both a National and a State Monument, walking tour maps can be picked up at the Historical Center, where a museum fee includes tours of a few other buildings. It's an easy walk along the town's main street from the museum to the Lincoln Courthouse at the western edge of town. You'll pass the Montano Store, the San Juan Mission, the Wortley Hotel, Dr. Wood's house, the Tunstall Museum, the saloon frequented by Billy the Kid, and El Torreon, a rock tower erected by Lincoln's first Spanish settlers. A picnic lunch can be eaten at the wooded picnic area by the stream.

Either NM 48 or US 70 leads to Ruidoso, a busy all-season resort town in the Sacramento Mountains, and home of Ruidoso Downs Racetrack and the richest quarter-horse race in the United States. Outdoor recreation and ski resorts are nearby. Then cruise down the highway past pistachio orchards to Alamogordo, location of the International Space Hall of Fame.

Oliver Lee Memorial State Park

Whether your interest is natural history excursions, relaxing in peaceful and scenic surroundings, hiking into mountains, or delving into human history and even some personalities, Oliver Lee Memorial State Park south of Alamogordo is a gem in New Mexico's park system. The campground is situated at the mouth of Dog Canyon, smack against the west-facing escarpment of the Sacramento Mountains, with shaded picnic enclosures and a view of the Tularosa Basin past White Sands National Monument to the mountains beyond. Sunsets are great and mornings may begin with the song of a cactus wren, a visit from a roadrunner, or a rare peregrine falcon flying overhead. This spot is a good base for exploring nearby White Sands.

It is no wonder that archeological research has revealed human occupation in Dog Canyon for at least 6,000 years. This desert site has the essentials for survival and enjoyment, including perennial freshwater springs, tillable land, and a natural fortress of rocky cliffs for easy defense. The canyon even provided the right materials for making essential stone tools—some 170,000 stone artifacts have been found here.

We know more about the recent inhabitants. Emigrating from southeastern France, Francois-Jean "Frenchy" Rochas homesteaded at the mouth of Dog Canyon. Although his exact arrival date is not known, by the late 1880s he had acquired some 400 cattle and six horses and lived in the two-room rock-and-adobe home he constructed. About 1893, Frenchy and a prominent Tularosa Basin rancher named Oliver Lee cooperated in the construction of a cement flume that channeled water into ditches across Frenchy's homestead and south to Lee's ranch headquarters a mile away. Unfortunately, Frenchy was found shot dead in his cabin soon after Christmas of 1894. He was probably murdered, but the mystery was never solved. Shortly before his death at 51, he wrote a letter saying he was working in his vineyard and had planted olive, fig, apple, cherry, plum, and peach trees.

On Frenchy's death, Oliver Lee secured title to this lovely box canyon. Cattleman Lee further increased his land holdings to nearly one million acres of rangeland—

amid intermittent hostilities and political rivalries—and served in both houses of the New Mexico State Legislature. The park commemorates the colorful life of this pioneer. Guided tours to Lee's ranch house, completely rebuilt from ruins and authentically furnished, are regularly scheduled.

A nature trail leads from the visitor center to the lush springs and picnic area situated among cottonwood and ash trees; it continues via a boardwalk and stairs to additional lower canyon views. Maidenhair ferns cling to the moist canyon walls, and remnants of the old flume are visible, with prickly pear, yucca, and mesquite just a few steps away. Yet orchids grow by the stream, and the diverse plant life of Dog Canyon includes a rare penstemon and several other threatened and endangered plant species. The animal life is equally varied.

The strenuous 4.2-mile (6.8-km) Dog Canyon National Recreational Trail begins at the visitor center and climbs into the mountains and Lincoln National Forest, gaining 3,000 feet (914 m) in elevation to FR 90B on Joplin Ridge. This trail was used by Indians for thousands of years and continues southwest to the Guadalupe Mountains. Autumn is the time to hike this trail as you'll avoid the intense summer heat. If you're not up to the 8.4-mile (13.5-km) round-trip, do the 2.4 miles (4 km) to Lee's line cabin, in a canyon oasis of trees along a small creek. From the trail near there, you can see the narrow Eyebrow Trail edging along the top of the ridge and a series of waterfalls cascading from the cliff tops. This canyon area, however, also served as a trap into which to lure enemies, knowledge used by the Mescaleros Apaches.

White Sands National Monument

You'll quickly suspect that the sand is different at White Sands National Monument. It is said that these white dunes are one of the last recognizable landmarks when astronauts race toward the moon. In fact, they are so blindingly white that you can barely open your eyes at midday, so make sure you wear sunglasses. The dune formations form

a dazzling wave of moving hills that is the world's largest gypsum dunefield. This ecological island of some 275 square miles occupies the sun-drenched northern edge of the Chihuahuan Desert.

The sand is pushed here by southwest winds from crusty Lake Lucero, a dry lake bed most of the year. The grains of gypsum sand skip and hop as they land on other grains, and the entire dune surface flows or creeps to the northeast. The major sand movements occur during spring storms; breezes are milder the rest of the year.

Insider's Tip:
Because the White Sands Missile Range completely surrounds the monument—and continues to be an important testing site—both the monument and nearby US 70 are closed for one to two hours on an average of twice a week.

Pick up a map at the visitor center and begin the 16-mile (26-km) round-trip drive on the Heart of the Sands Loop, first stopping at the 1-mile (1.6-km) Big Dune Trail for a self-guiding nature jaunt. As you climb the dunes, listen for birds and look for tracks of lizards, pocket mice, roadrunners, and the cryptic prints of the darkling beetle. Notice how soaptree yucca and cottonwood trees have adapted to the moving sand. Did you smell the sweet scent of hoary rosemary mint?

As you enter the main dunefield, the road becomes hard-packed gypsum. Pull over only in established areas to explore on foot; do not stop on the road. White Sands is a place where you won't experience mys-

White Sands National Monument, NM.

tic emotions unless you walk into the dunes, climb them, observe the patterns and textures of the sand, and notice the way the dunes play with light. These dunes are not so high that climbing them is difficult. It's an emotional journey to surrender to this landscape, a joyful one of solace in a surrealistic scenario. A sunset stroll across the dunes is a delight; in addition to the color show, the timing is good for sighting wildlife. Imagine the charm of the white dunes under a full moon.

Although kit foxes, coyotes, badgers, porcupines, rabbits, and skunks hunt in the fringe areas around the dunes, more than 90 percent of the animal species inhabiting the monument are birds and insects, and these are also the most obvious. An interesting camouflage adaptation is seen in the white dunes habitat. Natural selection favors animals that are difficult to see because they can escape predation. Two species of lizard and some mice are almost pure white. Many other animals are lighter in color than expected, a nearly transparent cricket, for example.

Aguirre Springs National Recreation Area

After the drive south through the flat Tularosa Valley, the turnoff to Aguirre Springs National Recreation Area east of Las Cruces leads to the ultimate backcountry picnic-lunch experience, which could easily extend into an overnight. The campground is nestled in a curve of the Organ Mountains at an elevation 5,540 feet (1,689 m), high enough for varied high desert vegetation and wildlife, small shade trees of juniper and oak, and even a few late wildflowers in early autumn. Getting there involves a 5.5-mile (8.8-km) steep and somewhat winding drive—particularly the last part—on a

Special Event:
Three-hour tours to the source of the white sands, Lake Lucero, are held in White Sands National Monument one day each month.

paved road, although it is nothing really difficult unless your rig is big and long.

The Baylor Pass National Recreation Trail begins at the Aguirre Spring Campground and provides 6 miles (10 km) of hiking, horseback riding, and mountain biking. The Pine Tree Trail is for hiking only, a loop trail of 4.5 miles (7 km) that also begins at the campground. It's fun to just wander about the spacious campground, however, after a picnic lunch and admire the looming closeness of these mountain peaks on an autumn day with cumulus clouds lingering in the sky and twisting about in the high crevices, with the smooth, shiny granite surface of one peak dominating the view.

State Parks and Reservoirs Along the Rio Grande River

Deliberately last on the tour is the stretch of the Rio Grande River north of Las Cruces, where a string of state parks offer camping during the fall bird migration. At these southern and lower elevations, days are often perfect for being outdoors. Take Interstate 25 if you wish to bypass Las Cruces, and then head west to Radium Springs and take the scenic back road, NM 185, and then NM 187, north. Traveling involves noticing how and where the natives live, not the speedy view from the interstate. This is the region where New Mexican farmers grow chiles and, in autumn, this route passes verdant fields of this crop. In fact, the Rio Grande Valley of New Mexico—centered at Hatch—produces the biggest chile crops in the world on some 22,000 acres. And New Mexicans do love to eat their chiles.

Stop at Fort Seldon State Monument for a stroll among the crumbling ruins of this flat-roofed adobe fort built to protect the settlers from raids by Apaches and desperadoes. Included in the monument are the remains of General MacArthur's boyhood home and museum exhibits. Adjacent Leasburg State Park is located south of the dam that channels irrigation water to Mesilla Valley, and offers canoeing, kayaking, fishing, and camping. Trails lead to cactus and wildflower gardens. Percha Dam

State Park has more fishing and camping along the river below the dam, while Caballo Lake State Park offers camping both on the edge of the reservoir and below the dam. Caballo is a wintering location for bald eagles, so scan for them perched in trees or in flight over the water.

The most northerly park choice is Elephant Butte Lake State Park, the largest and most popular lake in New Mexico. Named after a rock formation across the lake, the park has a marina and the setting for every imaginable water sport, plus all types of campsites. I camped on a beach and woke in time to watch a fiery sunrise top the mountains across the lake—not a bad way to begin the day. A visitor center contains a tyrannosaur fossil, petrified wood, bones of an elephant ancestor, and other items. Some RVers stay a while here, and a trail connects to Desert Cove and nearby services.

The nearby city of Truth or Consequences was renamed for the popular radio show. Used by the Apache Indians before the area was settled, 110-degree mineral springs bubble up to the surface here. Commercial bathhouses have been constructed around the thermal waters.

Bosque del Apache National Wildlife Refuge

The warm New Mexican sunshine and the fertile riverine environment of 57,191-acre Bosque del Apache National Wildlife Refuge attract enormous numbers of migrating birds that arrive in autumn and spring. The Bosque is famous for the many sandhill cranes and snow geese that begin arriving in late October and leave the first of March, two of the 329 bird species that live in or migrate through the refuge.

Begin a visit by stopping at the visitor center to view the park video, pick up information, check out the current scoreboard for bird sightings, and obtain a map for the one-way, 12-mile (19-km) auto tour (cycling and walking also permitted), which has a couple of cutoffs that shorten the route. You may also borrow an audio cassette to accompany you on the drive. Ask which nature trails along the tour are accessible when you visit. A wheelchair-accessible ramp for viewing a wetland pond is located near the beginning of the drive; several other observation decks, some with spotting scopes, offer panoramic views backed by mountain scenery. Bring binoculars; photographers often use their vehicles as blinds to avoid spooking the birds. Qualified guides lead tours of the refuge most weekends between December 1 and March 1.

The tour route has ample room for pulling over, so be patient and take your time to get the feel of the refuge. The longer you take, the more birds—and their behavior—you'll observe. Even a relatively short tour during autumn might net you sightings that include white pelicans, Canada geese, egrets, cormorants, great blue herons, bald eagles, red-winged blackbirds, doves, hawks, pheasants, coots, various ducks, kingfishers, and many more. A rare sighting is an endangered whooping crane. I watched an osprey devouring a fish.

For a different perspective of the refuge surroundings, hike the moderately strenuous 2.2-mile (3.5-km) Canyon Trail a short distance south of the visitor center along NM 1. Along the path are Bosque Refuge Overlook, Canyon Overlook, a natural arch, and the wild things of the Chihuahuan Desert.

It will become obvious as you travel that "Bienvenidos" is Spanish for "We welcome you." New Mexico extends that invitation to you, so take advantage of it and you'll discover why residents call it "the land of enchantment."

Winter Trips

Adventurous RVers can experience dynamic happenings along the Oregon coast in winter. Good days for observing wild surf and whale migrations are interspersed with exhilarating winter storms, yet the weather is temperate enough for hiking the spectacular Oregon Coast Trail. December is the peak season for Dungeness crabs, which are delicious edibles. Travelers wanting more relaxed waterfront camping and a sunnier clime might choose Baja Sur, in the midst of exploring the Sonoran Desert. Or you can visit the same latitudes in Big Bend National Park, a

Tall sunflower
(Helianthus giganteus)

magical place of river canyons, Chihuahuan Desert, star gazing, and mountains. Wildlife enthusiasts can follow the Rio Grande from Big Bend to the Gulf of Mexico, a birder's dream trip.

To catch the transition from winter back into spring's joyfulness yet travel in pleasant weather throughout the trip, begin north near Death Valley and follow the wildflower and cactus blooms south through Mojave National Preserve, Joshua Tree National Park, past birds at the Salton Sea, to Anza Borrego Desert State Park. The sum total of this transition from winter to spring, as well as from Mojave to Sonoran deserts, will reveal whether deserts can be addictive landscapes for you. Perhaps they have already captured your wandering spirit.

CHAPTER 13

Southern Oregon Coast:
Dynamic Merging of Land and Sea

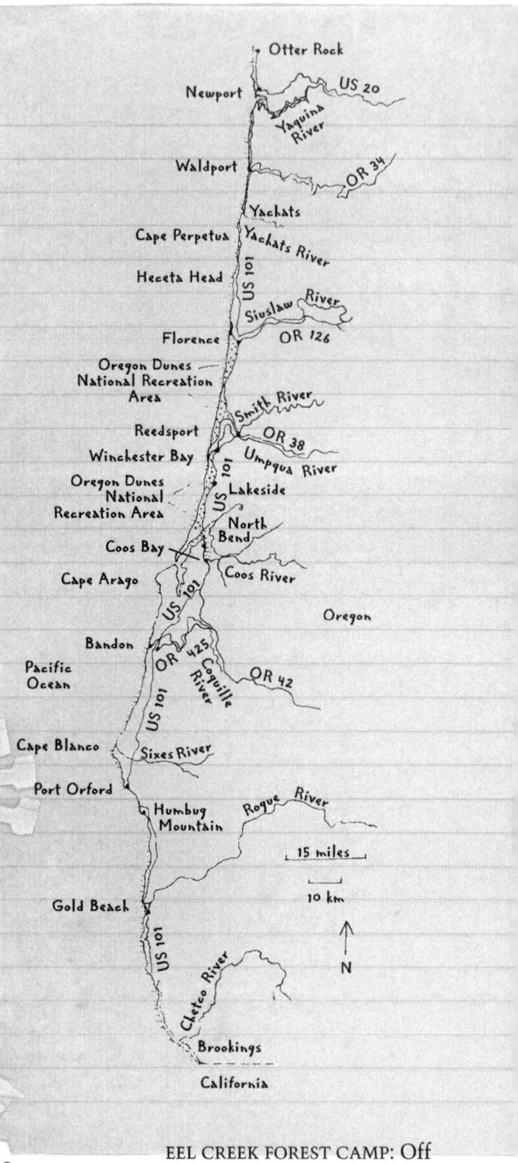

MILEAGE

About 220 miles (354 km) on US 101.

RESOURCES

- For ticket information for the Performing Arts Center, call (541) 265-ARTS.
- Greater Newport Chamber of Commerce: (800) 262-7844.
- Oregon Tourism Division: (800) 547-7842.
- Oregon Fish & Wildlife: in Newport: (541) 867-4741; in Charleston: (541) 888-5515.
- Oregon Parks & Recreation Department, 1115 Commercial Street NE, Salem, OR 97310-1001; (800) 551-6949.

CAMPGROUNDS*

BEVERLY BEACH STATE PARK: Off US 101, 7 miles (11 km) north of Newport; full hookups, electrical, and tent sites, restrooms with showers; yurts with heat and electricity that sleep five.

PACIFIC SHORES RV PARK: in Newport at 6225 N. Coast Highway 101, Pacific Shores has campsites (no tents) overlooking the beach and Yaquina Head Lighthouse. A swimming pool, exercise room, lounges, game room, and lighted nature trails to the beach are some of the amenities. Reservations: (800) 333-1583.

SOUTH BEACH STATE PARK: Off US 101, 2 miles (3 km) south of Newport; electrical sites, restrooms with showers; yurts with heat and lights sleep five.

JESSIE M. HONEYMAN STATE PARK: Off US 101, 3 miles (5 km) south of Florence; full hookups, electrical, and tent sites, restrooms with showers; yurts with heat and lights sleep five.

UMPQUA LIGHTHOUSE STATE PARK: Off US 101, 6 miles (10 km) south of Reedsport: hookup and tent sites, restrooms with showers, yurts, cabins.

EEL CREEK FOREST CAMP: Off US 101, at Lakeside; RV and tent sites, restrooms.

SUNSET BAY STATE PARK: Off US 101, 12 miles southwest of Coos Bay; full hookups, electrical, and tent sites, restrooms with showers, yurts.

*These campgrounds are open year-round with special off-season daily and monthly rates at state parks; reservations are rarely needed in winter.

BULLARDS BEACH STATE PARK: Off US 101, 2 miles (3 km) north of Bandon; full hookups and electrical sites, yurts, horse camp, restrooms with showers.

HUMBUG MOUNTAIN STATE PARK: Off US 101, 6 miles (10 km) south of Port Orford; electrical and tent sites, restrooms with showers.

HARRIS BEACH STATE PARK: Off US 101, north side of Brookings; full hookup, electrical, and tent sites, yurts, restrooms with showers.

Did you ever wish you could watch the merging of land and sea at its most dynamic? You can do that if you travel along the southern Oregon coast in winter. It requires a somewhat adventurous spirit, but the rewards are many. Some people believe nothing happens here in winter except rain, and that the residents have adapted with webfeet. I won't kid you; it does rain a lot and there are violent winter storms, so it's not a time for tent camping or for bringing rigs that are ready to fall apart in the wind.

The truth is that winter includes many sunny days when rainbows ride the surf and there is little wind. Summer visitors don't see the wonderful wild surf and high waves that are so hypnotic as they burst around sea stacks and reflect off headlands. Winter storms are so thrilling to watch that many residents and visitors find places with views so they can be warm inside but not miss the action. Beachcombing is invigorating after a storm, when the air is charged with freshness and strollers can see what the waves have swept ashore. I've walked on the beach when the scene looked like a blizzard, with foamy bubbles flying inland and depositing what looked like several inches of fresh snow, although it was really smashed marine microorganisms. Even on milder days, these bubbles come in with the surf and you can walk among small pools of rainbow colors that burst underfoot. Winter is also the best time to hunt for agates in the sand.

The southern Oregon coast is one of the few places in the contiguous states with mild winter temperatures, a fact that is just being discovered by RVers. The trails I'll tell you about are ones you can use year-

round; it's rare when it snows on this tour. And if you want a little more warmth, head for the sand dunes on a sunny day, where the sunshine reflects off the sand. Winter is also the time when whales migrate down the coast. People don rain gear and head for high points to view them.

The prime season for Dungeness crabs is in winter, when they're fresh and plump and meaty. These invertebrates have become a specialty associated with the Christmas season, which is also when you can visit a botanical garden decorated with festive lights atop coastal cliffs.

I will point out some sheltered storm-watching and camping areas, but the trick is to keep on top of what's happening with the weather and plan excursions accordingly. Winter storm winds blow from the southwest, so choose RV campsites with this in mind. Naturally, bring along some indoor games and those books you've been saving for a rainy day. I'll also suggest some indoor visits for those times when the rain falls and the wind blows.

Safety at the Beach

The beauty of the beach sometimes overwhelms your sense of caution. Surf is powerful and can lift logs around and drop them on you; children should be warned not to walk on logs or play on them. Be aware of incoming tides and don't become stranded on offshore rocks or rounding headlands. Always keep an eye on the waves; a sneaker wave can sweep you out to sea. Although it's a cold ocean along this coast, people do go out into it (not the locals). Be alert for outgoing underwater currents. Obtain a tide table; walking is best at low tide, but know when it turns, because much of the beach disappears. Keep back from the edges of unstable cliffs overlooking the sea.

Since the harvesting of shellfish (not oysters, however) and marine invertebrates is allowed year-round without a license in certain intertidal areas, it's best to check limits and special regulations with the Oregon Fish and Wildlife Department. At certain times, there is a public alert against

Oyster farming along Yaquina River near Newport, OR.

harvesting bivalves—clams, mussels, and scallops—or even Dungeness crabs because of toxic growths in the sea. This is carefully monitored and precautions are posted in the specific area. Check with the Oregon Fish and Wildlife Department.

Newport on Yaquina Bay

In the mid-1800s, succulent Yaquina Bay oysters lured the first white settlers to the area of Newport, and today the town is an important coastal port with a sportfishing marina. The working waterfront along the bay is a great place to watch commercial fishing boats unloading their catch of scrambling Dungeness crab and stroll past markets selling fresh-from-the-sea fish. Huge murals of coastal seascapes and marine mammals decorate the walls. Fine galleries and gift shops—with their seascape paintings, wood products, and jewelry inspired by coastal themes—reflect the artistic talent of the people who live on the coast. Restaurants feature delicious fresh seafood.

The active Yaquina Head Lighthouse still shines out to sea at the northern edge of Newport, part of the outstanding Yaquina Head Natural Area that features an interpretive center and trails. The viewpoint overlooks rocky offshore islands—a national wildlife refuge—and allows close

views of the many sea birds. A stairway leads down to a cobble beach and intertidal area. A side road to the lower level of the headland leads to the world's first barrier-free walkway through a tide pool area. A former rock quarry has been reclaimed by the sea with the help of astute design and engineering. Visitors get to see nature re-establish itself.

Newport is a great place for getting answers about the marine environment and for seeing creatures of the ocean up close. The world-class Oregon Coast Aquarium

Official Whale-Watching Sites

Gray whales migrate yearly from the Arctic to lagoons in Baja California Sur, where they mate and give birth in winter. In spring they head north again to the rich feeding grounds of the Arctic. During the last week in December, the Hatfield Marine Science Center (HMSC) and Oregon Parks and Recreation send volunteers to selected viewing sites along the Oregon coast to answer questions and point out whale behavior. When you see the sign "Whale Watching Spoken Here," why not stop and see what's happening? Whale films are shown during the week at the U.S. Forest Service Cape Perpetua Visitor Center and at HMSC, a great activity for rainy days.

opened in 1992 along the south side of the bay. One of the favorite displays is the huge cylindrical tank of moon jellies, so beautiful and delicate and graceful, yet so difficult to glimpse swimming in their natural habitat. The sea otters are another star attraction in their outdoor rock-encircled pool as they entertain visitors by cracking crabs apart and laying back in the water to eat them. Sea lions and seals swim in their own rocky enclosure. A vast mesh-covered cage contains North America's largest seabird aviary. Not intimidated by curious visitors, tufted puffins swim underwater— an activity that is difficult to see in the wild. Many people came to see the recent arrival, Keiko, the killer whale of movie fame, but he has now been flown to Icelandic waters. From frogs to fossils, bring your marine curiosity to the aquarium.

Adjacent to the Oregon Coast Aquarium is the renovated public wing of the Hatfield Marine Science Center (HMSC), which is part of Oregon State University's coastal research facility. In addition to a live octopus that you can touch, tide pool animals, and other fish in tanks, interactive exhibits let you touch base with the latest in marine research, from chaos theory, the geology of underwater hot springs, and whale sounds, to diagnosing fish and crab diseases. Check to see if there is a current Seatauqua program with workshops on such subjects as winter steelheading, tide pools at night, bay crabbing, sand dune ecology, coastal geology, Indian crafts, cooking sea vegetables, birding, coastal fossils, the art of clamming, coastal plants, and the art of Japanese fish printing.

People from around the world visit the official whale-watching sites along the Oregon coast during gray whale migrations— the last week of December and during spring break. They learn about mammal behavior from HMSC and state park volunteers.

SITES WITH VOLUNTEERS (NORTH TO SOUTH):

Yaquina Head Lighthouse *
Don A. Davis City Kiosk * **
Yaquina Bay State Recreation Site *
Seal Rock State Recreation Site *
Yachats State Park *
Devil's Churn Viewpoint
Cape Perpetua Overlook
Cape Perpetua Interpretive Center * **
Cooks Chasm Turnout *
Sea Lion Caves Turnout *
Umpqua Lighthouse *
Shore Acres State Park * **
Face Rock State Scenic Viewpoint *
Cape Blanco Lighthouse *
Battle Rock Wayfinding Point *
Cape Sebastian State Scenic Corridor *
Cape Ferrelo *
Harris Beach State Park *

* Wheelchair-accessible
** Enclosed observation building

One of Oregon's most visited places, the Yaquina Bay Lighthouse overlooks the ocean at the mouth of the Yaquina River. After it was no longer used, tales spread that the structure was haunted by the ghost of Muriel, a girl who disappeared while visiting the light at night, leaving only blood stains. The lighthouse is now restored, with a museum and gift shop, and is on the National Registry of Historic Places as part as Yaquina Bay State Park. At Christmas it is ablaze with holiday lights.

Three large campgrounds provide choices for shelter and activities in the Newport area. Beverly Beach State Park is halfway between the wild wave action at Devil's Punch Bowl in Otter Rock and the Yaquina Head Lighthouse, and it offers access to forest and beach walks. Pacific Shores RV Park is near Yaquina Head Outstanding Natural Area and has lots of

Special Events:
Located in historic Nye Beach in the center of Newport, the Performing Arts Center and Visual Arts Center have a year-round flow of exhibits and entertainment. The Seafood and Wine Festival in February is at the Newport Marina.

amenities. South Beach State Park has trails to the forest, beach, and the south jetty of Yaquina Bay, where you can watch birds and boats at sea.

South to Florence

In addition to the natural wonders of the coast, every town along the highway has special attractions. Waldport is proud of the dramatic new bridge across Alsea Bay and the visitor center that commemorates it. In Yachats, residents fought hard to preserve a trail that borders booming surf along a swatch of scalloped cliffs and offshore rocks. This is a 0.75-mile (1.2 km), wheelchair-accessible paved walk at Smelt Sands Wayside. Some viewing places are more spectacular than others, and the surf action is not always the same at any one place because of variations in wind, tide, currents, and weather, so try more than one place when you go out.

The approach to Cape Perpetua is postcard pretty, with ridges of misty mountains edging the sea. The fury of winter waves meeting the rocky shore is overwhelming at several stops where Cape Perpetua jogs into the sea. Trails of all lengths and difficulty weave through this area, some down paths that lead to churning coves, a spouting horn, and rocky shelves of tide pools. Other trails climb up Cape Perpetua, lead to a giant spruce tree, and one loops high and long into the coastal forest. Maps and exhibits are available at the forest service visitor center. A road also leads to the top of the 803-foot (245 m) cape to the short Whispering Spruce Loop Trail, where views stretch vast and wide over miles of ocean, coastline, and wildlife sightings.

The Heceta Head Lighthouse is one of Oregon's most photogenic lights; you've probably seen photos of it perched on Heceta Head at the north end of sweeping swells moving into Cape Cove. A short trail in Devil's Elbow State Park climbs gently to the lighthouse, with smashing vistas of the rocky coastline. You'll see the Heceta House en route, an 1893 Queen Anne-style residence that is now a historic landmark and, according to local rumors,

haunted. The television movie *Cry for a Stranger* was filmed here.

The best place to photograph the lighthouse is at pullouts south of the Conde McCullough bridge and the tunnel to the steep, craggy cape that includes Sea Lion Point.

Wild Steller's sea lions—the males grow to 2,000 pounds—are the attraction at popular Sea Lion Caves on this cape. Also called northern sea lions, they are a threatened species and strictly protected. Sea birds and these mammals are active outside the cave in spring and summer. Elevators carry you 208 feet underground to view the huge cave at the edge of the cliffs where the sea lions spend time in winter.

Forty Miles of Coastal Sand Dunes

Another coastal town at the mouth of a river, Florence, features an old town bayfront of walking dimensions along the Siuslaw River, complete with tourist shops and good clam chowder. Across the picturesque bridge is the beginning of the Oregon Dunes National Recreation Area (ODNRA).

When I first visited the Oregon coast, I thought this 40 miles (64 km) of coastal sand dunes just prevented me from getting to the beaches. Now I'd just as soon explore the sand dunes as visit a beach; they are equally fascinating. Mile-long oblique formations of sand stretch to the sea, providing golden curves and ocean panoramas for anyone who walks atop them. Lakes sparkle. Translucent blue pools lie in valleys. A patch of flowers on the sand catches the eye. Wavy patterns, textures, even the tracks of animals seem like mystical writings on the sand. Wildlife is here, although it is often elusive. Ospreys fly to their nests in the broken tops of trees. Deer move through early and late in the day. In fact, 425 species of wildlife find habitats in the ODNRA. Included in the scattered 26 distinct habitats are wetlands, salt marsh, and rhododendron-splashed coastal forest.

Strangely, it is a landscape where you can observe plant succession happening quite easily, from pioneer plants to coastal

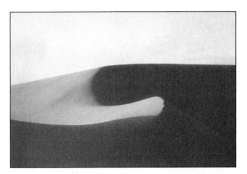

Dune formations in Oregon Dunes National Recreation Area.

forests. Plants and trees struggle on the sand hills; some live, some die. But always the landscape moves and changes. In winter sunshine it's an enchanting place, but you need to venture into the magic, to walk into quiet and solitude in this open landscape—a terrain of solace. Take note of orientation clues, however, to avoid getting lost. Then see what you discover. Try to find a transverse dune, an oblique dune, a forest island, a deflation plain, a foredune, and a parabola dune.

A good base for exploring the dunes is Honeyman State Park, just south of Florence. In the 1950s, *Life* magazine called this one of the outstanding state parks in the United States. It's a popular picnicking and camping spot, with good representation of those elements that constitute the Oregon Dunes. Trails in the park edge three lakes—Cleowox, Lily, and Woahink—where water activities dominate in warmer months. But the fun is in climbing the massive dunes; it's definitely aerobic exercise. Canada geese often hang out at the edge of Woahink Lake.

Reedsport is sheltered by a long arm of sand dunes edging the mouth of the North Umpqua River, which is a major contributor to the sand supply of the dunes. Centrally located, the ODNRA visitor center offers maps complete with trail locations, lakes, picnic spots, and campgrounds, as well as information on history, geology, dune formations, and fishing.

Before heading south to more dunes, consider a side trip a few miles east of Reedsport on OR 38 to the Dean Creek Elk

Viewing Area. A stop there almost guarantees seeing several Roosevelt Elk in the bottomlands near the river.

Several trails in the ODNRA begin in coastal forest and then wander up and down across open sand to foredunes on the ocean; some have posts in the sand marking the way at intervals. Siltcoos Dunes and Estuary, Oregon Dunes Overlook, and Tahkenitch areas all feature several trails. Carter Lake offers a trail for physically impaired persons. The Umpqua Dunes Scenic Area, which is accessible from the Eel Creek campground (open year-round), has particularly high dunes and good representative habitats edging the sand; it is an outstanding place to explore. Climb a sand dune to watch the sunset. Notice how the ocean blazes a rich melon hue across the sand and then the color of the afterglow slowly shifts to a soft lavender that paints the sand hills and circles of water.

 Insider's Tip:
If quiet, safe hiking is on your itinerary, be warned that off-highway-vehicles are allowed in some areas; they are prohibited at Eel Creek, Tahkenitch, and the Oregon Dunes Overlook areas.

Another year-round campground edges the dunes near the active Umpqua River Lighthouse, just south of Winchester Bay, which has a popular sport-fishing marina. The first Oregon lighthouse here was sited on the north spit of the river in 1857, but that location was a bit unstable and the lighthouse fell into the river four years later. Another lighthouse was placed here in 1894 at a more secure location.

Oregon's Bay Area

The dramatic bridge spanning the Coos River marks the southern edge of the ODNRA and your entry into the twin cities of North Bend/Coos Bay—the coast's largest population center. This is Oregon's bay area, one of the world's largest timber ports. The cities are proud of their fine arts, crafts, myrtlewood shops, and the Oregon

Coast Music Festival (which is held in July).

This metropolitan area ends with an abrupt change of terrain to the south, a wild mixture of cliffs, coves, booming surf, and rugged forested slopes, around which US 101 detours. You can reach this area from Coos Bay, where signs point the way to Charleston, a fishing town on the South Slough arm of the bay. The mudflats here are thick with clammers during a good low tide. The major attractions, however, are a trio of coastal state parks reached via the Cape Arago Highway: Sunset Bay, Shore Acres, and Cape Arago.

It is hard to imagine that these three park jewels once comprised the family estate of California shipping magnate and the founder of North Bend, Louis J. Simpson. And although the palatial homes where he entertained famous visitors are now gone,

South Slough National Estuarine Sanctuary near Charleston, OR.

Oregon Coast Trail

Begun in 1971, the Oregon Coast Trail was the dream of Samuel L. Dicken, a geography teacher at the University of Oregon who explored the proposed route for the trail. When completed, the Oregon Coast Trail will eventually cover the coast of the entire state. Still a priority for the state parks system, it is approximately 60 percent complete. For a brochure on completed sections and connections to these along the entire coast, write the Oregon Parks and Recreation Department.

much of the magic remains. Sunset Bay features a protected ocean cove that is shallow enough for calm, warm water. In the forest across the highway a year-round campground provides access to a 3-mile (4.8-km) section of the Oregon Coast Trail along the cliff-tops. It connects the three parks and provides views of the Cape Arago Lighthouse.

Shore Acres is the site of a botanical garden started by Simpson and maintained by the park system. Although the gardens are not so colorful in winter, they still provide a soothing walk among the graceful plantings and bronze herons in the lily pond of the sunken oriental garden. During

the Christmas holidays, colored lights decorate trees and the geometric plantings. The original Garden House welcomes visitors at this time for refreshments among its antique furnishings and historic photographs. If you arrive before dusk, you might catch a luminous sunset complementing this fairyland of festive colors. Thousands of people come from around the world to be part of this holiday scene.

A glass-enclosed observation building, which offers protection for winter visitors while they scan the ocean for gray whales, sits on the former homesite. This is one of the premier spots for watching the winter surf fanning out from its collisions with offshore rocks and sandstone cliffs. The walkways are sometimes inundated by the powerful assault of sea spray. Cove after cove has been sculpted by dramatic ocean encounters and the constant shaping of the rocky coast. Surf booms everywhere.

The geology here is an exquisite collage of shapes. Layers of rock are exposed, some

Special Event:
During the last three weeks of December, Friends of Shore Acres welcome visitors to the Holiday Lights Celebration at Shore Acres Botanical Gardens that features 100,000 lights. Also check out the parade of lighted boats in Coos Bay.

tilted sideways, some thrown flat with long creases. Groups of punched holes and rounded knobs add patterns and textures. Red-billed black oystercatchers move easily on the steep walls. Take care of yourself, however; the steep, slippery, and eroding cliffs pose dangers for any humans climbing about.

At road's end is the third park, Cape Arago, where ribbons of rain pour down the high cliffs as waterfalls. Three separate coves are rich with intertidal life. Great blue herons move in at low tide to partake of the riches that consist of tide pool sculpins, sea stars, giant green anemones, sea urchins, black turban snails, tiny porcelain crabs, three species of chitons, and much more. Offshore is Simpson Reef, a stretch of rocks that is home to seals and sea lions. You can't miss their barking.

Seven Devils Road running south from Charleston provides a connecting highway back to US 101 and access to the South Slough National Estuarine Sanctuary—the first of its kind—in 4 miles (6.4 km). Some of the rich wetlands of the bay area have been preserved. The sanctuary includes a visitor center, hiking trails, fishing, educational workshops, and canoeing routes from Charleston. It's a fascinating place full of Indian and pioneering history that is now reverting to a more pristine landscape and research preserve.

Oregon's Oldest and Wildest Coast

Coastal towns vary in ambiance and especially in the allure of their beaches, but few can claim to match the spectacular beach at Bandon. Miles and miles of sand attract beachcombers to walk among the ever changing profusion of sea stacks and tide pools, perhaps scanning for agates, jasper, and other rocks, or looking for glass floats and other artifacts tossed ashore by winter storms. It's never just boring sand and ocean here. Oregonians get spoiled; they expect the dramatic in their special beaches.

A wheelchair-accessible walkway was built recently atop the cliffs at Bandon's Coquille Point as part of the Oregon Islands

National Wildlife Refuge. This trail is complete with interpretive panels overlooking offshore seabird colonies. This is accessed, along with a Face Rock viewpoint and other state waysides, via the town's Beach Loop. Several stops have trails downhill to the long stretch of beach.

Bandon also boasts an old-town walk past fine galleries, crafts, shops, restau-

Surf action at Shore Acres State Park.

rants, and a seafood market along the Coquille River where you can buy fresh fish. A striking and much photographed feature of the area is the Coquille River Lighthouse, located on the north bank of the river. Bullards Beach State Park, with trails to the lighthouse and beach, is in the same area; horse trails wander north from the park. This lighthouse was abandoned and then restored as an historic museum. Now it features great old photographs of days when ships sailed up the river and serves as a place from which to watch winter storms. It is awash with lights during the holiday season.

Special Events:
Instructional programs about local points of interest are conducted each Saturday during winter by the Bandon Stormwatchers. You are also invited to join them for storm watching.

A stop at the West Coast Game Park south of Bandon is always fun. Sometimes you'll see a baby tiger or lion, but there are always many tame and often exotic animals that you can feed and pet in the walk-through area. More dangerous animals are safely caged. The park boasts more than 75 species and 450 animals including camel, bear, cougar, leopard, tiger, and lion.

If the weather's not too windy and wild, a side trip to Cape Blanco promises a view to the oldest standing active lighthouse, the state's most westerly point, a state park (with winter camping for the brave), trails, and lots of beach exploring on both sides of the cape. You can dig for razor clams at low tide on the north beach. Be warned, however, that the storm winds blow harder here than anywhere else on the coast. Along this road is the renovated historic Hughes House; unfortunately, it is not open during the winter, but follow the park road past it down to the Sixes River for picnicking and excellent bird-watching.

Port Orford is the oldest townsite on the Oregon coast, founded with visions of gold mining success and later dreams of a famous port. It was the only natural deep-water harbor on the coast, although southwest winds and the lack of proper breakwater construction have kept it just one of Oregon's small ports. The port is unique, though; in winter, commercial fishing boats are hauled in and out of the water daily with a big hoist to prevent them from being swept ashore in storms. Adventurous people park nearby at a viewpoint to watch the surf hit the breakwater as their vehicles rock in the storm winds.

Sunny days often follow high winds. On such a day one Sunday in November, I sat on the headlands behind the port facing west and saw several whales playing in the kelp bed. They stayed for hours and were so close I could hear their loud intakes of air before I saw them surface. (In May of another year, I spotted a gray whale and her calf spouting in the shallow waters next to the harbor.)

I think of this coast as a connection to the wild. Although we ride in boats out into the sea, we are not at home there, not

Windsurfer near Port Orford, OR.

even on that corridor that is the constantly changing meeting place of land and sea. Yet we can walk out from the harbor of our civilization and encounter wonderful and unexpected wild things at this ragged seam where the water, air, and land meet. You might see a squadron of sanderlings scurry back and forth with the waves. Seagulls are sometimes like moving poems and at other times screaming scavengers. Surf scoters ride the incoming waves and then dive beneath the surface as the waves break. It takes time to observe other lives near the coast, but surely these wild things are part of the total experience of this environment. To see how wildlife responds to winter storms is a great eye-opener.

The popular town beach near Battle Rock (ask about the history of this) is long and stunning in its views and provides access to a nice tide pool area where you can walk though a slot in a rock formation. Writer Peter Farb once called this one of the world's great seascapes; see what you think. During the winter solstice here, I have watched the sunset and then turned around to see a moonrise. What you see depends on the weather.

Six miles (9.7 km) south is 1,748-foot (533-m) Humbug Mountain, the only mountain on the south coast that slopes right into the ocean. A 3-mile (4.8-km) trail climbs to the summit through a rare pocket of old-growth rain forest that includes myrtlewood and Port Orford cedar trees; this is a wonderful hike in any season. I've lunched often at the grassy plateau on top, but it faces south, so it is not a place to be during storms. A walkway goes under the highway from Humbug Mountain Campground to this trail.

The highway between Port Orford and the California border hugs the coast all the way and is a spectacular drive. This section of the coast is quieter—with less visitors and development—and is warmer year-round, so it is often called the "banana belt." It passes the famed Rogue River at Gold Beach, where jet boats now travel up-river even in winter. One of the most impressive vistas is at Cape Sebastian State Park—a steep uphill side trip for small rigs with enough power. I've been there when I was above the low-lying clouds—a mystical feeling. A Japanese submarine was also there at such a time. The boat surfaced to recharge its batteries and a caretaker heard only the foreign voice of a crew member. On a good day, consider the 2-mile trail down to the beach; the view on top to the west can blow you away on a windy day.

The highway downhill from Cape Sebastian provides a superb panoramic vista of the Myers Creek beach area of Pistol River State Park. It's difficult to resist a walk among the whale-size rocks on the beach.

The remaining miles to Brookings offer one superlative stop after the other in the Samuel H. Boardman State Park, perhaps the choicest piece of real estate on the Oregon coast. And that is fitting since Boardman, the first state parks' superintendent, played a major role in park development. If you like to hike, put on your walking shoes. Seven miles (11 km) of the Oregon Coast Trail are found in the park, with many access points for shorter hikes. This section is an up-and-down excursion along cliff tops and through the forest, with some descents to the sand. Watch for posts with signs for the trail.

The geology along the trail in Boardman is wonderfully diverse. Mack Arch and Arch Rock are the first fine introductions, with a picnic area at the latter. The north trailhead is not easily spotted, nor are there any signs, so I suggest hiking this area from the easier access at Natural Bridge Viewpoint, where you head north after viewing the bridge. Hike past Thunder Cove for 2 miles (3.2 km) to the trail's end at Miner Creek, a sandy beach cove where you may find deer tracks. A waterfall plunges down to the sea from the creek and spruce-topped offshore sea stacks add to the scenic composition. You could not imagine a more idyllic spot.

The trail continues to the southern trailhead at Cape Ferrelo, sometimes taking to the road for a spell. Other appealing short hikes are north from Indian Sands to the 345-foot-high (105-m) Thomas Creek Bridge or south from Indian Sands to Whalehead Cove. Watch for peregrine falcons, gray whales, and sea birds. If you walk little, however, you won't be disappointed at the many viewpoints along the road where you can pull over and feast your eyes. The perfect base for spending time in this area is Harris Beach State Park, which has its own share of ocean and beach enticements.

Across the Chetco River from Brookings is the busy local port at Harbor, where sailboats, charter boats, and a commercial fishing fleet make harbor walks intriguing. The prelude to the Dungeness crab pot-fishing season, which usually begins December 1, is an exciting time to explore the port. The boats are being readied for sea, and if you look high in the rigging you might find a fisherman at work.

The southern Oregon coast is special in winter. The wild things, the fresh sea air, the staggering complexity of nature's rocky shores, the seafood delicacies, the solitude, the sighting of a gray whale, the sand dunes at sunset, the patterns of driftwood on the beach, and the sights and sounds of wild surf will touch your inner self.

CHAPTER 14

Baja:
The Native Essence of Baja Sur

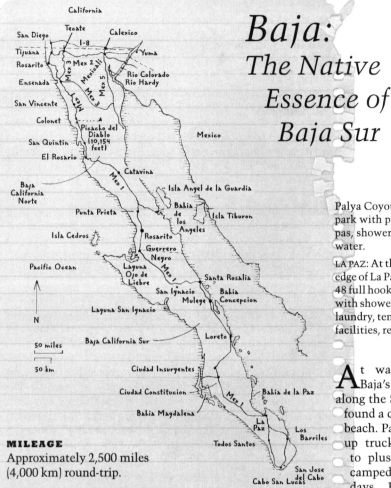

Palya Coyote has an RV park with pit toilets, palapas, showers, and drinking water.

LA PAZ: At the western edge of La Paz on Mexico 1; 48 full hookups, restrooms with showers, pool and spa, laundry, tennis court, beach facilities, restaurant and bar.

At water's edge on Baja's prettiest bay along the Sea of Cortez, I found a campsite on the beach. Parking my pickup truck camper next to plush RV buses, I camped free for a few days. First light on Bahia Concepcion came seductively, then blazed into a gold-speckled, burnt orange as Mexican fishermen emerged from their palm-thatched shack, launched a small boat, and carved a shimmering wake into the sunrise. Brown pelicans in breeding plumage posed majestically on the water, backed by the silhouettes of mountains. A white egret stalked breakfast a few feet from my site in the gentle surf that swirled around a collection of sea shells. A stillness made the whole scene a collage of magical

MILEAGE
Approximately 2,500 miles (4,000 km) round-trip.

RESOURCES
- Mexico's federal tourist bureau, the Secretaria de Turismo (SECTUR), has its main offices in Mexicali and La Paz. Branch offices are in Tijuana, Ensenada, Tecate, Rosarito, San Felipe, San Quintin, and Loreto. Brochures, maps, hotel and restaurant lists, and information on local activities are usually available.

CAMPGROUNDS
RVers will find plenty of campgrounds. Some are primitive, but most developed areas have some with hookups. You can also pull off the road and camp outside the cities with few restrictions. Consider adding a solar panel to assist in boondocking.

ORCHARD RV PARK: In Mulege; tent and RV sites along the river; restrooms with hot showers, dump station.

BAHIA CONCEPCION: From north to south: Punta Arena is 2.5 miles (4 km) from Mexico 1, with palapas and popular with windsurfers; Playa Santispac is the most developed, with showers, toilets, and kayaks for rent; Playa El Burro has palapas;

forms and colors that were ever so soothing to the human spirit. It was January and the weather was perfect.

How many RV destinations can be so rewarding, so much an excursion into the carefree life of the traveler? I know of no such place in the United States so totally undeveloped, yet accessible and inspiring in its beauty, as Baja. True, you must drive there through a foreign country whose language you might not speak, but a little planning and essential information will easily equip you for the trip. The main highway is not so different from many secondary highways in the United States.

Except for a few large cities, which are easily avoided if you so desire, Baja has few people. It's mostly landscapes to explore— a place where you have space and nature, a place where you have time to contemplate and to quietly observe. The southern half of the peninsula, Baja California Sur, is Mexico's least populated state. It seems a place for which the self-sufficient RV rig was designed. More than 50 percent of visitors to Baja choose camping. And although you should always be alert and cautious, I traveled the length of this peninsula alone at age 55 and never felt unsafe, camping all the way. I found the people to be warm and friendly.

Although the first maps created by sixteenth-century Spanish explorers depicted Baja as an island, it is a peninsula connected to the Mexican mainland at its northern extremity, the Sea of Cortez separating the land masses that were split apart by movement along the San Andreas Fault. Until 1973, travel through this "forgotten peninsula" was a matter of rough roads and four-wheel-drive vehicles, but that changed with the completion of the Transpeninsular Highway (Mexico 1), which journeys south to Cabo San Lucas in 1,704 km (1,059 miles). Surrounded on three sides by water, Baja is 193 km (120 miles) in width near the United States border and narrows to 45 km (28 miles) near La Paz. Therein lies one reason why Baja is so fascinating. Although two-thirds of this land is Sonoran Desert— with intriguing plant species—you are never far from the often-wild Pacific coast,

with its lagoons and coves, nor many miles from the Sea of Cortez (the Gulf of California) and its tranquil bays. The gulf is biologically the richest body of water on the planet, an added attraction for kayakers, snorkelers, and scuba divers. Birders should note that around 300 species are seen in the vicinity of Baja. And the peninsula is justly famous for its year-round fishing.

Winter is a great time to visit Baja. Not only is the weather usually fine the length of the peninsula, with little rain (except in the northwest area), but winter is also when many Americans and Canadians es-

Before You Go

No visa is required for U.S. or Canadian citizens. For a stay longer than 72 hours or travel south of Ensenada, a validated "tourist card" is necessary. A tourist card is good for stays of up to 180 days and can be obtained free of charge at a Mexican consulate or tourist office, at many U.S. travel agencies, or at the border. Validation is done by a Mexican immigration officer, most conveniently at the border, or in Ensenada. Do have proof of citizenship or a passport. No vehicle permits are required for Baja, only for the mainland.

U.S. automobile insurance is not valid in Mexico; acquire short-term insurance for Mexico at agencies in the States before entering Baja and carry a copy of the policy.

cape cold weather and snow storms. In the interior, you'll see such travelers more often than the natives.

Mexican money is the nuevo ("new peso"), which is worth one thousand times the value of the old peso. Banks offer the best exchange rates.

Night travel is not advised because of all the livestock that wanders onto the highway; be especially alert going around blind curves. The speed limit on most highways is 80 kilometers per hour (48 mph); the relatively narrow roads are 6–8 m (19–25 feet maximum) wide. Knowledge of sign shapes comes in handy and knowing the following words is helpful: *Curva Peligrosa* (Dangerous Curve); *Despacio* (Slow);

Zona de Vadoss (Dip Zone); *Desviacion* (Detour); *No Tire Basura* (Don't Throw Trash); *No Rebase* (No Passing); *No Hay Paso* (Road Closed); *Alto* (Stop); *E* (Parking); *Circulacion* (One Way); *Ceda el Paso* (Yield); *Solo Izo* (with an arrow curving left—Left Turn Only); *Parada* (Bus); *Conserve su Derecha* (Keep to the Right); and *Llantera* (Repair Shop).

Automotive fuel is sold only at government-owned Pemex stations (no credit cards accepted); leaded (*Nova*), higher-octane unleaded (*Magna Sin*), and diesel are available. Be prepared for long stretches without services. Consider carrying some spare vehicles parts. Rest a little easier knowing that the Secretaria de Turismo operates a fleet of 275 green pickup trucks called *Angeles Verdes* (Green Angels) that patrol the highways looking for vehicles in trouble. They are equipped to remedy problems or to get you to help.

Most side roads are dirt and are not easy to travel for most RVs. Mountain bikes are great for dirt road explorations. Although some areas offer boat rentals, consider carrying an aluminum skiff, sea kayak, canoe, or inflatable atop your pickup or small rig. It is best to limit RV caravans to two or three vehicles. For detailed information on side trips, carry a detailed map.

Pets may not be welcome in many places, so leave them at home unless this is unavoidable. A certificate signed by a veterinarian stating that the pet is in good health and has had rabies and distemper shots must be obtained within 30 days before entering Baja.

The Border to Ensenada

Baja has five official border crossings (west to east): Tijuana, Otay Mesa, Tecate, Mexicali, and Algodones. For this tour, the three western crossings are nearest to the route. Tijuana, however, is a large city and very congested—not a good place to begin confronting Mexican drivers. Otay Mesa bypasses the downtown area of Tijuana. Tecate is one of Baja's most relaxed border crossings, an inviting old town without industrial pollution. At any crossing, try to avoid busy hours by crossing at midday and during the week.

The drive from Tecate to Ensenada on Mexico 3 weaves through mostly uninhabited chaparral country of rolling hills along the slopes of Sierra Juarez, and traffic is usually light. The route passes Mision Guadalupe and vineyards. The alternate route from Tijuana heads to Ensenada via a toll road (Mexico 1D) or Mexico 1; this is a busy, tourist section of Baja more typical of southern California. The highways do pass Rosarito, fish camps, and beach stopovers, although access is limited on the toll road.

Buying Supplies

Although most residents of Baja away from the large cities don't speak English, it's easy to learn enough Spanish to keep you well fed. Plan on doing your own cooking in the sparsely populated areas away from restaurants, where even the smallest markets can provide bottled water and the ingredients for an easy-to-fix meal, especially one with some Mexican flavors, such as avocado, queso fresco (fresh cheese), pan dulce (sweet pastry), or bolillos (European-style rolls). Choices are more varied in larger towns where government-sponsored markets, CONASUPO or CONASUPER, are found. Privately owned supermarkets are called supers or supermercados, while smaller stores are tienda de abarrotes (abarrotes means "groceries"). The best place to buy bakery items is at a panaderia, where they are made. Knowing the names of a few food items is helpful: carne de res (beef), pollo (chicken), puerco (pork), pescado ("catch of the day"), camarones (shrimp), langosta (lobster), abulon (abalone), and taco de pescado (fish taco—Baja's number-one seafood specialty).

Unpeeled fruits and vegetables purchased at markets are the best ones to add to your diet. For health reasons, don't eat peeled, raw fruit and vegetables; it's impossible to disinfect such produce. Restaurants and hotels serve purified water; tap water should not be consumed. Some people do get intestinal upsets (turista) because the gastrointestinal flora of the area are different from those to which most tourists are acclimated. Eating and drinking in moderation will help prevent the symptoms of nausea and diarrhea, which shouldn't last but a day or two.

In addition to being the largest port in Baja and a trade center for fishing and agriculture, Ensenada is a bustling coastal city frequented by millions of weekend and summer tourists. It is a fine city for strolling, but many of the popular scenic attractions are a few miles south.

A good road branches off Mexico 1 to the tip of Punta ("point") Banda, where *La Bufadora* ("Buffalo's Snort") is an attraction. It is named for the sound produced as incoming waves rush into an underground cave and are then spewed out noisily some 25 to 30 meters (82 to 98 feet) high through a blowhole. Scan for gray whales. Many visitors come to scuba dive, kayak, or camp; some set up house on the beach and watch the many birds fly by.

Ensenada to El Rosario

South of Maneadero, the highway weaves through green valleys dotted with a succession of small villages, farms, olive groves, and vineyards. From here to El Rosario, you are not far from the ocean, and a tangle of unpaved roads head for beaches, fish camps, and surfing spots.

To the east are mountain ranges that form the northwest-southeast spine of the peninsula, mostly fault-block mountains, but a few are volcanic. These are the same sierras that run south from the Aleutian Islands through the United States to land's end at Cabo San Lucas. Adventurous RVers, with the necessary rig and gear, might head east to the conifer-topped granite peaks of Parque Nacional Sierra San Pedro Martir, one of Mexico's national parks that is reached via a 78-km (47-mile) unpaved but graded road south and east of Colonel. At the end of the park access road, a national observatory at 9,286 feet (2,830 m) offers tours every Saturday at 11 A.M. Hikers will find exciting trails. Snow sometimes closes the road in winter, but passenger cars can negotiate the road most of the year.

Back on Mexico 1, the highway runs near the ocean through more farm communities that produce vegetables and fruit. Colonia Vicente Gurrero is becoming an agricultural center with good services for

travelers and access to the beach, where you can find pismo clams and watch brilliant sunsets brushing the sea. Mision Santo Domingo lies north and east of the town.

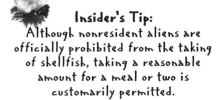

Insider's Tip:
Although nonresident aliens are officially prohibited from the taking of shellfish, taking a reasonable amount for a meal or two is customarily permitted.

Weather at the farming community of Valle de San Quintin is influenced by the insulating character of its three bays, and the climate is similar to that of San Francisco, with foggy summers and temperatures in December to January in the mid-50s. It is chiefly a destination for anglers and hunters. It has many unpaved roads, but the complex coastal environment of bays, tidal flats, volcanic cones, and salt marshes attracts those interested in clamming and scuba diving. South of the town, Mexico 1 is quite close to the ocean, with beach access and campgrounds for enjoying the Pacific side of the peninsula. Windsurfers and surfers have long explored this Pacific coastline for favorite spots.

The highway enters a more arid region and climbs through coastal hills to a mesa that drops steeply into El Rosario. You may also notice mounds of sea urchin shells along the road, remains of a local industry that harvests sea urchins and extracts the gonads. Ninety percent of the harvest is quickly flown to Japan, where it is considered a tasty addition to their sushi fare.

Not long ago, El Rosario was the last place along the route where you could communicate by telephone. It was also considered the last outpost before entering the wilds of Baja. Another claim to fame are the ten tons of bones from a giant duckbill dinosaur found in the area. In the 1960s, El Rosario became a checkpoint for the Baja 1000 off-road race and the first landing site of the Flying Samaritans, volunteer North American doctors. The family of Mama Espinosa—who contributed greatly to the initial success of both of these endeavors—has operated the small restaurant, Espinosa's Place, since before the Transpeninsular Highway was completed, and their burritos, from bean to lobster, have fed a good number of the travelers who came this way.

The Vizcaino Desert

As the highway heads inland and southeast from El Rosario, many travelers feel they are entering "the real Baja," the desert landscape they've read and dreamt about, which is extravagantly edged with mountains. From here south is where you want to be in winter. Although still part of the Sonoran Desert, different locations and weather factors support specific flora and fauna, so each area has its own charisma. This is the Vizcaino Desert, a landscape thought such a classic desert habitat by the designers of Biosphere II (an ecological research laboratory in Arizona) that they modeled their dome's desert biome after it.

Not too many miles farther, weird-looking plants resembling huge feathery, upside-down carrots (some grow to 18 m or 60 feet) dot the landscape. When geographer Godfrey Sykes discovered this odd plant, he said, "Ho, ho! A boojum, definitely a boojum!" And so, inspired by Lewis Carroll, he named it the boojum tree. Cardon is "king" of the cactus, larger even than the saguaro. Ocotilla, Baja fairy duster, tree yucca, mesquite, ironwood, paloblanco ("white stick"), and the striking elephant tree are some of the plants you'll see along desert walks. The pitaya cactus was a most favored Indian food. John Steinbeck wrote that the sound of the Baja Sonoran Desert was the crackling of mesquite and ironwood seeds by mice and rats. Animal life in the peninsula's desert is often more bizarre than the flora. The chuckwalla lizard stores fresh water that gurgles as it walks, but it can desalinate salty water if necessary. Centipedes leave tracks.

One reason I find the Baja desert so much fun is the ease of wandering freely across the desert from the road—no fences prohibit you from doing so. One place in particular is outstanding: the Catavina Boulder Field, just north of Catavina. Wander about and check out the various desert plants (even blooming flowers), a colorful shrine, and petroglyphs. Winter weather is perfect for off-road desert excursions by foot. You'll find campgrounds at Catavina.

Desert fascinations continue past small summits and through arroyos, valleys, and dry lakes to near Punta Prieta, where Mexico 1 splits. The east fork is a pretty drive through three scenic canyons and several washes. It also provides a great view of the intensely blue water and rumpled mountains of offshore islands as you come into Bahia de Los Angeles, a small serene natural harbor on the Sea of Cortez. Although anglers have been flying into the town for some time, it is still a quiet place without telephones. The bay is sheltered by Isla Angel de la Guarda, and several species of whales, dolphins, and sea turtles are frequently spotted in its waters. Offshore fishing in winter is best for yellowtail; panga (small boats) rentals and guided fishing trips are available. Because of all the coves and numerous small islands offshore, kayaking is a fine way to spend a day. Novice kayakers should check the free guidelines at Guillermo's Restaurant. Brown pelicans in mating plumage flock in to grab the fishing debris when the catch is brought to shore. Several campgrounds with varied amenities are located north and south of town and offer some fine primitive sites near the beach.

Guerrero Negro, Scammon's Lagoon, and Whale Watching

Almost immediately after crossing the 28th parallel on the main fork of Mexico 1—and entering Mountain Time and Baja California Sur—a road to Guerrero Negro heads west. The town is named after a Hawaii-ported whaling vessel, the *Black Warrior*, that was so overloaded with whale oil in 1858 that it sank while being towed out to sea. Charles Melville Scammon discovered the mating and birthing place of the gray whales—Baja coastal lagoons—in the 1940s. He estimated that 10,000 gray whales were killed between 1846 and 1874. After the gray whale became an endangered

San Ignacio Mission, San Ignacio, Mexico.

species, conservation efforts have revived their numbers to some 21,000. Baja is the southern terminus of their annual migration from the Arctic, and January to March is when you can visit Scammon's Lagoon (Laguna Ojo de Liebre) to observe these giant cetaceans.

Both Malarrimo Restaurant (which features great lobster and other kinds of seafood) and Grupo Mario's (which can be contacted at Restaurant Bar Mario's) in Guerrero Negro organize small group tours of Scammon's Lagoon via a panga, with lunch included on Isla Arena, which is a large sandbar island covered with exquisite white dunes.

Although these whale-watching tour groups are taken by van from Guerrero Negro, I drove out one day to an old salt wharf on the bay, 7 miles (11 km) west from the center of town on C. Allendre. This wide gravel road offers great bird-watching. Long-legged egrets, curlews, and tricolor herons move silently through the grasses of wetlands. Take binoculars and consider doing this at sunset for some outstanding photographic opportunities. I found Mexican children dancing near the wharf, local fishermen twirling lines (without any poles) to catch fish, and ospreys building nests on abandoned concrete towers.

A less expensive way to tour Scammon's Lagoon is to travel the 15-mile (24-km) road that intersects Mexico 1, 5.5 miles (9 km) south of town. However, this very slow route alternates between rough washboard and sandy surfaces passable by passenger car in dry weather. The road passes through a salt company checkpoint at 3.5 miles (6 km), where you often must wait for an attendant to open the gate. Pangas are usually available for tours on the lagoon. No private boats, kayaks, sailboards, or inflatable rafts are allowed on the lagoon during the whale season. This location is in Parque Natural de la Ballena Gris, the world's first gray whale sanctuary. Writer Erle Stanley Gardner loved to explore the nearby desert and coastal terrain.

Primitive camping is allowed in the park along the shore of the lagoon. Overnighting here—and the white dunes tour—were highlights of my Baja trip. Being one of a few humans among wild things was wonderful. A flock of willets flew by and gathered food, and I walked into the surrounding desert contemplating how long ago the gray whale was called the "desert whale" by the Indians. Seen from the distance, the spouts of these whales seem to rise out of the desert vastness. The sunset was brilliant and the next morning I was treated to the sight of a full moon setting over the water.

San Ignacio to Mulege

On the January morning I drove the highway east across the peninsula to San Ignacio, an overnight rain had left expanses of yellow and rose wildflowers carpeting the desert floor. I couldn't resist stopping to walk a vehicle track that curved through the scene. A bleached cow skull and a piece of weathered desert wood among the colors made excellent subjects for a still-life photograph.

A palm-tree lined street that crosses Rio San Ignacio takes you into San Ignacio, a charming small town with pastel buildings around a tree-shaded plaza. The town gives the impression of being an oasis in the desert—and indeed, dates are a good buy here. But the main attraction is the picturesque, bougainvillea-draped Spanish mission with its stone steps, recessed statues, four-foot-thick walls of volcanic stone, and intricately carved doors. Whale-watching tours are available from here to Laguna San Ignacio, and also to the famous rock art in caves and arroyos north of San Ignacio in the Sierra de San Francisco.

The highway to Santa Rosalia winds through rolling hills quite close to the Tres Virgenes, three distinct volcanic cones that rise above the yucca and cardon cactus. It's a delightful landscape, particularly when crowned by white clouds. The road climbs into a range of eroded hills before it descends to a coastal plain and the mining town of Santa Rosalia.

Mulege and Bahia Concepcion

Another oasis—and a favorite stopover—is Mulege, located by the estuary of the Santa Rosalia River along the Gulf of California, with its outstanding fishing. Mulege embodies the essence of being comfortable and old but picturesque, and it has all the amenities and necessities you'll need. With its crops of dates, figs, bananas, oranges, and olives, it was a regional market center long before the Transpeninsular Highway brought tourists to the area. Far enough south and located by the water, it has the feel of the tropics.

Mulege dates back to 1705 and the founding of Mission Santa Rosalia de Mulege, which is just upstream from the bridge over Mexico 1. A pathway to the mission passes through lush vegetation bordered by banana plants, to a terrace where a tower offers a lovely hilltop view of the date-palm-edged river, the town, and the hills to the south. Several choices for campsites invite stays, but excellent facilities and surroundings are at Orchard RV Park. Along the river, campers can enjoy free fruit (mangoes, dates, figs, oranges, and limes) from the orchard. You should walk to town from the riverfront parks; the streets of Mulege are too narrow for RV rigs.

A few miles south of Mulege is the long western shoreline of Bahia Concepcion, which is a magnet for campers. Its many

coves, sandy beaches, spits, islands, and cobalt-blue water offer breathtaking and constantly changing views. Bayfront camping is mostly primitive but varied, and the fun is finding a place that pleases you, not a slot in an RV park. Boating, kayaking, diving, fishing, sailing, and windsurfing are all popular. Checking the birds, the sea shells, and the underwater life—which includes sea turtles—is equally rewarding. Sunrises are enchanting. One of the cleanest marine bay systems in the world, the bay is now a national marine preserve. Do your part to keep the water clean.

Loreto and Puerto Escondido

To drive into Loreto, park, and stroll the streets on a Sunday morning, as I did once, is to experience an intercultural connection as a quiet observer. From the cobblestone plaza, I had an excellent view of Mission de Nuestra Señora de Loreto ("Our Lady of Loreto") as the bells rang for the morning service and people entered though the high arched doorway. Children played ball outside until the last minute, when they were welcomed and hugged by the priest. It was an expression of the warmth of the culture that can be found in this rugged interior that comes from the heart and affects the traveler.

Mulege Campground on the Santa Rosalia River.

Founded in 1697 with the establishment of a Spanish mission—which was not completed until 1752—Loreto is the oldest permanent European settlement in the Californias which, at that time, included considerable land in what is now the United States. Loreto was the capital of this area for over 130 years until a hurricane demolished much of the town; the capital was then moved to La Paz. Loreta was rejuvenated by anglers who learned of the exceptional gulf fishing and flew in to try their luck, although it is still a peaceful place away from crowds.

The Fondo Nacional de Fomento al Turismo (FONATUR), a project funded by the government, has attempted to create a mega-resort in the area and to change sleepy Loreto. Although the Loreto Inn, tennis center, and golf course at Nopolo Bay, along with the new marina at Puerto Escondido (now Puerto Loreto) are the beginnings of development south of the town, Loreto itself has remained relatively unspoiled. Several campgrounds with hookups are located in Loreto, and the port has long attracted sailors.

In its continued attempt to lead travelers to the best of Baja, Mexico 1 now heads west across the Magdalena Plains toward Bahia Magdalena, passing green fields, range cattle, perhaps a caracara hawk, and going through a couple of commercial agricultural centers with their good markets and restaurants. Bahia Magdalena is the third lagoon heavily inundated with gray whales during the winter season. Paved roads lead to both Puerto Lopez Mateos and San Carlos—the only other deep-water port on the Pacific coast besides Ensenada—where whale watching information and panga tours are found. Birds are numerous by the water.

Our tour now crosses a lonely stretch of 134 miles (216 km) traversing the interior to La Paz; the only Pemex station is about midway at El Cien. When I stopped there a few years ago to photograph a small church, a group of smiling young children rushed out to greet me. Warm and welcoming, they happily posed for me and added human interest to the photo. Such are the travel experiences that become treasured memories.

La Paz and the East Cape

After the recent lonely cross-country journey, you might want to overnight in La Paz, where several campgrounds with enticing amenities are found along the western edge of the city off Mexico 1. As the sun sets over the bay and sailboats move across the water, a walk along the city's seaward promenade ("meleco'n") is a great way to spend an evening. La Paz is an easygoing large city that's little changed since writer John Steinbeck saw it in 1941 and called it "a lovely place." Thousands of pearls were once harvested from oysters along this coast, and it was here that Steinbeck heard a tale that inspired his novel *The Pearl*. To reach the ferry port to the mainland, head east along the bayfront via Mexico 11 to Pichilinque.

 Insider's Tip:
A vehicle permit is needed on the mainland of Mexico, so be sure to have one before trying to obtain a ferry ticket.

South of La Paz, the highway climbs into the foothills of the Sierra de la Laguna, the mountainous heart of the Cape Region. These "islands in the sky" receive the greatest rainfall in Baja, and are habitat for a rare mix of plant species and many wild animals that live here undisturbed by civilization. The only way to observe this area and get into the high canyons and among the granite peaks is to hike or backpack; you'll need topographic maps. The area is being considered for national park status.

When Mexico 1 jogs back to the gulf coast, it meets the town of Los Barriles, where the winds blow so well and so frequently that windsurfing is a popular sport; Bahia de Palmas is usually a moving rainbow of colorful sails. Board rentals and lessons are easy to obtain.

The world-famous "Tuna Hole" is south of Punta Pescadero and noted for year-round catches of large yellowfin tuna by skilled anglers. Guided trips can be arranged at bay area hotels.

Land's End at Los Cabos

Below the Tropic of Cancer and approached from Mexico 1, San Jose del Cabo is the first of the two towns included in our destination called Los Cabos ("The Capes"). This is the rounded tip of the peninsula where the waters of the ocean and the gulf mix. Dating back to 1730 as an agricultural and cattle-raising center, San Jose del Cabo is still a sleepy, wonderfully situated place that now attracts visitors for its peaceful qualities. Succulent tropical fruits, including mangos and coconuts, are still grown, and visitors delight in selecting huge cantaloupes and papayas at the markets.

Fishermen at sunrise, Bahia Concepcion.

The harbor at the other cape town, Cabo San Lucas, was a hiding place for English pirates who plundered Spanish galleons in the 1500s. In fact, one privateer was known to say that this area of sensational offshore rock formations was a "great place for larceny but no place to live." A place of rich natural diversity, however, a Hungarian naturalist, Janos Xantus, collected some 92,000 specimens of the flora and fauna for the Smithsonian Institution from 1859 to 1861; he also fathered a lot of children. When John Steinbeck sailed into Cabo San Lucas in 1941, he found only a tuna cannery and a few houses, marveled at the beauty of the tide pools, and wrote that the "great rocks at the end of the peninsula are almost literary. They are a fitting Land's End."

When this small village was discovered in the 1950s and 1960s by sportfishers who flew or sailed there, it was on its way to becoming known as the "marlin capital of the world." Once the highway was completed, Cabo San Lucas began attracting automobile and RV travelers for many reasons, including 360 days of sunshine, warm waters, and beaches that form a corridor between the two cape towns. An international airport has increased the influx of fun-loving people arriving to spend time here. Although Cabo San Lucas is undergoing vigorous development, it is still small enough for easy travel.

With an excellent harbor for sportfishing and recreation boats, Cabo San Lucas is a magnet for tourists. A ticket on a glass-bottom boat is all you need for the short ride to view El Arco ("The Arch"), the 200-foot-high (62 m) offshore rock formation that is almost symbolic of the town. Two tall pinnacles named Los Frailes ("The Friars"), and a smaller one, Roca Pelicanos ("Pelican Rock"), are examples of the varied geology seen on such a ride. This is also a nature preserve, with sea lions, brown pelicans, and marine life including coral, sea fans, sea urchins, and colorful tropical fish.

The surf pounds on the quiet beach at the south end of town by the Hotel Solmar, and magnificent frigate birds and blue-footed boobies fly overhead. Some private beaches can be reached by boat, and pangas are available for rent. If you don't try the marlin fishing, walk down to the sportfishing dock when the catches are unloaded and view these enormous fish. Diving and horseback riding are other activities, and shops and open-air restaurants and bars are plentiful. Campgrounds are nicely situated along the highway just before you enter Cabo San Lucas.

I traveled to Mexico chasing the gray whales that migrated there past the Oregon coast. But the year I traveled to Baja the grays were slow in arriving at Scammon's Lagoon and, although I did see some whales, it was the unexpected joys of the Baja landscapes that caught me by surprise. Baja is a place to be a bit adventurous. It's also a place to enjoy the leisurely pace of life where a smile is universal.

CHAPTER 15

Southeastern California and Nevada: Enigmatic Deserts

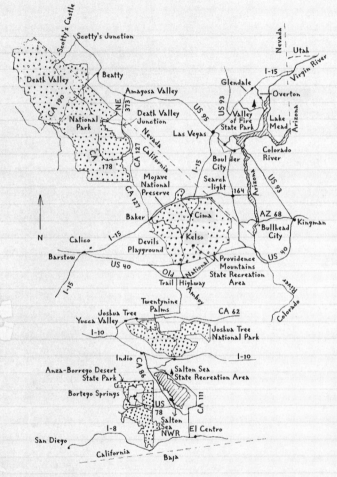

MILEAGE

Approximately 1,200 miles (1,930 km).

RESOURCES

- Valley of Fire State Park: (702) 397-2088.
- Lake Mead National Recreation Area: (702) 293-8990.
- Death Valley National Park: (760) 786-2331.
- Mojave National Preserve: (619) 255-8801.
- Joshua Tree National Park: (760) 367-7511.
- Palm Springs Aerial Tramway: (619) 325-1391.
- Anza-Borrego Desert State Park: (760) 767-5311.

CAMPGROUNDS

VALLEY OF FIRE STATE PARK: 55 miles (88 km) northeast of Las Vegas via Interstate 15 to NV 169; campsites in two campground areas, one with showers in the restrooms.

DEATH VALLEY NATIONAL PARK: At Furnace Creek Area; campsites at Furnace Creek Campground with restrooms (pay showers available at nearby Furnace Creek Ranch), reservations via Destinet at (800) 365-2267; campsites (first-come, first-served) at Stovepipe Wells with restrooms (pay showers available at Stovepipe Wells motel); check at visitor center for information on other park campgrounds.

MOJAVE NATIONAL PRESERVE: From US 40, north on Cedar Canyon Road to Black Canyon Road to Hole-in-the-Wall Campground; campsites with pit toilets and limited water.

JOSHUA TREE NATIONAL PARK: Black Rock and Cottonwood campgrounds have flush toilets and water, seven other campgrounds have chemical toilets and no water; Phone MISTIX at (800) 365-2267 for reservations at Black Rock Canyon and Indian Cove.

ANZA-BORREGO DESERT STATE PARK: Adjacent to Visitor Center, Borrego Palm Canyon has RV sites with hookups and tent sites, restrooms with showers; Tamarisk Grove has campsites, restrooms with showers; call MISTIX at (800) 444-7275 for reservations.

One desert runs into another in southeastern California. Hot scorching lands in summer, these enigmatic and fragile environments become hospitable to humans in winter. Wildflowers and cactus burst into bloom late in the season. Sunshine is the norm, but rain creates the magic. Trails lead to hidden oases. Occasionally glimpsed are animals that adapted to this harsh land with curious and sometimes bizarre mechanisms. The clarity of the night sky affords excellent stargazing.

The desert landscape is often flat and seemingly barren, and just as often full of intriguing vegetation and startling geologic features that rise in convoluted complexity. Jumbo rocks attract rock climbers. Expanses of sand dunes urge hikers to ascend them, noticing along the way the fascinating textures and tracks imprinted upon the mobile grains.

These are the Mojave and Sonoran deserts—warm deserts compared with the cooler Great Basin Desert that connects to the north—with elevations below sea level in Death Valley and Imperial Valley, and mountains rising in places to over 11,000 feet (3,300 m). Travelers have to exert some energy here to learn a few of the deserts' secrets, yet many people return again and again. Their reasons are varied and individualistic, but often compelling. Nothing is rushed in the desert. The desert waits and grows when conditions are right.

Among other delights along this tour, you'll visit two national parks, a national preserve, a national recreation area, Nevada's first state park, and California's largest state park. These destinations include the recently designated Mojave and Colorado Desert Biosphere Reserve, 27 million acres preserved as internationally significant "samples" of Earth's biodiversity. It sounds like a worthy RV trip, doesn't it? (Don't be confused by the name Colorado Desert, which is an area in the larger Sonoran Desert.)

For reasons of temperature, begin in the north and time your visit to be in Anza-Borrego Desert State Park in early March for the added enchantment of the wildflower blooms, although any time in winter should be good for exploring. The dry desert air gets cool at night, especially in winter, and temperatures change quickly when the sun goes down. Bring some warm clothing—layers are good—in case days bring an unexpected change.

What's Special About the Mojave and Colorado Desert Biosphere Reserve?

The Joshua tree, the Panamint daisy, and the elephant tree are examples of unique plant species of the reserve. Bighorn sheep, desert tortoise, and desert pupfish are representative of the diverse animal life. Ecosystems include rugged canyons, fragile wetlands, native palm oases, and curious sand dune environments, all home to endemic species of organisms such as sand-dwelling fringe-toed lizards. Protecting this area is akin to taking care of your backyard since, in a broader sense, as a traveler and as an American, it is your backyard.

The Northeastern Mojave Desert

Not far from the neon-lit streets and wildly popular casinos of Las Vegas, a couple of places at the extremity of the Mojave Desert are appealing. The first is Valley of Fire State Park, northeast of the gambling terrain via Interstate 15. The park's campground is one of my all-time favorites as a temporary homesite. It is nestled among cavelike recesses of red rock outcrops, which were once wind-blown sand dunes. One time I found a site complete with a flowering plant that attracted hummingbirds and had entertainment at my doorstep.

For thousands of years, prehistoric people came to the Valley of Fire region to harvest wild plants and hunt bighorn sheep with a notched stick called an atlatl. The Basketmakers gradually learned pottery skills as they evolved into the Pueblo Anasazi and left behind petroglyphs, the rock art that is so intriguing yet difficult to interpret.

The low desert that dominates this 46,000-acre park offers great orienteering excursions for closer observation of its natural history. Such walks are enhanced by the profusion of red rock formations that feature wrinkled, etched, angled, and scoured components, mostly created by the weathering and fracturing of the fiery Aztec Sandstone. See if you can find the magnificent arch not far from the campgrounds. A self-guiding trail leads to petrified logs, with longer trails to Petroglyph Canyon and Fire Canyon/Silica Dome.

Flowering plants—beavertail and cholla cactus, desert rhubarb, datura, indigo bush, and desert primrose—are especially photogenic in the coral-colored sand. Peak blossoming, however, is in mid-April, so they are not a major feature of the park during a winter excursion. You'll want to come again anyway.

Many of the park attractions—the Bee-

hives, Elephant Rock, the Cabins, and the Seven Sisters—are a few steps off the main park road, but two scenic driving loops are worthwhile. A 2-mile (3.2-km) road leads to the campgrounds and a petroglyph display at the Atlatl Rock Picnic Area. A longer 7-mile (11-km) round-trip excursion from Rainbow Vista takes you to the White Domes area, where you'll see a marvelous mosaic of layers and swirls, textures and patterns in the rocks, sometimes with straight raised seams indicating joints cemented by quartz and calcite. The range of delicate colors—purples, golds, mauves, creams, and oranges—are alone worth the trip. Most people can't resist naming the rock formations. A short trail takes you to Duck Rock, and you'll find yucca in this area.

Rather than taking the interstate back to Las Vegas, try a scenic route that rims the Lake Mead National Recreation Area along NV 167. Reservoir enthusiasts will find marinas and campgrounds along Lake Mead at Overton Beach, Echo Beach, and Callville Bay. These are the waters impounded by 726-foot (221-m) Hoover Dam, the engineering marvel that tamed a section of the once-mighty Colorado River. Now, sailboats moving with the wind are encircled by the harsh environment of the Mojave Desert. Yet the desert has its allure, as seen along this Northshore Scenic Drive. The Black Mountains edge the blue colors of the lake, with brilliant red boulders, rock formations, and wildflowers accenting this merging of river water with desert terrain. Migrating birds and ducks know the way here, and white pelicans, egrets, herons, cormorants, ospreys, and bald eagles frequent the area.

The Desert Tortoise

The prime activity period of the desert tortoise in this area is March through May. At this time, a few lucky observers might see one of these endangered animals foraging for plants or prowling the desert for a mate. For much of the rest of the year, these tortoises spend their time underground in shallow holes or deeper burrows. To glimpse their wrinkled necks and solemn eyes, while their short legs paddle them slowly along underneath massive shells, is the essence of the desert experience.

Found in both the Mojave and Sonoran deserts, the desert tortoise often lives more than a hundred years. They are a success story dating back 175 million years to the time of dinosaurs. Yet they are now endangered, and humans are their greatest threat. General George Patton conducted training maneuvers for World War II atop their homes. Since then, motorcyclists have crushed them, nuts with guns have riddled them, cattle and sheep have diminished their food supply, and recently they've caught a deadly respiratory illness from pet tortoises. The result: areas of the Mojave and Sonoran deserts once populated by 1,000 desert tortoises per square mile now have no more than 200 per square mile in the best of these sites. And every year there are fewer.

Death Valley National Park

West of Las Vegas, US 95 leads to several routes into Death Valley National Park and the northwestern reaches of the Mojave Desert, but the best choice for this tour is west into the park from Death Valley Junction. Stop at the Death Valley Visitor Center and Museum in the Furnace Creek area to orient yourself for further exploring. Should you wish a few amenities, you'll

"Beehives" at the Valley of Fire State Park, NV.

find a complete array of services, including camping, horseback and carriage rides, a golf course, tennis courts, swimming pools, food, and gas. Check out the outdoor exhibit of old-time wagons and vehicles while learning the history of borax prospectors.

Death Valley is a place of extremes. Badwater, the lowest elevation in the country, is 280 feet (85 meters) below sea level. Given this and the geographic latitude, it is not surprising that the highest recorded temperature—in the shade at Furnace Creek—was 134 degrees Fahrenheit one year, a rather unpleasant temperature that you'll avoid by a visit in late winter, when daytime temperatures are more likely in the 70s. From the 5,475-foot (1,669-m) perspective at Dantes View (no bus-like RVs or trailers allowed), you can overlook this incredible low area and the 200 square miles (500 square kilometers) of the Death Valley Salt Pan. This smooth vast whiteness is backed by the towering snow-peaked Panamint Range, where long-lived bristlecone pines grow on 11,049-foot (3,368-m) Telescope Peak. An alkali flat, salts continue to accumulate in this basin that once contained meltwater from Sierra Nevada glaciers. The park's more than 2 million acres contain a nearly complete record of Earth's geologic past, although it is jumbled out of sequence from all the faulting, folding, vulcanism, erosion, and deposition.

The mountains rarely allow precipitation to penetrate this sunken basin. When this does happen, a garden of wildflowers blossoms, usually in March in the lower valley. Government botanist Frederick Vernon Coville explored the area on a six-

month expedition in 1891 and collected hundreds of plants, which he called "the weird flora of the Mojave Desert."

One of the most popular excursions in Death Valley is a trek over the miles and miles of sand dunes against a backdrop of the Kit Fox Hills and the more distant Grapevine Mountains. Enter the dunes either 2 miles (3.2 km) east of Stovepipe Wells or from Sand Dunes Picnic Area, 19 miles (31 km) from the visitor center. Plan your wandering for early or late in the day to get the best views of these wonderful curving shapes full of textures and tracks. Locate landmarks, perhaps a certain mountain feature, to guide your way and pick your own route across the transverse and barchan dunes composed mostly of grains of quartz.

Most of the dune vegetation is found in low areas. Look for pickleweed, four-wing saltbush, creosote bush, and mesquite plants. White salt deposits from an old clay lakebed, or playa, form surface deposits in certain places. Be alert for desert dwellers—lizards, kangaroo rats, and sidewinders—that might share your stop in a shady cool place at the edge of the dunes. Tracks on the sand usually are easier to find; perhaps you'll see those of a beetle that resemble a tiny bulldozer or the paw prints of the elusive kit fox.

If one night is the extent of your stay in the park, plan one evening for the dunes and reserve early the next morning for a hike in Golden Canyon, a sculpted formation created by water and erosion. Observe the alluvial fans, tilted rock layers formed by faulting, ripple marks left by an ancient

Sand dunes in Death Valley National Park, CA.

lake, deposits of borax and gypsum, bad-lands, and swirled chocolate and cream lay-ers of pinnacles. An optional extension of the trail continues to Zabriske Point—which is also accessible by road. This is a strenuous and often steep and difficult trail to a great viewpoint of nearby badlands and striated jagged points.

Other intriguing side trips are available to those who stay longer. Scotty's Castle is 53 miles north of the visitor center and was once the desert retreat of Albert Johnson, a wealthy midwesterner. The site in Grape-vine Canyon was suggested by Walter E. Scott, who was known as "Death Valley Scotty," and who was a frequent guest and later spent his last years living in this Mediterranean-style castle and complex. Learn its history and walk the nature trail to Scotty's grave. Stop along the way to hike the Salt Creek Nature Trail and hope for a glimpse of a desert pupfish that are often seen in spring. These rare creatures can live in water that is two to three times saltier than the sea and up to 112 degrees Fahrenheit. They retreat to mud burrows when it is cooler.

Another suggested side trip is a hike to view the polished marble narrows atop an alluvial fan in Mosaic Canyon, past Stovepipe Wells. Scan the cliffs with binoc-ulars for bighorn sheep.

Insider's Tip:
Although summer is the usual season for dramatic thunderstorms, always be alert for the possibility of flash floods after a rainfall. In any of these desert parks, don't enter dips in the road if they contain water.

From the park map, it soon becomes ob-vious that mining was important in the his-tory of Death Valley. Although borax is the main mining story, other minerals, includ-ing gold and silver, are chapters. The park is a repository of gold rush legends, improba-ble truths, fact, and fiction.

Continue south out of the park via CA 178 and skirt the salt pan, passing the Artist's Drive Loop (restrictions may

Furnance Creek Inn in Death Valley, CA.

apply), and then take a short unpaved road that visits the Devil's Golf Course, with its rock-salt pinnacles. Past Badwater the road wiggles to Mormon Point and later reaches Ashford Mill Ruins, where gold from the Black Mountains was processed. Jubilee Mountain Pass offers good scouting for wildflowers. Take CA 127 past the Dumont Dunes and dry lakes to Baker, site of the world's tallest thermometer.

Before heading into the Mojave Nation-al Preserve, consider a side trip to the refur-bished ghost town of Calico, east of Barstow. This authentic silver-mining town was a busy place from 1881 to 1907. Today, you can walk through streets replete with old wooden structures now turned into shops featuring leatherwork, pottery, art, bottles, spices, antiques, rocks, and other wares. The old schoolhouse still looks the same, com-plete with desks. Ride the Calico-Odessa Railroad, take the Maggie Mine Tour, or check out the riding stables. Restaurants and a campground are available.

Mojave National Preserve

To prepare yourself for a trip into the lone-ly terrain of Mojave National Preserve, stop at the visitor center in Baker and pick up maps and detailed information. Part of the Mojave Desert public wildlands, this 1.4-million-acre preserve ranging in elevation from 1,000 to 8,000 feet (305 to 2,438 m) was created by the Desert Protection Act, which was signed into law in late 1994. Management of the area, therefore, is fairly recent, with about half of the land officially designated wilderness. This rugged landscape appeals to explorers who need little in the way of services—a full gas tank and a gallon of water per day per person are essentials. A vastness of dramatic and varied landforms, the Mojave requires considerable travel and searching before you can form an intimacy with the place, but even a cursory visit is rewarding. Although several of the roads in the preserve are paved, many unpaved roads provide access to interesting areas; you'll want to check their current condition. Then head south on Kelbaker Road, which initially passes through flat scrub desert and then edges to an area of lava and volcanic cinder cones before reaching views of mountain ridges. I found these mountains wreathed with a provocative misty haze that delineated the geometric outlines of the ridges in early morning.

 Insider's Tip:
A glance at the preserve's detailed map reveals the enormous number of jeep roads that invite exploration by mountain bike or by hiking. However, travel cross country by bike is prohibited. Avoid the dangers of abandoned mines and watch where you put your hands on rocks or bushes; some of the tiny critters are not friendly. Using metal detectors is illegal in the preserve.

After the primitive undeveloped nature of the drive into the preserve, it is surprising to find the spacious Spanish architecture of Kelso Depot, which was built in 1924. The surroundings here are so quiet it is almost a haunting experience to step outside and walk about this railroad station that was once so important on the Las Vegas-to-Los Angeles route of the Union Pacific Railroad. This location was chosen to water the steam engines at the bottom of the steep Cima grade. In the 1940s, nearly 2,000 people lived in the area and trains regularly rolled through carrying more than 2,500 tons of iron ore, heading from the Vulcan Mine to the Kaiser Steel Mill. The station housed various amenities, including a restaurant nicknamed "The Beanery." By the 1950s, diesel engines erased the need

for this watering station and Kelso declined into the ghostlike affair seen today. However, that may change. In 1992, the Bureau of Land Management bought the depot and an adjacent lot for one dollar. Now the National Park Service hopes to restore this gracious structure as a visitor center.

One travel option is to take the paved Kelso-Cima Road at this intersection. Continuing on the Cima Road leads to the almost perfect rounded Cima Dome, a mass of rock rising 1,500 feet (457 m) and covering 75 square miles that is the site of the world's largest stand of Joshua trees. Located here is the trailhead for the 4-mile (6.6-km) round-trip hike to 5,755-foot (1,754-m) Teutonia Peak. (You might prefer taking this route to the Kelso intersection from Interstate 15.)

Just south and west of the Kelso Depot are the popular Kelso Dunes. Rising more than 700 feet (213 m) above the desert floor in a huge area, these dunes of rose quartz grains have been blown here by southeast winds. A 3-mile (4.8-km) rough road provides access to dune parking. Pick the easiest route to climb these sand hills and wander freely in the openness for a satisfying adventure. If there's been some rain, yellow, white, and pink wildflowers may edge the lower dune area. Sometimes, in the dry desert air, the sliding dunes produce vibrations, even a "booming" sound. The dunes are closed to vehicles.

From US 40, some choice recreation areas can be reached via the Essex Road. The first of these is Providence Mountains State Recreation Area, a mountainous terrain that includes the large flat-topped Wildhorse Mesa, the title and locale of a Zane Grey book. You'll find the short Mary Beal Nature Trail and some campsites here, but the major attraction is the Mitchell Caverns Trail, a 1.5-mile (2.4-km) guided tour through limestone caves.

The easiest approach to the preserve's Hole-in-the-Wall Campground (elevation: 4,500 feet [1,372 m]) is to take the Black Canyon Road northeast from Essex Road. (The unpaved road that enters from the north is not recommended for motorhomes or trailers.) Limited water, a telephone, a dump station, and spacious, although un-shaded, sites are found in the campground, as well as a picnic area with an unusual trail challenge. This moderately strenuous trail descends into a maze of volcanic rock formations where ring holds must be used to negotiate the passage through slots be-tween the rocks, a difficult technique that some can't manage. I watched hikers ap-pear to vanish into the rocky depths. This camp area is also the trailhead for the 7-mile (11-km) hike through Wild Horse Canyon to the more isolated Mid Hills Campground. It's a route that's popular with desert lovers, complete with dramat-ic volcanic formations, juniper trees, and perhaps a sighting of a bighorn.

When you look at the detail of the park map, it seems obvious that many have ex-plored this fascinating preserve and learned it secrets. The numerous springs and wells pinpointed on the map are crucial for the elusive wildlife here. The desert tortoise, mule deer, coyote, and golden eagles are a few of the 300 wildlife species in this area. Many of the bird species live in the canyons and washes. Mining ruins, remnants of cat-tle ranches, and rock art are part of the cul-tural history.

 Insider's Tip:
Some roadside camping is allowed in the preserve. Use existing sites and don't destroy critical desert habitat. A listing of some of these sites is available from the visitor center in Baker.

Joshua Tree National Park

Not many miles of desert separate Mojave National Preserve from its neighbor to the south, Joshua Tree National Park, but they are pretty empty miles with few people and services. With my bent for back roads, I continued on Essex Road to the Old Trail National Highway, but I admit that a better choice is Interstate 40 and then south on Kelbaker to Amboy. From there the 47 miles (75 km) south to Twentynine Palms roll through dry-lake areas where salt is commercially harvested.

Kelso Depot in Mojave National Preserve, CA.

After many miles of few services, trav-elers may need to replenish food and sup-plies before entering the 800,000 acres of Joshua Tree National Park. You can cer-tainly make do with the small markets in Twentynine Palms, and I enjoyed a tasty Chinese lunch there, but I was surprised to find that Yucca Valley was a real shopping center with a number of supermarkets and retailers and a modern mall. On my map, Twentynine Palms, Joshua Tree, and Yucca Valley looked similar in size, yet Joshua Tree has few services, so you might prefer to enter the national park from the west en-trance station, one of four entry roads on the park's north side along CA 62. Be warned, however, that the most scenic and fun campgrounds in the park's interior have no water, so bring enough to last your visit or stock up at the few places on the periph-ery of the park; check your park map for specifics.

With all the fascinating stops along the main route, it's easy to spend at least a day moving diagonally across Joshua Tree Na-tional Park. Much of the park away from the road is designated wilderness, so it takes even more time to explore its hidden and delightful desert aspects. You can't miss the many Joshua trees that only grow at this elevation and are symbolic of the Mojave Desert, which is somewhat moister and cooler than the lower desert. Actually, these small trees with their distinctive shape are yuccas that produce huge clusters of greenish-white flowers in late spring that are pollinated exclusively by the pronuba moth.

Although the park is named after this

small tree, be prepared for the magic of its rock formations, with their infinite series of chaotic seams and creases. At first unimpressive as you travel Park Boulevard from the west entrance—the smallest rocks appear disposed of here in piles—the scenery quickly changes at the Quail Spring Stop, where rock climbers gather to practice. The park is famous for the jumbo rocks that are perfect for learning the skills needed for this sport. No bolts are allowed and climbers should assume that those already in place are unsafe; ask for the park climbing brochure if needed.

Hidden Valley is a wonderful, inviting place, where an easy short path leads through rock openings to a site where rustlers once hid cattle. Today, you are more likely to find people scrambling atop the rock formations surrounding the circular path. Hidden Valley is a favorite picnic stop, and you'll quickly learn that shade in the park (remember this at campgrounds) is provided by huge boulders rather than trees.

For finding birds or rock art, try the Barker Dam Loop Trail. One of the earliest Southwest cultures, the Pinto people lived here and harvested pinyon nuts, mesquite beans, acorns, and cactus fruit.

For a panoramic vista of valley, mountains, and desert, take the side road to Keys View. The long distance California Riding and Hiking Trail intersects this road, with backcountry registration available. The Ryan Campground accommodates horses. Back on the main road, a strenuous 1.5-mile (2.4-km) trail ascends 5,461-foot (1,665-m) Ryan Mountain for some fine views. Four-wheel drive or a mountain bike is recommended for the 18-mile (29-km) self-guiding Geology Tour Road.

I happily chose Jumbo Rocks as my campground for a couple of days and was not disappointed. I even located the self-guiding Skull Rock Trail near my site. This campground offers lots of sheltering rocks, which are great for making hidden discoveries. Campers scramble among the slots and rocks and find places to climb without ropes or technical equipment. These are intriguing rock structures, huge blocks and ovals of rocks joined together by seams,

sometimes like a row of fossilized teeth in a monster. At this location, jumbo rocks are so numerous they dominate the desert vegetation (but spring brings some flowering cactus). Some chunks of rock have been catapulted atop other rocks to form a high bridge; some top a jumbo formation with shapes like loaves of bread. Campers discover narrow passageways and cozy dead-ends for shaded privacy, taking a chair and a book for some time alone, or a companion for conversation. At sundown, a walk along the road reveals richly lit rocks that glow with a pumpkin-like hue. You might glimpse a jackrabbit or a roadrunner .

 Insider's Tip:

If you're afraid to venture out across the terrain because you fear that most things in the desert are "deadly," don't be. In fact, deserts are safer than much of the country. Most desert animals move about at night to avoid the heat. However, food particles can attract tiny things that creep and fly; make sure to check or shake out paraphernalia before wearing or using it in case of scorpions.

As Pinto Basin Road heads toward the south entrance station, it passes through a transition from the Mojave Desert to the Sonoran Desert, a transition determined primarily by elevation. At less than 3,000 feet (915 m), creosote bush, ocotillo, and creosote predominate. A self-guiding nature trail loops through the Cholla Cactus Garden, and the Ocotillo Patch may be in bloom.

Cottonwood Spring, Joshua Tree National Park.

Trails in the Cottonwood Spring area lead to mill sites and to Mastodon Peak. A demanding but memorable 4-mile (6.4-km) hike heads for Lost Palms Oasis, one of the most beautiful native fan palm oases in California. More than 110 of these tall, water-seeking trees are found there in a deep canyon nourished by an underground spring and surrounded by walls of quartz monzonite. This remote place is one of the best places to find bighorn sheep and other wildlife. If you don't feel up to this trek, visit the easily accessed Cottonwood Spring and walk among the lush green oasis of cottonwoods and fan palms. This was an important stop for the explorers, cattlemen, and miners who came this way in the late 1800s. The earliest wildflower blooms, in February, are in the Cottonwood area, where desert dandelion, lupine, chia, and phacelia are some of the species that pop out into color.

Consider a change-of-pace side trip before visiting the next desert area. It's a short jaunt heading west on Interstate 10 to Palm Springs, where CA 111 intersects the road to the Palm Springs Aerial Tramway. On the tramway you'll travel from desert terrain at 2,653 feet (809 m) to alpine forest at 8,516 feet (2,596 m) in the San Jacinto Mountains. At the top are 50 miles (80 km) of wilderness trails, although you can just relax and enjoy the spectacular perspective of the surrounding landforms. My son and I were excited to find we had gone from warm weather to a snowy landscape, with huge boulders and trees covered by a recent snowfall.

Anza-Borrego Desert State Park

From Palm Springs, travel south on CA 86, to the Salton Sea, which has a rather unusual history. During the Pleistocene Period, this valley between the Santa Rosa and the Chocolate mountains was under the waters of Lake Cahuilla, but the lake dried up some 500 years ago and left huge salt deposits. Although the valley was quite alkaline and not the best soil for crops, an irrigation canal was built in 1902 to bring water from the Colorado River to attract more settlers. The canal silted up by 1909

and its headworks later were breached by heavy rains that flowed into the Salton Sink. Great effort and a large amount of material finally stanched the flow of the river, but the water remained as a salty lake, four times the salinity of the sea, and now evaporating at about five feet each year. This sea does have its charm, however, and a couple of beach areas are fun stops. The Salton Sea National Wildlife Refuge edges the southwestern shore and offers a visitor center, wildlife viewing sites, good spring birding, and hiking trails.

Either CA 78 or S 22 will take you west into the center of Anza-Borrego Desert State Park and to the visitor center west of the town of Borrego Springs. Called the "erosion road," this entry route into Anza-Borrego follows California's most active fault line; a free brochure is available.

Considering how most of southern California has become inundated with people, buildings, and highways, Californians were wise to preserve 600,000 acres of the Borrego Desert, a jewel of a park where both local residents and travelers can find solitude and room to explore in the Sonoran Desert. But it is especially important as a refuge for wild things.

RVers will find a range of campgrounds (including a horse camp), even one with hookups. They will also find the unusual policy of allowing open camping throughout the park, as long as your vehicle is within one car length of the dirt road, and as long as no damage to native plant life can occur; exceptions are near water holes, the visitor center, and developed campgrounds. Check the park regulations.

Good reasons exist for choosing Borrego Palm Canyon Campground as your base. Although there is no shade (tent sites have shade ramadas), it's adjacent to both the visitor center and the most popular park trail, Borrego Palm Canyon. This self-guiding nature trail (3 miles [4.8 km] round-trip) winds past red-flowering ocotillo and golden wildflowers to a native palm grove and year-round stream. Scan for bighorn sheep on the high cliffs.

If you'd prefer camping under some tall trees—an unusual find in the desert—consider Tamarisk Grove south of Yaqui Pass on S 3. I liked the cool shade there and camped next to a couple who came every year in early spring to watch the twenty or so long-eared owls that nest in the trees, which they verified for me with lots of photos. Great birding is just across the road via the short Yaqui Well Trail. If plant study is your aim, the Cactus Loop Trail is also across from the campground. Younger children can look for cactus wrens, ravens, lizards, and coyote tracks in the wash behind the campsites.

Of the four North American rain-starved major deserts, the Sonoran is the richest in its diversity of life forms and habitats. Here in Anza-Borrego, primeval reptiles, coyotes, mountain lions, and roadrunners scurry amid fossil remains of sabertooth cats and mammoth elephants. The geology is varied, with several mountain ranges, badlands, alluvial fans, a sandstone canyon, and washes that are favored terrain for wildflowers and birds. The park is so large and relatively unknown that rangers and scientists keep adding to their storehouse of discoveries.

Insider's Tip:
Although an encounter with a mountain lion is highly unlikely, avoid hiking alone, make noise (perhaps by singing), keep children in sight, and carry a good walking stick, which can be useful as a defense. Respect the cougar's wildness and never approach this animal. Stay calm; do not run, which might trigger a predator instinct to attack. Pick up small children and stand tall yourself and face the lion. Throw rocks, branches, or whatever and fight back if attacked. Report any sightings.

Good roads access many of the attractions, but those with four-wheel-drive vehicles could explore new territory for days and days. Some bipedal energy is needed, or horses and mountain bikes, to travel trails and back roads and make individual special finds. Check out the geology along the Narrows Earth Trail east of Tamarisk Grove, walk to the entrance view of Split Moun-

tain and visit rare elephant trees, walk to a pictograph site off S2, or continue farther southeast on this road to explore Mountain Palm Springs and nearby Carrizo Badlands Overlook. County Road S 2 is rich in human history. From Scissors Crossing southeast to Palm Spring, a self-guiding auto tour follows the southern Emigrant Trail and the route of the Butterfield Overland Stage; a brochure will help you visualize some of the associated history.

Insider's Tip:
Peak wildflower bloom is usually from late February until sometime in April; the best time to visit is the first of March. Late in the season, try the higher elevations at Blair Valley, Culp Valley, or Indian Gorge. Call the wildflower hot line at Anza-Borrego at (760) 767-4684 for up-to-date information on the season.

Although you can visit many attractions on your own, the park has an extensive list of ranger-led activities that will enhance your education and fun. Rangers will take you to see mammoth, camel, and zebra fossils; to a birding hot spot; and for a hike to the wind caves overlooking the Carrizo Badlands. They also host some stargazing woven around Indian legends and lead the Animal Tracks Workshop. Check the park newspaper for times and places.

Given enough time to wander in these special parks in two major deserts, you may go home with a new outlook on deserts. Your knowledge about the survival of wild things will be enriched by witnessing firsthand the physical stresses of the desert in this most gentle of its seasons. Not only will you have a deeper feeling for your affinity for being in wild deserts, you'll also learn about your own resourcefulness and powers of observation when you are away from crowds of humanity. Writer Joseph Wood Krutch once commented, "Not to have known—as most men have not—either the mountain or the desert is not to have known one's self."

CHAPTER 16

Big Bend and the Lower Rio Grande Valley:
A Wildlife Corridor

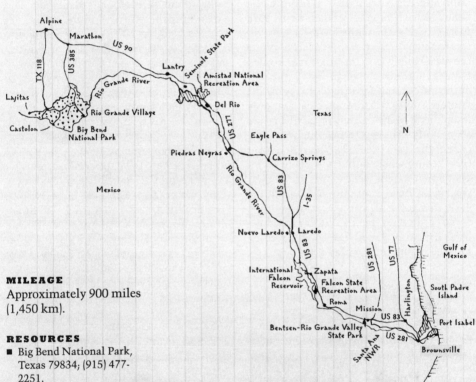

MILEAGE

Approximately 900 miles (1,450 km).

RESOURCES

- Big Bend National Park, Texas 79834; (915) 477-2251.
- Santa Ana National Wildlife Refuge, Route 2, Box 202A, Alamo, Texas 78516; (210) 787-3079.

CAMPGROUNDS

BIG BEND NATIONAL PARK: 40 miles (64 km) south of Marathon on US 385; campsites and restrooms at Rio Grande Village Campground, concession showers, laundry, and full hookups in the store area; campsites at Chisos Basin with restrooms; campsites at Cottonwood with pit toilets; reservations not accepted.

FALCON STATE RECREATION AREA: 25 miles (40 km) south of Zapata via US 83; Campsites with hookups, restrooms with showers, dump station; reservations at (512) 389-8900, Monday through Friday.

BENTSEN–RIO GRANDE VALLEY STATE PARK: 6 miles (10 km) southwest of Mission off FM 2062; campsites, restrooms with showers, dump station; reservations (see Falcon).

Look at a map of the United States. Does it surprise you that the southern tip of Texas is the southernmost extension of western landscapes in this country? South Texas has latitudes similar to those of Baja, a fact already deduced by many winter travelers. Some take short trips there when snow and ice in the north send them looking for warmer weather; others spend much of the winter in the delightful country that borders the Rio Grande River—the second longest river in the United States. The quiet time in January that follows the hectic holiday season is an excellent time to recharge your inner batteries and unwind just north of the Mexican border.

Although some of this landscape is isolated and desolate, a tour along the Rio Grande River from Big Bend National Park to its mouth at the Gulf of Mexico encounters many natural treasures. Nature is at a crossroad along this international border. Flora and fauna converge here from the north and the south, particularly during the winter; some wildlife species are only found here. Many intriguing creatures are about, but the most entertaining and abundant of these are the birds. You'll marvel at their beauty and joyfulness. If you'd rather visit when wildflower blooms are at their peak in Big Bend, wait until March, but the park changes with the influx of visitors. Some of the desert plants flower in the lowlands in February, with the color spreading into the mountains by May.

Big Bend National Park

A green island of mountains in a desert sea. Brilliant stargazing at night. A desert amphibian and rare and wonderful bird sightings. A soak in natural hot springs. These are a few of the Texan treasures found in Big Bend National Park, but the essential ingredient is the Rio Grande River.

Enfolded by the great arc of the Rio Grande River that is the origin of its name, Big Bend National Park is reached by routes through isolated country that enter the park via two highways: US 385 and TX 118. I'd suggest taking the US 385 approach south from Marathon because a ranger station with information is situated at the northern entrance. You'll enter the park at Persimmon Gap in the Santiago Mountains, a route once on the Comanche War Trail.

The fossil bone exhibit displays fossil skulls and other bones of mammals that roamed this land 50 million years ago when it was a savanna and swamp with croco-

diles, hippopotamus-like creatures, and miniature horselike animals. Millions of years older, however, is the most famous of the park's fossils, the Big Bend pterosaur, a flying reptile with a 51-foot (15.5 m) wingspan—possibly the largest animal ever to fly above Earth's surface. Magic windows into the past, fossilized remains are still being found in the park's badlands. The park's human history is more recent, yet extends back 10,000 years to prehistoric big-game hunters, followed by hunter-gatherer Indians of the Desert Culture, who lived here about 6,000 B.C. Today we come in motorhomes, our refrigerators and cupboards full of survival sustenance that permits us to roam pretty much where we wish.

Route choices must be made at Panther Junction, where the park headquarters and a visitor center are found. Depending on the temperature and weather, head for Rio Grande Village, the Basin in the Chisos Mountains, or the Castolon area; all have campgrounds. Since elevations and temperatures vary considerably throughout the park, check weather conditions and predictions before proceeding; abrupt changes can occur.

RIO GRANDE VILLAGE

The road from Panther Junction to Rio Grande Village descends almost 2,000 feet (610 m) in elevation through the Chihuahuan Desert to an excellent riverfront camping area among cottonwoods on the floodplain of the river. Camping supplies and groceries are available at the store. A cross-country walk in the nearby desert might produce glimpses of javelinas (collared peccary); don't approach them. Coyotes often come to Rio Grande Village at dusk.

Insider's Tip:
In this isolated park, gasoline can be found at Rio Grande Village, at park headquarters at Panther Junction, and at Castolon. Groceries can be purchased at all three major campground areas; the Basin has a restaurant.

A discovered place at sundown in Rio Grande Village, Big Bend National Park, TX.

Dusk is the best time to walk the Rio Grande Village Nature Trail, which starts at the campground. The path leads through varied riverine vegetation to a desert hill with a 360-degree view of the river, the campground, the Chisos Mountains, the isolated farmhouses across the river in Mexico, and the sun setting the Sierra del Carmen cliffs afire. Swifts fly overhead, and sometimes a falcon can be seen. The river floodplain provides good rewards for birdwatchers; at least 434 species have been identified in the park. Summer tanagers, painted buntings, vermillion flycatchers, yellow-bellied sapsuckers, and cardinals are a few of the colorful birds. Join a ranger-led birding walk to increase your skills.

Stargazing at the village is great entertainment and is frequently featured at the evening campground programs. When I was there in January, we found dim Mercury just above the horizon; straight above was brilliant Venus, then the crescent moon, and higher still, Jupiter. The red star Betelgeuse, Orion's Belt, and the brightest star, Sirius, are easy to find.

BOQUILLAS CANYON

Over the ages, the Rio Grande River—a "gravity-powered belt sander"—has carved wondrous limestone gorges along the 107 miles (172 km) that now form the lower border of the park. The first of these three canyons is Boquillas, which is a short distance east of the village. It is a quiet 33-mile (53 km) stretch of the river, a place of sandy beaches, sunlight, side canyons, and easy floating for canoes. Commercial operators offer trips to all the canyons throughout the year and you can do your own river trip with a permit. Walkers can experience the mouth of the canyon via a 1-mile (1.6-km) round-trip trail that climbs over sea shell fossils embedded in limestone.

BOQUILLAS, MEXICO

A short spur road leads to the Boquillas Crossing, where a rowboat will ferry you across for a visit to the small Mexican village of Boquillas. The last I heard, they were still awaiting the arrival of electricity in Boquillas. Tacos, cold Mexican beer, and hand-spun yarn bracelets are often for sale. Towns once thrived on both sides of the river when lead, zinc, and silver were mined in the adjacent Sierra del Carmen cliffs. The Mexicans frequently obtain supplies from their American friends at Rio Grande Village.

HOT SPRINGS ALONG THE RIO GRANDE

On almost any day, think hot springs and either take the trail from west of Rio Grande Village or drive the short distance on the unpaved spur road to the springs along the river. The village trail begins at the picnic area at the old Daniels Ranch, where an adobe home with a reed roof is located a few steps from the river. This trail offers a wonderful perspective of the river, its floodplain, and the adjacent low rock formations. Take time to discover mortar holes used by Indians for grinding mesquite beans and seeds. The trail is edged by a variety of cactus: purple-tinged and long, brown-spined prickly pear; tiny button cactus; the tasajillo, or Christmas cactus, with its red fruit lingering through this winter season; the interesting candlelilla, or wax plant; and the chief indicator of the Chihuahuan Desert, the tall, dagger-bladed lechuguilla plant.

Enclosed in a rocked-in pool next to the river, the 105-degree mineral waters are soothing. Wear a bathing suit beneath your clothes so you can enjoy the waters if the water level is right; it varies from year-to-year. Notice the artistic swirls and textures of the rose- and cream-colored rocks. Heated geothermally by igneous rocks, research indicates the hot water arises from a pocket of "fossil water" deposited at least

Casa Grande peak in the Chisos of Big Bend, TX.

20,000 years ago that is not being replaced.

J. O. Langford, an early settler, came here to recover from bouts of malaria—and he did. He built a home, a post office/trading post, a motel, and even arbors with willow tree posts and river-cane roofs for campers. Pictographs on the layered limestone cliffs are reminders of earlier occupants. Continue on past the hot springs to view the resort remains along the Hot Springs Historic Walk.

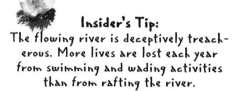

Insider's Tip:
The flowing river is deceptively treacherous. More lives are lost each year from swimming and wading activities than from rafting the river.

If you'd like a short trip on the river, slip your boat into the river here at the Hot Springs and float the 2.5 miles (4 km) to Rio Grande Village.

MARISCAL CANYON

No experience will infuse you with the river essence of the park better than the 7-mile (11-km) float trip through Mariscal Canyon, the canyon with the big bend, the great U-turn that spawned the park's name. This canyon can be floated easily in one day if you travel the long, four-wheel-drive River Road to the launch site early enough in the day. Ask the folks at the Rio Grande Village store about commercial operators, or maneuver the roads yourself in an appropriate vehicle. Some skill is required for this trip on the water, so check conditions with a ranger. The launch site is at the remote backcountry campsite at Talley.

Slip the tough skin of your raft, canoe, or kayak into the gravity-induced movement of the water and soon enter the steep limestone walls of the canyon. I did this in January and the weather was perfect. This float is mostly a calm, spirit-soothing ride, with some controlled paddling required only at a small rock slide and at the ten-foot gap between huge blocks of rock called the Tight Squeeze. The remains of a hermit's structure and debris from floods can be seen high up in the rocks. Beaver live in bank burrows along the river. Timing is usually right for a picnic lunch stop on the Mexican side of the river. Ever-changing rock formations, riparian vegetation, wildlife, the interplay of light and shadow, and reflections of oranges and blues upon the green water are enchanting in the canyon. The take-out is at the Solis back-country campsite. If you've never floated a river, try this one.

THE CHISOS MOUNTAINS
Mountain lovers can head for the Chisos (pronounced "chee-sos") Mountains, a volcanic area of striking spires and peaks with a scattering of trees and grasses, a surprising contrast to the surrounding Chihuahuan Desert. These isolated mountains were once hiding places for Apache Indians. Access is via a steep, winding road into the area called the Basin (not recommended for trailers over 20 feet [6 m] and motorhomes over 24 feet [7 m]). Those who negotiate the hairpin curves will find a scenic campground with the magnificent Casa Grande Peak to the east and the Window to the west. Or you can leave your rig parked elsewhere and drive in for the day. With this area's wetter climate, two or three snowfalls occur annually in the high Chisos, although temperatures are usually comfortable.

Indians say that the Great Spirit simply dumped all the leftover rocks in Big Bend. Some geologists find this volcanic rock so inverted, jumbled, mixed, intruded, and extruded that they call it the "eggbeater formation." To me, these rocky peaks look like the work of a giant sculptor who chisels away, but seldom is successful in getting an image to work. Occasionally he comes close and you'll see a unique shape, but mostly it's a scramble of angles and cracks that is random yet pleasing. The colors of the rocks are varied—golds, oranges, browns, grays, greens, mauves, purples, and bluish-blacks.

Good hiking trails of varying lengths are found in the Chisos. A favorite day hike is the 5.3-mile (8.5-km) round-trip trail to the Window, a V-shaped notch in the rim of mountains where all the surface water

A view of Juniper Canyon ridges from Lost Mine Trail, Big Bend, TX.

from the Basin drains into the desert. Another fun hike is the 4.6-mile (7.4-km) Lost Mine Trail, which begins at Panther Pass; pick up the informative trail guide. Why not pack a lunch and relax while you enjoy the sweeping mountain views at trail's end? The Pinnacles Trail weaves past lichen-encrusted spires as it ascends to panoramic views in the Chisos. Backpackers find an extensive system of interconnecting trails in the high Chisos that reach nearly 8,000 feet (2,438 m). Weather can change abruptly, so be prepared, and make sure you carry water.

Big Bend offers striking examples of various landscapes that, along with the climate, define the habitats of wildlife. Many of the trees—ponderosa pine, Arizona cypress, Douglas fir, quaking aspen, and bigtooth maple—are at their most southerly distribution in the Chisos. These mountains are the only location in the United States where the Colima warbler is spotted; it nests here in spring after wintering in Mexico. Wildlife abounds in the Big Bend. In addition to the rare Sierra del Carmen white-tailed deer, intriguing roadrunners, smelly javelinas, coyote, and black bear, be aware that the Chisos Mountains are mountain lion country. Exercise caution, but don't panic—attacks on humans are rare. Both the panthers and peregrine falcons are monitored in the park. Twelve nests for these endangered falcons are recent discoveries, and seventeen young were counted in 1997—an exciting increase over past years.

ROSS MAXWELL SCENIC DRIVE

The third road to branch off into the park interior is the Ross Maxwell Scenic Drive, with a wealth of interesting historical, scenic, and geologic stops along the east side of Burro Mesa. Windmills still turn in the breeze at the Old Sam Nail Ranch as they pump water and attract birds. A path leads to the adobe ruins of a ranch house in an oasis of vegetation. At Blue Creek Ranch, a path winds down to the comfortable-looking old homestead ranch house complete with a veranda facing the mountains. The Dodson and Blue Creek trails climb into the Chisos Mountains from here. The Blue Creek Trail was made by the ranchers who lived here to move their sheep up to a cooler summer range.

Coyote at Rio Grande Village, Big Bend, TX.

Stops at Sotol Vista and Mule Ears viewpoints offer fine views of the complex park geology. (Past Sotol Vista, vehicle recommendations are the same as those for entering the Basin.) From a spur road, the Burro Mesa Pour-off Trail leads to the walls of a canyon created by a lava flow, with the pour-off standing as a huge dry waterfall. It was in the region to the west that the U.S. Army experimented with using camels in the summer of 1860. It was a smart idea in this hot, dry landscape, and the experiment was successful—the camels left horses and mules in the dust. But then came the Civil War, followed by the railroad, and camel travel became obsolete.

Tuff Canyon is a lovely surprise, a picturesque bit of water-carving between walls of tuff. A short trail leads to an over-look of a scenic canyon directly below, and a longer trail enters the canyon wash.

CASTOLON

The scenic drive continues past Castolon Peak about a mile to the historic village of Castolon. Buildings that were originally built as permanent quarters for cavalry troops—although they became stores and residences—are still in good condition. The old La Harmonia store—once a meeting place of Texas Rangers, ranchers, trappers, and travelers—is still operated as a park concession, and is a good place to imagine old times among the antiques and to buy ice cream on a warm day.

Across the river sits the Mexican village of Santa Elena. The floodplain of Castolon Valley was long home to Native Americans. Corn, beans, tomatoes, and other vegetables have been farmed for some time. Mexicans still cross the river in small johnboats to shop at Castolon's general store. On this side of the Rio Grande River, the Cottonwood Campground is situated in the lush riverine thread of vegetation.

SANTA ELENA CANYON

Santa Elena Canyon is upriver another 8 miles (12.8 km), past crumbling adobe homes of old farming settlements. Rubber rafts leisurely float in and out of the canyon mouth on fine days, adding a human element to the beauty of the tall canyon walls that begin to abruptly enclose the river here. The short Santa Elena Canyon Trail lets you enter the mouth of the canyon via steep steps cut into the rock. The path eventually drops down past huge boulders to river level, where the river is squeezed between narrow walls. A high point along the trail provides great views of the Chisos Mountains.

River runners put in at Lajitas on the west side of the park for this 17-mile (27-km) river segment, a challenging and inspiring one or two day trip. The first 11 miles (17.6 km) traverse rugged desert mesa country interspersed with colorful insertions of limestone and igneous rocks. The river then slips into the deep, narrow slot of Santa Elena Canyon that has been carved through Mesa de Anguila. Most demanding is the Rock Slide, a class IV rapid that requires scouting and then possibly portaging or guiding your raft or canoe through with ropes. The remainder of the float is fairly gentle. The take-out is just outside the mouth of the canyon, where Terlingua Creek enters the Rio Grande near the Santa Elena parking lot.

Big Bend is a large isolated park, with a vast backcountry for four-wheel-drive expeditions and primitive camping (permits are required). What seems like desolate countryside has yielded curious relics of ancient organisms stitched into today's vibrant natural history.

Judge Roy Bean Visitor Center

Although the Rio Grande exits from Big Bend as a "wild and scenic river" that meanders past inviting side canyons, the route east from the park on US 90 is through miles of boring, sparsely inhabited country. Eventually the river and highway converge again and the terrain becomes more scenic. The first good stop for stretching and entertainment is the Judge Roy Bean Visitor Center in Langtry. Inside are interesting historical dioramas with audios; outside you can stroll past the Eclipse windmill to a cactus garden.

The highlight of this stop, however, is the original "Jersey Lilly" structure with a Texas Highway Department sign that reads, "On this exact site and in this very building Judge Roy Bean dispersed hard liquor and harsh justice, all a part of his 'Law West of the Pecos'." So wild and lawless was this area that by 1882 both the Texas Rangers and railroad authorities urged the appointment of a Justice of the Peace for Pecos County. And Roy Bean was ready. Using a 1879 Revised Statutes of Texas and a good amount of his own interpretation of the law—with a six-shooter lying on the table—he was swift in meting out justice: "I'm fining you $45 and a round of drinks for the jury, and that's my ruling!"

During the last part of the nineteenth century, Judge Roy Bean was the law in these parts, ruling in a combination courtroom/saloon/billiard hall built of wood siding with a front porch. Inside is the original wooden furniture, the bar, a billiard table with massive carved figures for legs, interesting notices on the wall, and photos of Lillie Langtry, an English actress known as "the Jersey Lily" who fascinated Bean. Apparently he never met Lillie, although he might have seen her perform in San Antonio, but he named this structure after her.

Where Judge Roy Bean meted out justice at Langtry, TX.

An itinerant misspelled "Lily" on the ancient sign that still hangs by the entry door.

Pecos River Scenic Overlook

Fifteen miles (24 km) east of Langtry, an historic marker at Dead Man's Gulch commemorates the silver spike that joined the transcontinental tracks of the Sunset Route (now the Southern Pacific) from New Orleans to San Francisco on January 12, 1883. This route spanned the steep walls and treacherous waters of the Pecos River and provided a way to haul buffalo hides back east.

An impressive highway bridge spans the rugged terrain of the Pecos River a few miles farther east. Pioneers heading west had to contend with finding a way across the Pecos without the luxury of a bridge. Today, recreational boaters come here for some fun on the blue water. A scenic overlook and roadside picnic area on the east rim of the spectacular limestone canyon is great for picnicking and admiring the view. The formation of Amistad Lake has deepened the water to some 80 feet.

Seminole Canyon State Park

Two thousand acres of sparse vegetation and deep canyons are at Seminole Canyon State Park, just east of the overlook. If your timing is right (Wednesday through Sunday at 10 A.M. and 3 P.M.), you can take one of the strenuous guided tours to the Fate Bell Rockshelter on the canyon floor to see the 8,000-year-old pictographs. The landscape at that time was much like it is today, with arid-adapted plants and small animals such as lizards, snakes, mice, fresh-water mussels, and fish serving as food for the Native American gatherers who left these pictographs.

Another hike requires even more time: a long trail to a 200-foot-high (61-m) overlook of the Rio Grande River at the mouth of Seminole Canyon. Panther Cave, on the opposite side of the canyon, is the site of more pictographs (accessible by boat from Amistad Lake). The creative efforts of these ancient people has a distinctive style limited to this region. People who visited this area some 12,000 years ago roamed a quite different landscape, before the more recent climate change. They were hunters in an area of pine, juniper, and oak woodlands in the canyons and luxuriant grasslands on the uplands, where animals species included elephant, camel, bison, and mammoth. Camping and a visitor center are available.

Amistad National Recreation Area

Both the railway and the highway now lead toward the midpoint of the wavering "V" of water created by the damming of the Rio Grande just below the Devils River tributary. The waterways form the International Amistad Reservoir, a joint project between Mexico and the United States that started storing water in 1968. The reservoir is named with the Mexican word for friendship; symbolizing the cooperative spirit are bronze eagle sculptures in the middle of the dam. How different this international border is than it was 150 years ago. It is peaceful now, with no Indians fighting or obvious clashes between Mexicans and Texans.

Boating is popular in the Amistad National Recreation Area and some nature trails are found. Free primitive campsites near the water are available at several locations; these can be beautiful in early morning with mists and ghostlike great blue herons in the distance. A toll-free access to the Mexico Marina is across the dam.

Lower Rio Grande Valley

South of Laredo, via US 277 and US 83, is another international reservoir, the 60-mile-long (97-km) Falcon Reservoir, which marks the beginning of the Lower Rio Grande Valley (the delta), defined as the last 190 miles of the river. It is actually a flat alluvial plain resulting from thousands of years of flooding and silt deposition by the Rio Grande. The valley is a winter garden of citrus, cotton, sorghum, sugar cane, and vegetables, with dikes and levies resembling hills, an occasional farm building, and a scattering of tiny villages spawned by railroad crossings that become almost a seamless urban strip along the highway.

Although the fertile soil and long growing season have encouraged development of the riverine environment, a string of parks and wildlife refuges offers varied recreation choices in an area where prime habitat still lures wildlife in this international biological crossroads. Various units of the Rio Grande Valley National Wildlife Refuge are helping to provide wildlife corridors. Probably no other part of this country is so rich in biological value and yet so under threat from development. Even so, birders will think they are in paradise. John James Audubon visited here in 1848 and sketched the roadrunner that appears in *Birds of the Southwest*. Ocelots and jaguarundi hide among the tangled brush, but you will probably only spot an armadillo or collared peccary.

FALCON STATE RECREATION AREA

Along our tour, the river has dropped in elevation from 1,850 feet (564 m) at Rio Grande Village to 948 feet (289 m) at Del Rio, and is now at 311 feet (95 m) at Zapata. This is a new version of the town that was flooded by the Falcon Reservoir. South of Zapata, Falcon State Recreation Area includes a prime bird-watching campsite that fronts the lake; the park offers a birding field checklist. Water sports, boating, and fishing are popular—black and white bass, crappie, stripers, and huge catfish are plentiful. A lighted asphalt airstrip (50 feet wide [15 m] and 3,000 feet [914 m] long) is located near the park entrance.

The trick to relaxed birding is luring them with food. Try making homemade

Bird-watching in Big Bend, TX.

feeders by cutting off the tops of liter-size soda bottles, filling them with bird-seed and, along with halved grapefruits or oranges, hanging them on nearby vegetation. The tangy pulp will attract the beautiful alta mira (or Lichtenstein's) oriole, golden-fronted woodpeckers, cardinals, pyrrhuloxia, and mockingbirds, and the scene surrounding the RVs will be punctuated with brilliant colors flashing through the air. These alert wild creatures take a quick suck of juice, check for competitors, and then grab another quick slurp of grapefruit.

At the lake, white pelicans soar overhead and then dive down to the water; great blue herons stalk along the shore. Serious birders may want to visit the woodlands just below the dam, where birding is exceptional along the river. Look for least grebe, green kingfisher, black-bellied duck, and the ringed kingfisher, with its loud, harsh, and rattling call.

BENTSEN–RIO GRANDE VALLE STATE PARK

Continue southeast on US 83, following the river on its way to the sea. You'll pass through small towns with more Hispanic character than the usual American ones, although they also exude a Texan flavor. Homes and businesses with Spanish arches as well as cowboy hats are numerous. Texas beef is featured in restaurants and markets. Many roads lead to Mexico on this lower stretch of the Rio Grande. One historic crossing has an old, original ferry, long used for trips into our neighbor country. Roadside stands feature great buys on Texas grapefruit and oranges.

Another place where RVers hang out is Bentsen–Rio Grande Valley State Park, a few miles from Mission. This is an area that caters to "Winter Texans" to the point that a special newsletter is published, since these winter visitors increase the area population by roughly 50 percent. Birds and a couple of hiking trails are the attractions.

If you have never seen a green jay, this exquisite flying poem is as colorful as a Walt Disney creation. The multicolored birds, along with the chicken-like chachalacas and the great-tailed grackles, produce an audible picture show that resembles a tropical jungle. Look high and you might discover the nest of a great horned owl up in a tree, or you might see a golden eagle. Fox squirrels are friendly and even crawl through the bird feeders. A blue bunting, a clay-colored robin, a tufted titmouse, or even a scissor-tailed flycatcher might fly in for breakfast. If you need any help with bird identification or scouting tips, many friendly, experienced birders also inhabit the park.

Some campsites front on a "resaca." or oxbow, an arm of the river cut off in its meandering change of direction through the years. These are places to watch tangerine sunsets. For a better introduction to the vegetation, walk the two trails here. The mesquite-prickly pear brush and riverbottom woodlands have done the initial job of providing the habitat that attracts so much wildlife to this park. A detailed guide will inform you as you walk along the Rio Grande Trail, a loop with numbered stations and a spur trail that provides access to the river. Look for Texas tree snails glued on tree trunks and ant lions, or doodlebugs, along the Singing Chaparral Trail. Listen for both mourning and white-winged doves.

SANTA ANA NATIONAL WILDLIFE REFUGE

The next wild unit south along the Rio Grande River has the largest remnant of delta woodlands—the Santa Ana National Wildlife Refuge. From late November to mid-April, an open-air, interpretive wildlife tram provides rides; private vehicles can travel the 7-mile Refuge Drive when the tram isn't operating.

Foot travel is allowed at any time during daylight hours, and 12 miles (19.2 km) of trails provide plenty of choices for looping through the refuge on bird-watching walks. Choose among—or combine—three self-guiding nature trails that begin at the visitor center. The paved, wheelchair-accessible Santa Ana Trail loops down to Willow Lake and back. The Santa Ana's Communities Trail makes a bigger sweep of that same lake. The Wildlife Management Trail heads east and weaves around the Pintail Lake area. Feeding stations let you watch the birds easily, and two pho-

tography blinds can be reached along the nature trails. Eight more trails are accessible via the Terrace Trail or Refuge Drive. Egrets, Kiskadee flycatchers, and pygmy owls are possible sightings, but always be alert for a rare bird wandering into the area.

PORT ISABEL AND SOUTH PADRE ISLAND

When the first Europeans arrived here in the sixteenth century, they found 80 miles of impenetrable palm jungle fringing the riverbanks of the Rio de las Palmes, their name for the Rio Grande. A small remnant stand of these native sabal palms can be seen at Sabal Palm Grove Sanctuary in Brownsville.

Way down south in the land of Texas, the Rio Grande empties into the Gulf of Mexico. Just north of the mouth is Port Isabel, with its shrimp boat fleet and the *Lady Bea*, a dry-docked shrimp boat open to visitors. The most prominent scenic attraction, however, is the Port Isabel Lighthouse, a state historic structure, where you can climb the spiral staircase to fine views of the coastal plain and South Padre Island in the Gulf.

A long causeway from Port Isabel spans Laguna Madre and takes you to this narrow strip of land called South Padre Island. This resort community has high-rise luxury hotels, seaside cottages, restaurants featuring the fine area fish, campgrounds, and an inviting strip of beach for strolling. You can take a horseback ride north on secluded beaches with sand dunes, sea oats, and morning glories, or set out on foot to look for sea shells. Craft shows offer other entertainment here. The county campground is huge, with enough campers for a small town. Watch for rust on your rig if you stay for any length of time in this salty air.

Many travelers get hooked on this harsh yet beautiful landscape bordering the nurturing Rio Grande River and return year after year to spend time exploring. They find the beauty of flowers after a rain, a hoarfrost on Panther Pass, or a sunset framed by a "Window" in volcanic rocks, and certainly a treasure of bird species. The magic comes and goes. Look, smell, touch, and listen and you will find your own.

Appendix:
Sources for Further Reading

NATURAL HISTORY

Allen, John Eliot. *The Magnificent Gateway: A Layman's Guide to the Geology of the Columbia River Gorge*. Portland, Oregon: Timber Press, 1979.

Atkinson, Richard. *White Sands: Wind, Sand and Time*. Tucson: Southwest Parks and Monuments Association, 1987.

Carefoot, Thomas. *Pacific Seashores: A Guide to Intertidal Ecology*. Vancouver: J.J. Douglas Ltd., 1977.

Elias, Thomas S. *The Complete Trees of North America: Field Guide and Natural History*. New York: Van Nostrand Reinhold, 1980.

Harris, Stephen L. *Fire & Ice: The Cascade Volcanoes*. Seattle: The Mountaineers, 1980.

Kozloff, Eugene. *Plants and Animals of the Pacific Northwest: An Illustrated Guide to the Natural History of Western Oregon, Washington, and British Columbia*. Seattle: University of Washington Press, 1978.

Kricher, John C., and Morrison, Gordon. *A Field Guide to the Ecology of Western Forests*. Boston: Houghton Mifflin, 1993.

Matthiessen, Peter. *Wildlife in America*. New York: Viking Press, 1987.

McCall, Karen, and Dutcher, Jim. *Cougar: Ghost of the Rockies*. San Francisco: Sierra Club Books, 1992.

McKenny, Margaret. *The Savory Wild Mushroom*. Seattle: University of Washington Press, 1971.

Morris, Percy A. *A Field Guide to Pacific Coast Shells, Including Shells of Hawaii and the Gulf of California* (currently out of print). Boston: Houghton Mifflin, 1974.

Peterson, Roger Tory. *A Field Guide to Western Birds*. Boston: Houghton Mifflin, 1961.

Pough, Frederick H. *Peterson Field Guide to Rocks and Minerals*. Boston: Houghton Mifflin, 1996.

Redfern, Ron. *The Making of a Continent*. New York: Times Books, 1983.

Ricketts, Edward F., and Calvin, Jack. *Between Pacific Tides* (4th ed.). San Francisco: Stanford University Press, 1968.

Savage, Candace, *Peregrine Falcons*. San Francisco: Sierra Club Books, 1992.

Whitaker, John O., Jr. *The Audubon Society Field Guide to North American Mammals*. New York: Alfred A. Knopf, 1980.

Wiedemann, Alfred M., Dennis, La Rea J., and Smith, Frank H. *Plants of the Oregon Coastal Dunes*. Corvallis: Oregon State University, 1982.

Wood, Wendell. *A Walking Guide to Oregon's Ancient Forests*. Portland: Oregon Natural Resources Council, 1991.

OUTDOOR AND TRAVEL GUIDES

Bannan, Jan Gumprecht. *Sand Dunes*. Minneapolis: Carol-Rhoda Books, 1989.

Bannan, Jan. *Oregon State Parks: A Complete Recreational Guide*. Seattle: The Mountaineers, 1994.

Bannan, Jan. *Utah State Parks: A Complete Recreational Guide*. Seattle: The Mountaineers, 1995.

Bannan, Jan. *The West Less Traveled: The Best and Lesser Known Parks, Monuments and Natural Areas*. Golden, Colorado: Fulcrum Publishing, 1996.

Cummings, Joe. *Baja Handbook*. Chico, California: Moon Publishers, 1994.

Foreman, Dave, and Wolke, Howie. *The Big Outside: A Descriptive Inventory of the Big Wilderness Areas of the United States*. New York: Harmony Books, 1992.

Hinchman, Sandra. *Hiking the Southwest's Canyon Country*. Seattle: The Mountaineers, 1990.

Kaysing, Bill, and Kaysing, Ruth. *Hot Springs of the Great West*. Santa Barbara: Capra Press, 1993.

Kirk, Ruth. *Exploring the Olympic Peninsula* (3rd ed.). Seattle: University of Washington Press, 1980.

Mueller, Marge, and Mueller, Ted. *Washington State Parks: A Complete Recreation Guide*. Seattle: The Mountaineers, 1993.

Riley, Laura, and Riley, William. *Guide to the National Refuges*. New York: Macmillan, 1993.

Rockwell, David. *Glacier National Park: A Natural History Guide*. Boston: Houghton Mifflin, 1995

Ross, Cindy, and Gladfelter, Todd. *A Hiker's Companion: 12,000 Miles of Trail-Tested Wisdom*. Seattle: The Mountaineers, 1993.

Sierra Club Guides to the National Parks of the Desert Southwest. New York: Stewart, Tabori & Chang, 1996.

Sullivan, William L. *Exploring Oregon's Wild Areas: A Guide for Hikers, Backpackers, Climbers, Cross-Country Skiers, and Paddlers*. Seattle: The Mountaineers, 1994.

Warren, Scott S. *Exploring Colorado's Wild Areas: A Guide for Hikers, Backpackers, Climbers, Cross-Country Skiers, and Paddlers*. Seattle: The Mountaineers, 1992.

RV BOOKS

Abraham, Marilyn. *First We Quit Our Jobs: How One Work-Driven Couple Got on the Road to a New Life.* New York: Dell Publishing, 1997.

Baker, Kim, and Baker, Sunny. *The RVer's Bible: Everything You Need to Know about Choosing, Using, and Enjoying Your RV.* New York: A Fireside Book, Simon & Schuster, 1997.

Groene, Janet, and Groene, Gordon. *Living Aboard Your RV: A Guide to the Fulltime Life on Wheels.* Camden, Maine: Ragged Mountain Press, 1993.

Groene, Janet. *Cooking Aboard Your RV.* Camden, Maine: Ragged Mountain Press, 1993.

Miller, Richard W. *Mountain Directory for Truckers, RV, and Motorhome Drivers: Locations and Descriptions of Over 250 Mountain Passes and Steep Grades in 11 Western States* (3rd rev. ed.). Los Angeles: R & R Publications, 1996.

DESCRIPTION & HISTORY

Abbey, Edward. *Desert Solitaire: A Season in the Wilderness.* New York: McGraw-Hill, 1968.

Abbey, Edward. *Down the River.* New York: E. P. Dutton, 1982.

Ackerman, Diane. *The Moon by Whale Light: And Other Adventures among Bats, Penguins, Crocodilians, and Whales.* New York: Vintage Books, 1992.

Berger, Bruce. *The Telling Distance: Conversations with the American Desert.* Portland, Oregon: Breitenbush Books, 1990.

Bird, Isabella. *A Lady's Life in the Rocky Mountains.* Norman: University of Oklahoma Press, 1960.

Bowden, Charles. *Blue Desert.* Tucson: University of Arizona Press, 1986.

Carrighar, Sally. *One Day at Teton Marsh.* New York: Ballantine Books, 1947.

Dietrich, William. *The Final Forest: The Battle for the Last Great Trees of the Pacific Northwest.* New York: Simon & Schuster, 1992.

Duncan, Dayton. *Out West: American Journey along the Lewis and Clark Trail.* New York: Penquin Books, 1988.

Egan, Timothy. *The Good Rain: Across Time and Terrain in the Pacific Northwest.* New York: Alfred A. Knopf, 1990.

Grey, Zane. *Rainbow Trail.* Santa Barbara: Santa Barbara Press, 1985.

Grey, Zane. *Riders of the Purple Sage.* New York: Pocket Books, 1974.

Grey, Zane. *Rogue River Feud.* New York: Pocket Books, 1975.

Kappel-Smith, Diana. *Desert Time: A Journey through the American Southwest.* Tucson: University of Arizona Press, 1992.

Lavender, David. *The Southwest.* Albuquerque: University of New Mexico Press, 1980.

Lefebvre, Irene Sturm. *Cherokee Strip in Transition.* Enid, Oklahoma: Cherokee Strip Centennial Foundation, 1993.

Lopez, Barry Holstun. *Desert Notes: Reflections in the Eye of a Raven.* New York: Avon Books, 1990.

Lopez, Barry Holstun. *River Notes: The Dance of Herons.* Kansas City, Kansas: Andrews & McMeel, 1979.

McPhee, John. *Rising from the Plains.* New York: Farrar, Straus & Giroux, 1986.

Meloy, Ellen. *Raven's Exile: A Season on the Green River.* New York: Henry Holt, 1994.

Naar, Jon, and Naar, Alex. *This Land Is Your Land: A Guide to North America's Endangered Ecosystems.* New York: HarperPerennial, 1993.

Nabhan, Gary Paul. *The Desert Smells Like Rain: A Naturalist in Papago Indian Country.* San Francisco: North Point Press, 1982.

O'Brien, Dan. *Equinox: Life, Love, and Birds of Prey.* New York: Lyons & Burford, 1997.

Payne, Roger. *Among Whales.* New York: Scribner, 1995.

Peacock, Doug. *Grizzly Years: In Search of the American Wilderness.* New York: Henry Holt, 1990.

Powell, John Wesley, *Exploration of the Colorado River of the West and Its Tributaries.* New York: Dover, 1961.

Ryden, Hope. *Lily Pond: Four Years with a Family of Beavers.* New York: William Morrow, 1989.

Schullery, Paul. *Mountain Time.* New York: Simon & Schuster, 1988 ed.

Stegner, Wallace. *Where the Bluebird Sings to the Lemonade Springs: Living and Writing in the West.* New York: Random House, 1992.

Steinbeck, John. *Sea of Cortez.* New York: Viking Press, 1941.

Teale, Edwin Way. *Autumn Across America: A Naturalist's Record of a 20,000-Mile Journey through the North American Autumn.* New York: Dodd, Mead & Company, 1956.

Trimble, Stephen. *The Bright Edge: A Guide to the National Parks of the Colorado Plateau.* Flagstaff: Museum of Northern Arizona Press, 1979.

Wood, Nancy. *Taos Pueblo.* New York: Alfred A. Knopf, 1989.

Zwinger, Ann Haymond. *Run, River, Run: A Naturalist's Journey Down One of the Great Rivers of the American West.* Tucson: University of Arizona, 1975.

Zwinger, Ann Haymond. *The Mysterious Lands: A Naturalist Explores the Four Great Deserts of the Southwest.* New York: Truman Talley Books/Plume, 1989.

Index